CONTENTS

Acknowledgements

My thanks are due in the first place to my students for their advice and encouragement. I would also like to acknowledge with gratitude the assistance of Professor H. C. Barnard, Roger Bilboul, Peter Cunningham, Professor Eric Eaglesham, Kathleen Hyndman, Edith Moorhouse, Tony Richardson, Kenneth Rose, Joy Rummey, Stuart Sexton and Robin Tanner. A great deal of time and help was given me by Edmund Sackett, John Warmington and the rest of the staff at Westminster College library and by the staff of the Official Paper and Lower Reading Rooms of the Bodleian Library. Mrs M. Bailey and Mr R. Sadler generously gave me permission to quote from the manuscripts of Sir Robert Morant and Sir Michael Sadler.

The publishers listed below were kind enough to allow me to use extracts from books and other copyright material:

The Bodley Head Ltd.
Charles Scribner's Sons
Critical Quarterly Ltd.
The Garnstone Press Ltd.
Hamish Hamilton Ltd.
The Hamlyn Publishing Group Ltd.
Hodder & Stoughton Ltd.
Humanities Press Inc.
Longman Group Ltd.
Michael Joseph Ltd.
Macmillan (London & Basingstoke) Ltd.

N.F.E.R. Publishing Co. Ltd.
Organisation for Economic Co-operation and Development
Oxford University Press
Penguin Books Ltd.
Pergamon Press Ltd.
Prentice-Hall Inc.
Putnam & Co. Ltd.
Routledge & Kegan Paul Ltd.
Thames & Hudson Ltd.
Times Newspapers Ltd.

Extracts from Crown-copyright publications and transcripts of Crown-copyright records in the Public Record Office appear by permission of the Controller of Her Majesty's Stationery Office.

CHAPTER 1

INTRODUCTION : EDUCATIONAL ATTITUDES IN THE LATE EIGHTEENTH AND EARLY NINETEENTH CENTURIES

Is is not always easy to look with sympathy upon the policies and actions of the educationalists of a hundred and fifty or two hundred years ago; basic attitudes have changed too much in the meantime. By today's standards their beliefs may seem retrograde in the extreme; but to many at the time they appeared generous and even dangerously radical: as one Member of Parliament rhetorically declaimed, 'What produced the French Revolution? Books.'[1]

So not for nothing did Hannah More write feelingly that she had been 'battered, hacked, scalped, tom-a-hawked . . . for three years, and continue to be'[2] on account of her work in schools. It is unlikely that her views on educational theory and practice would be considered seditious nowadays. For as she herself pointed out, her adherence to the doctrine of original sin was bound to lead to accusations of unnecessary severity and an unjustly ill opinion of mankind. Once accepted, however, the concept of original sin inevitably exerted a powerful influence upon educational theory:

> The foundation of the Christian religion, out of which the whole structure may be said to arise, appears to be the doctrine of the fall of man from his original state of righteousness; and the corruption, guilt, and helplessness of human nature, which are the consequences of this fall, and which is the natural state of everyone born into the world. To this doctrine it is important to conciliate the minds, more especially of young persons, who are peculiarly disposed to turn away from it as a morose, unamiable, and gloomy idea: they are apt to accuse those who are more strict and serious, of unnecessary severity, and to suspect them of thinking unjustly ill of mankind.
> (H. More, *Strictures on the Modern System of Female Education*, etc., 1799, Vol. II, p. 252)

No doubt a similarly genuine conviction regarding the innate predisposition to sin of mankind in general and children in particular had been behind the more specific advice of John Wesley:

> A wise parent should begin to break their will the first moment it appears. In the whole art of Christian education, there is nothing more important than this. . . .

And Wesley could quote with apparent approval his mother's injunction to

> . . . make him do as he is bid, if you whip him ten times running to effect it. Let none persuade you it is cruelty to do this, it is cruelty not to do it. Break his will now, and his soul will live, and he will probably bless you to all eternity.
> (A. H. Body, *John Wesley and Education*, 1936, p. 51)

The aim of education, then, was to wrench childhood away from its naturally sinful proclivities and to guide it firmly but if necessary by no means gently along the paths of righteousness. With the Bible (or selected parts of it) as textbook and exemplar, the souls of the younger generation might be saved and the existing social system preserved by one and the same process. The social function of education is made clear in the following two passages, which span almost half a century. The first, written by Hannah More, is a straightforward statement of her ideas; the second, taken from a sermon delivered by William Branwhite Clarke in 1838 to raise money for the National Society for Promoting the Education of the Poor in the Principles of the Established Church, is more high-flown in style but identical in sentiment:

My plan of instruction is extremely simple and limited. They learn, on week-days, such coarse works as may fit them for servants.[3] I allow of no writing for the poor. My object is not to make fanatics, but to train up the lower classes in habits of industry and piety. I knew no way of teaching morals but by teaching principles; or of inculcating Christian principles without imparting a good knowledge of scripture. *(William Roberts, Memoirs of the Life of Mrs. Hannah More, 1836 ed., Vol. II, p. 66)*

. . .

. . . whilst (the National Society) does not unfit the poor from the discharge of those subordinate necessary claims which Providence has laid upon them, it, at the same time, fits them for that state of future bliss which is expressly promised to the 'poor in spirit'. No one need therefore fear, that, in subscribing to the funds of this Society, he is offering encouragement to pride, or lifting from their true condition, by acquaintance with pursuits which would unfit them for the lowly offices of private life, those whom the Scripture itself acknowledges as destined to be 'hewers of wood and drawers of water'. Whilst it teaches humility, and patience, and contentment, it proclaims to all the glories of redemption, the salvation of the Cross, emancipation from the burden of the flesh, the free and gracious gift of everlasting blessedness at God's right hand. *(William Branwhite Clarke, Claims of the Church of England to support from its Members, 1838)*

Views such as these were repudiated by a minority within the church. Richard Dawes, whose enlightened and forcefully expressed opinions may well have cost him preferment, bitterly resented the attitude of those who, as he put it, 'look upon the labourer as a machine which sleep winds up at night, to be set again in motion in the morning, and again run down on doing its daily work'.[4] In 1850 he publicly lashed out against the prevailing ethos of the National Society; his criticisms seem to have a note of exasperation about them. In retrospect it is easy to see why. Reaching far beyond contemporary standards of popular education both within and without the National Society, Dawes' ideas were foredoomed, constituting by their very transience one of the tragedies of mid-nineteenth-century education:

There are many things which make one despair of ever seeing the National Society carrying out a system of education of an effective kind, as connected with the Church . . .

The National Society, and perhaps a majority of the clergy, wish to introduce a system of education, which would establish in every parish a charity school for the education of the poor . . . keeping the labouring classes, in their education and habits formed in early life, entirely apart from the classes immediately above them. Now, this is making a distinction of a most invidious kind: the labouring classes feel no elevation of kind in being educated in this way: on the contrary, it has a most depressing tendency about it, and they feel that it is not a thing in which they take any interest themselves, but think it the duty of the clergy to write begging letters year after year, and to preach education sermons in order to provide it; and, after all, the result, hitherto, has been satisfactory neither to the clergy nor to the classes for whom it is intended; and the most which can be said of it is, that it is just better than nothing . . .

The National Society has, in some measure, been a national deception, retarding the cause of education rather than advancing it, by taking the place of a better system, and has been held up to the public, and supported by the subscriptions of the charitably disposed, as educating the children of the labouring classes in connexion with the church, when in reality its schools have been a failure . . .[5]

(R. Dawes, Remarks occasioned by the present crusade against the educational plans of the Committee of Council on Education, 1850, pp.6-11, passim)

The utilitarian view

Richard Dawes' condemnatory attitude towards the educational policies of the Church of England was fully shared by the utilitarians – a group of intellectually influential bourgeois economists, politicians, and philosophers who favoured state intervention in education. In their view, a traditional neglect of popular education on the part of the Church of England had long invalidated any claim which it might once have had to control working-class schools:

In other protestant countries, as in Scotland, at Geneva, in Switzerland, and Holland, the education of the lower orders was regarded as an object of the greatest importance, both in a religious and a political point of view. Careful provision was made for it. Parochial schools were established; funds were set apart for their maintenance; means for acquiring the first and most important parts of the literary branch of education were placed within the reach of all the people; all the people were actually taught them; and the lower orders, in all these several countries, as they have been the best educated, so have they been the most virtuous and orderly that existed upon the face of the earth. In England the case was widely different. The education of the lower orders was totally neglected. In general they could neither write nor read.

(James Mill, Schools for All, in Preference to Schools for Churchmen Only, in James Mill on Education, ed. W. H. Burston, 1969, p. 122)

Strong supporters of Joseph Lancaster's 'glorious design of extending the benefits of education to every member of the community', utilitarians such as James Mill and Jeremy Bentham had no time for the standard circumscribed approach to schooling.* Their deep belief in human

---

*Bentham's ideas on upper- and middle-class education were set out in his *Chrestomathia* (1816). Classics were excluded and science and technology strongly emphasized.

rationality caused them to reject absolutely the Anglican fears that excessive learning would induce the masses to subvert the social order. Education, James Mill stoutly maintained, far from causing social unrest, would serve irrefutably to persuade the working class to accept their subordinate position:

> . . . I have seldom met with a labouring man (and I have tried the experiment upon many of them) whom I could not make to see that the existence of property was not only good for the labouring men, but of infinitely more importance to the labourers as a class, than to any other.
> *(A. Bain, James Mill, a biography, 1882, p. 365)*

It was consequently an article of utilitarian faith that social stratification, far from being a decree emanating from an Old Testament deity, was in fact the result of logically inevitable and fundamentally beneficial economic forces:

> It is absolutely necessary for the existence of the human race, that labour should be performed, that food should be produced, and other things provided, which human welfare requires. A large proportion of mankind is required for this labour. Now, then, in regard to all this portion of mankind, that labours, only such a portion of time can by them be given to the acquisition of intelligence, as can be abstracted from labour. . . . There are degrees, therefore, of intelligence, which must be reserved to those who are not obliged to labour.
> *(James Mill, Education, in James Mill on Education, ed. W. H. Burston, 1969, pp. 106-107)*

The utilitarians, therefore, represented an approach to popular schooling which radically differed from that of most churchmen. The aim – the acceptance of subordination – was identical. But this was to be obtained not by limitation of imparted knowledge but by the cultivation of an understanding of basic economic realities. And it was the responsibility of the state to supervise the process.

EDUCATIONAL ATTITUDES 2

I went to the Garden of Love,
And saw what I never had seen:
A chapel was built in the midst,
Where I used to play on the green.

And the gates of this chapel were shut,
And "Thou shalt not" writ over the door;
So I turned to the Garden of Love,
That so many sweet flowers bore;

And I saw it was fillèd with graves,
And tombstones where flowers should be;
And priests in black gowns were walking their rounds,
And binding with briars my joys and desires.

The words of William Blake's 'Garden of Love' seem in many ways a fitting postscript to an episode of innovation and experiment in education which had begun with the enthusiastic reception of Jean Jacques Rousseau's book *Emile* by some of the more liberal-minded members of English intellectual society. By the end of the first decade of the nineteenth century, however, political circumstances and religious dogma had imposed rigidity and authoritarianism upon teaching which was to mask the achievements – and failures, it must be said – of the freethinking educationalists of the later eighteenth century.

The most prominent of these were David Williams, Thomas Day, R. L. Edgeworth, and Maria Edgeworth, his daughter. Their views held a common commitment to environmentalism and an absolute rejection of original sin. Unlike their sectarian contemporaries they would probably have endorsed Wordsworth's conviction that

> . . . trailing clouds of glory do we come
> From God, who is our home:
> Heaven lies about us in our infancy!

This was hardly compatible with conventional thinking; nor was the opinion, put forward here by David Williams, that

> We have clear and indisputable proofs that our reason and imagination are produced by experience; and not endowments and properties, which any beings, material or immaterial, bring with them, at the time they take possession of our bodies. Experience determines the nature of the passions, when they are produced, or when they are directed to necessary objects . . .

Although Williams himself had a deep admiration for Rousseau's intellect, he was not prepared, as some were, to accept his ideas *in toto:*

> Rousseau's observations have a tone of invective, and a spirit of acrimony, which do not commonly accompany experience; his system is too comprehensive, and its parts too harmoniously fitted, to be the result of actual observation: the whole has an air of romance, which has little influence on the judgement and understanding, however it may affect the fancy.
>
> . . .
>
> We repeatedly opened the Emile; but the advice and reasoning, which had often amused us, were then insipid. We perceived its system to be a collection of maxims suited to ancient Greece, blended with the customs of American savages.
> *(David Williams, Lectures on Education, 1789, Volume I, pp. 44, 84 and 141)*

Yet, like Rousseau, Williams rejected the morality of the world and saw in education a great potential force for its amelioration; but little, he thought, could be expected from the established schools, which, in his view, existed only to preserve the undesirable aspects of society:

> . . . it will be an everlasting rule in education – that a boy whose object is to be advancement, and not virtue, should be educated in the established schools of every

community. The reason is not so much for the connections he may make, or the celebrity he may acquire, as that his very soul will be moulded to the times, and he will come into the world perfectly fitted for it. In this view of things, education is the art of forming a citizen upon the principles and views of any particular government. His sentiments; his conscience; his mind, must be regulated by the laws of this institution; and nature must be warped by authority.
(David Williams, A Treatise on Education, 1774, pp. 12-13)

As might be expected, David Williams' concept of teaching was a humanitarian one, formulated, as were those of Day and the Edgeworths, with the assumption of small groups of pupils and adequate material resources.

If the subject of education was thoroughly understood, and proper people could be always employed in it, punishments and even rewards would be as unnecessary to lead a child to his business as to his food. The disposition to knowledge is as natural to the mind, as the desire of food is to the body. But when the taste is vitiated in either, we must have recourse to expedients; and among those that offer themselves, chuse the least injurious.
(David Williams, A Treatise on Education, 1774, p. 101)

Education, then, was seen by Williams to be an essentially natural process; children should require neither punishment nor the incentive of competition; equally undesirable was excessive formality, though, like the authors of the Plowden Report almost two centuries later, Williams was at pains to emphasize that 'freedom is in' does not imply that 'discipline is out':[6]

It is a vicious mode of reasoning, because children are improperly employed, they should run about idly and at hazard; or because children are formed into prating impertinent puppets, they should be suffered to sink into the inattention and stupidity of brutes . . .

The common method of confining children to formal lessons to be committed to memory, I will allow to be injurious to the understanding, as it is to health. But it does not follow, that children are to be left to their own devices, or to obtain information by accident.
(David Williams, Lectures on Education, 1789, Volume II, p. 307)

Richard and Sabrina: two cautionary tales for educational experimenters

R. L. Edgeworth is perhaps best known for his part authorship of the book *Practical Education;* Thomas Day wrote the classic *History of Sandford and Merton* in which his beliefs regarding education were presented in story form for the edification (and probably boredom) of whole generations of late eighteenth- and nineteenth-century children. But whatever doubts the cosmopolitan eccentricities of the two friends may seem to cast upon the ultimate soundness of their judgement, they certainly had the courage of their convictions. Both attempted to rear children according to the precepts in which they believed. The involuntary subject of Edgeworth's experiment was his eldest son; that of Day his own intended bride. First, here is Edgeworth's account of his son's education:

> . . . I formed a strong desire to educate my son according to the system of Rousseau. His Emile had made a great impression upon my young mind, as it had done upon the imaginations of many far my superiors in age and understanding. His work had then all the power of novelty, as well as all the charms of eloquence; and when I compared the many plausible ideas it contains, with the obvious deficiencies and absurdities, that I saw in the treatment of children in almost every family, with which I was acquainted, I determined to make a fair trial of Rousseau's system. My wife complied with my wishes, and the body and mind of my son were to be left as much as possible to the education of nature and of accident.
>
> . . .
>
> I dressed my son without stockings, with his arms bare, in a jacket and trowsers such as are quite common at present, but which were at that time novel and extraordinary. I succeeded in making him remarkably hardy: I also succeeded in making him fearless of danger, and, what is more difficult, capable of bearing privation of every sort. He had all the virtues of a child bred in the hut of a savage, and all the knowledge of *things*, which could well be acquired at an early age by a boy bred in civilized society. I say knowledge of *things*, for of books he had less knowledge at four or five years old, than most children have at that age. Of mechanics he had a clearer conception, and in the application of what he knew more invention, than any child I had then seen. He was bold, free, fearless, generous; he had a ready and keen use of all his senses, and of his judgement. But he was not disposed to *obey:* his exertions generally arose from his own will; and, though he was what is commonly called good-tempered and good-natured, though he generally pleased by his looks, demeanour, and conversation, he had too little deference for others, and he showed an invincible dislike to control.
>
> (R. L. *Edgeworth, Memoirs, 1820, Volume I, pp. 177-179*)

The boy refused to obey his tutor and was accordingly sent off to a Catholic seminary. The sequel is a sad one. He later ran away to sea and then settled in Carolina. There he died in his early thirties, leaving a wife and a young family.

Next, Thomas Day and Sabrina. Their quaint story is recounted wittily (and maybe a little waspishly) by Anna Seward, who knew them both:

> Ever despicable in Mr. Day's estimation were the distinctions of birth, and the advantages of wealth; and he had learnt to look back with resentment to the allurements of the Graces. He resolved, if possible, that his wife should have a taste for literature and science, for moral and patriotic philosophy. So might she be his companion in that retirement, to which he had destined himself; and assist him in forming the minds of his children to stubborn virtue and high exertion. He resolved also, that she should be simple as a mountain girl, in her dress, her diet, and her manners; fearless and intrepid as the Spartan wives and Roman heroines. There was no finding such a creature ready made; philosophical romance could not hope it. He must mould some infant into the being his fancy had imaged.
>
> With the late Mr. Bicknel, then a barrister, in considerable practice, and of taintless

reputation, and several years older than himself, Mr. Day lived on terms of intimate friendship. Credentials were procured of Mr. Day's moral probity, and with them, on his coming of age, these two friends journied to Shrewsbury, to explore the hospital in that town for foundling girls. From the little train, Mr. Day, in the presence of Mr. Bicknel, selected two of twelve years each; both beautiful; one fair, with flaxen locks, and light eyes; her he called Lucretia. The other, a clear, auburn brunette, with darker eyes, more glowing bloom, and chestnut tresses, he named Sabrina . . .

Mr. Day went instantly into France with these girls; not taking an English servant, that they might receive no ideas, except those which himself might choose to impart.

They teized and perplexed him; they quarrelled, and fought incessantly; they sickened of the small-pox; they chained him to their bed-side by crying, and screaming if they were ever left a moment with any person who could not speak to them in *English*. He was obliged to sit up with them many nights; to perform for them the lowest offices of assistance.

They lost no beauty by their disease. Soon after they had recovered, crossing the Rhone with his wards in a tempestuous day, the boat overset. Being an excellent swimmer he saved them both, though with difficulty and danger to himself.

Mr. Day came back to England in eight months, heartily glad to separate the little squabblers. Sabrina was become the favourite. He placed the fair Lucretia with a chamber milliner. She behaved well, and became the wife of a respectable linen-draper in London. On his return to his native country, he entrusted Sabrina to the care of Mr. Bicknel's mother, with whom she resided some months in a country village, while he settled his affairs at his own mansion-house, from which he promised not to remove his mother.

It has been said before, that the fame of Dr. Darwin's talents allured Mr. Day to Lichfield. Thither he led, in the spring of the year 1770, the beauteous Sabrina, then thirteen years old, and taking a twelve month's possession of the pleasant mansion in Stowe valley, resumed his preparations for implanting in her young mind the characteristic virtues of Arria, Portia, and Cornelia. His experiments had not the success he wished and expected. Her spirit could not be armed against the dread of pain, and the appearance of danger. When he dropped melted sealing-wax upon her arms she did not endure it heroically, nor when he fired pistols at her petticoats, which she believed to be charged with balls, could she help starting aside, or suppress her screams.

When he tried her fidelity in secret-keeping, by telling her of well-invented dangers to himself, in which greater danger would result from its being discovered that he was *aware* of them, he once or twice detected her having imparted them to the servants, and to her play-fellows.

She betrayed an averseness to the study of books, and of the rudiments of science, which gave little promise of ability, that should, one day, be responsible for the education of youths, who were to emulate the Gracchi.

. . .

Thus, after a series of fruitless trials, Mr. Day renounced all hope of moulding Sabrina into the being his imagination had formed; and ceasing to behold her as his future wife, he placed her at a boarding-school in Sutton Coldfield, Warwickshire. His trust in the power of education faltered; his aversion to modern elegance subsided.

(Anna Seward, Memoirs of the Life of Dr. Darwin, 1804, pp: 35-41)

The rest of the Gothick extravaganza is quickly told: Day, on a trivial excuse, dismissed Sabrina and married a young lady of conventional upper-class background. Sabrina herself became the wife of Day's old friend Bicknel, who died leaving her with two young children and no money, whereupon Day made over to her an annual allowance of £30 – a figure that Anna Seward evidently felt to be a parsimonious one. A further sum was raised by her late husband's colleagues, and Sabrina herself later took the position of housekeeper to Dr. Burney at Greenwich, being 'treated by him, and his friends, with every mark of esteem and respect due to a gentlewoman, and one whose virtues entitle her to universal approbation'.

Day's theories may have made Sabrina's life a misery at times; but they were to prove lethal to his own. Believing that horses could be tamed and broken in by kind words alone, he attempted to put his ideas to the test with a favourite foal of his. According to Anna Seward again: 'He was not a good horseman. The animal disliking his new situation, heeded not the soothing voice to which he had been accustomed. He plunged, threw his master, and then, with his heels, struck him on the head an *instantly* fatal blow.'

'Practical education'

We shall not imitate the invidious example of some authors, who think it necessary to destroy the edifices of others, in order to clear the way for their own.

These words from the preface to Practical Education by Maria and R. L. Edgeworth set the tone of enlightened and perceptive commonsense which distinguishes the work. Published in 1798, the book was intended as a blueprint for a scheme of education based upon the theories and experience of the Edgeworth family and their circle. The curriculum which it recommends is a wide one, ranging from clay modelling to the use of microscopes; but it is in its evaluation of play and its analysis of the role of the teacher that Practical Education is most forward-looking, providing in this respect a sharp sense of déjà vu for readers more familiar with present-day books on the subject:

When a pedantic schoolmaster sees a boy eagerly watching a paper kite, he observes, 'What a pity it is that children cannot be made to mind their grammar as well as their kites!' and he adds perhaps some peevish ejaculation on the natural idleness of boys, and that pernicious love of play against which he is doomed to wage perpetual war. A man of sense will see the same sight with a different eye; in this pernicious love of play he will discern the symptoms of a love of science, and, instead of deploring the natural idleness of children, he will admire the activity which they display in the pursuit of knowledge. He will feel that it is his business to direct this activity, to furnish his pupil with materials for fresh combinations, to put him, or to let him put himself, in situations where he can make useful observations, and

acquire that experience which cannot be bought, and which no masters can communicate.
(M. and R. L. Edgeworth, Practical Education, 1798, Volume I, pp. 18-19)

. . .

S . . ., a little boy of nine years old, was standing without any book in his hand, and seemingly idle; he was amusing himself with looking at what he called a rainbow upon the floor: he begged his sister M . . . to look at it; then he said he wondered what could make it; how it came there. The sun shone bright through the window; the boy moved several things in the room, so as to place them sometimes between the light and the colours which he saw upon the floor, and sometimes in a corner of the room where the sun did not shine. As he moved the things he said, 'This is not it'; 'Nor this'; 'This hasn't any thing to do with it'. At last he found, that when he moved a tumbler of water out of the place where it stood, his rainbow vanished. Some violets were in the tumbler; S . . . thought they might be the cause of the colours which he saw upon the floor, or, as he expressed it, 'Perhaps these may be the thing'. He took the violets out of the water; the colours remained upon the floor. He then thought that 'it might be the water'. He emptied the glass; the colours remained, but they were fainter. S . . . immediately observed, that it was the water and glass together that made the rainbow. 'But,' said he, 'there is no glass in the sky, yet there is a rainbow, so that I think the water alone would do, if we could but hold it together without the glass. Oh I know how I can manage.' He poured the water slowly out of the tumbler into a bason, which he placed where the sun shone, and he saw the colours on the floor twinkling behind the water as it fell: this delighted him much . . .

A rigid preceptor, who thinks that every boy must be idle who has not a Latin book constantly in his hand, would perhaps have reprimanded S . . . for wasting his time *at play*, and would have summoned him from his rainbow to his *talk*; . . .
(M. and R. L. Edgeworth, Practical Education, 1798, Volume I, pp. 55-56)

Robert Owen and the school at New Lanark

Finally, Robert Owen, whose many-sided career as a social reformer gives him an importance which transcends his work in schools. This, and the slightly later date of his work in education, tend to set him apart from the progressive educationalists so far considered; he also owed less to Rousseau and more to Helvétius than they seem to have done.[7] In 1800 he became partner and manager at the New Lanark Cotton Mills in Scotland. There, during the next quarter of a century, he was instrumental in creating a model industrial community which, together with his writings, was soon to establish him as a figure of international reputation. Deeply convinced of the importance of education in shaping a new and better society, he was able in 1816 to open his Institution for the Formation of Character; the school catered for children from the ages of about two up to eleven or twelve during the day and was open in the evening for young people. Owen himself was especially concerned with the work of the children under six in the infant school and selected its first teachers, James Buchanan ('a poor simple-hearted weaver') and Molly Young, a mill girl of about seventeen. In Owen's own words,

The children were trained and educated without punishment or any fear of it, and were while in school by far the happiest human beings I have ever seen.

The infants and young children, besides being instructed by sensible signs, – the things themselves, or models or paintings, – and by familiar conversation, were from two years and upwards daily taught dancing and singing, and the parents were encouraged to come and see their children at any of their lessons or physical exercises. *(The Life of Robert Owen, by himself, 1857, in Robert Owen on Education, ed. Harold Silver, 1969, p. 62)*

A detailed account of the school at New Lanark was published in 1824 by Owen's eldest son, Robert Dale Owen. Part of his description of the children is given here:

The general appearance of the children is to a stranger very striking. The leading character of their countenances is a mixed look of openness, confidence and intelligence, such as is scarcely to be met with among children in their situation. Their animal spirits are always excellent. Their manners and deportment towards their teachers and towards strangers, are fearless and unrestrained, yet neither forward, nor disrespectful . . .

The individual literary acquirements of the greater proportion of the older classes, are such as perhaps no body of children of the same age, in any situation, have had an opportunity of attaining. The writer of the present article has had frequent opportunities of examing them individually; and he has no hesitation in saying, that their knowledge on some of the subjects, which have been mentioned, as forming part of their instruction, is superior to his own.

A sufficient degree of friendly emulation is excited amongst them, without any artificial stimulus; but it is an emulation, which induces them to prefer going forward with their companions, to leaving them behind. Their own improvement is not their only source of enjoyment. That of their companions they appear to witness with pleasure, unmixed with any envious feeling whatever; and to be eager to afford them any assistance they may require. *(Robert Dale Owen, An Outline of the System of Education at New Lanark, 1824, in Robert Owen on Education, ed. Harold Silver, 1969, p. 164)*

Notes

1   See Robert Bell, *The Life of the Rt. Hon. George Canning*, 1846, p. 218.

2   William Roberts, *Memoirs of the Life and Correspondence of Mrs. Hannah More*, 1836 ed., Vol. II, p. 82.

3   In justice to Hannah More it must be pointed out that she was undoubtedly proud when her first scholar, John Hill, became a teacher and then a sergeant-major in the marines.

4   Richard Dawes, *Suggestive Hints towards Improved Secular Instruction, etc.*, 3rd ed., 1849, p. 152.

5   An interesting modern interpretation of the National Society's role in delaying the development of a state system of education can be found in J. Hurt, *Education in Evolution*, 1971, p. 92.

6   Plowden Report, paragraph 739.

7   For an analysis of Robert Owen's educational thought, see the introduction by Harold Silver to *Robert Owen on Education*, 1969, and W. A. C. Stewart and W. P. McCann, *The Educational Innovators*, 1967, Vol. I., pp. 53-74.

CHAPTER 2

THE SOCIETIES AND THEIR SCHOOLS
(ABOUT 1800-1861)

The monitorial schools

By the end of the eighteenth century, influential elements in both the Anglican and the nonconformist establishments had acknowledged the need to provide some form of systematic and simplified instruction for the children of the labouring classes. Decisive action, however, was being impeded by a chronic lack of resources. The Sunday Schools had made, and continued to make, a notable contribution to popular education: 'During the first half of the nineteenth century,' a recent writer on the subject has claimed, 'predominantly working-class students were taught primarily by working-class teachers in schools largely financed, and sometimes also run, by working-class men and women.'[1]

Long before educational committees of the Privy Council and British and Foreign Societies were heard of . . . the Sunday-schools were sedulously at work, impregnating the people with the rudiments of an education which, though always rude and often narrow and fanatical in its teachings, was yet preserving a glow of moral and religious sentiment, and keeping alive a degree of popular intelligence which otherwise would assuredly have perished in the rush and clatter with which a vast manufacturing population came surging up upon the land.
(Morning Chronicle (15.11.1849), Letter IX, col. 1, quoted in T. W. Laqueur, Religion and Respectability, 1976, p. 123)

But Sunday Schools alone could not provide an adequate substitute for full-time education; some other, more effective, means would have to be found.

By 1800 the secularizing doctrines of the French Revolution in continental Europe had tended to transfer responsibility for education from church to state. But the long war with France and her allies made such a step unthinkable to many in England. Uncompromising on this point at the beginning of the period, powerful elements of ecclesiastical opinion were to become increasingly intransigent as the Tractarian Movement got under way; state support for education, even when eventually offered, was regarded with suspicion and disfavour by certain sections of the Church of England. This belief in the church's ultimate and absolute responsibility for education was firmly buttressed by tradition. Bishops were issuing licences to teach even after the turn of the century. But it was severely undermined by the difficulty experienced in raising funds to gratify even the most unexacting aims: 'a Barn furnishes no bad model, and a good one may be easily converted into a School', wistfully observed the sixth report of the National Society.

In these circumstances it is hardly surprising that the monitorial system was uncritically adopted, offering as it did great economy in staffing, equipment and accommodation. Andrew Bell, an Anglican clergyman, and Joseph Lancaster, a Quaker, were its two most celebrated advocates; between them they evolved a programme of teaching which seemed tailored to contemporary conditions. From their work grew the two religious societies which, at least up to 1870, were to dominate the elementary school scene: the nonsectarian British and Foreign and the Anglican National Society.

Joseph Lancaster and the British and Foreign School Society

Joseph Lancaster confidently claimed that '. . . a boy who can read, can teach, ALTHOUGH HE KNOWS NOTHING ABOUT IT.'[2] His own skill as a teacher lent credibility to the regimented syllabus which he pursued at his famous school in the Borough Road and earned him the patronage of king and aristocracy. But the reckless dedication which enabled him to elevate an inherently arid method of instruction to a tolerable, even enjoyable one, was eventually to lose him control of the school. William Allen, the secretary of the British and Foreign Society, explained the situation as he saw it in 1816:

It appeared that as far back as the year 1798, Joseph Lancaster taught a few poor children in the Borough Road; himself and parents were in low circumstances, but he seemed to be actuated by a benevolent disposition, and to possess great talents for the education of youth; he was countenanced and supported by a few benevolent individuals, and as the subscriptions were limited to a very small sum, he was obliged to devise the most economical plans. By a series of improvements, he at length demonstrated the possibility of instructing even a thousand children (if so many could be collected together in one room) by a single master; he divided his school into eight classes, each of which was managed by a monitor, whose duties were exactly prescribed to him, and who was made responsible for the good order of his class; over these, a monitor-general was placed, who regulated the business of the whole school, under the immediate direction of the master. Upon Lancaster's plan, a single book was found sufficient for a whole school, the different sheets being put upon pasteboard, and hung upon the walls of the school. He avoided the expense of pens and paper in the first stages of education, by substituting slates; he also introduced the plan of teaching the younger children to form the letters in sand, which plan was borrowed, I believe, from Dr. Bell, who had imported it from India; he contrived to teach writing and spelling at the same time, and he made a single spelling-book serve for a whole school, however large. He taught arithmetic from lessons which he had constructed for the purpose, whereby the monitor might correctly teach the principles of it, even if he were not fully acquainted with them himself; in this case also, one book of arithmetic served for the whole school. So that the expense of teaching on this plan, consists in the salary of the master or mistress, the rent of the school-room, and from ten to twenty pounds per annum, according to the size of the school, for the necessary apparatus.
(Parl. Papers, 1816, Vol. IV, Minutes of Evidence on Education of Lower Orders of the Metropolis, p. 115)

Inflexibility was the bane of the monitorial system. With teachers whose formal training, if they had been lucky, consisted of a three month course at the Borough Road school, and with monitors whose knowledge hardly transcended the contents of the lesson which they were currently teaching,[3] it is not surprising that a slavish conformity to the book was explicitly required:

The next is the simple Addition class. . . . In the first place, when his class are seated, the monitor takes the book of sums – suppose the first sum is as follows:

(No. 1)   lbs.
             27935
              3963
              8679
             14327
             ─────
             54904

He repeats audibly the figures 27,935, and each boy in the class writes them; they are then inspected, and if done correct, he dictates the figures, 3,963, which are written and inspected in like manner: and thus he proceeds till every boy in the class has the sum finished on his slate. He then takes the key, and reads as follows:

FIRST COLUMN. 7 and 9 are 16, and 3 are 19, and 5 are 24: set down 4 under the 7, and carry 2 to the next.

This is written by every boy in the class, inspected as before, and then he proceeds.

. . .

The whole of a sum is written in this manner, by each boy in the class: it is afterwards inspected by the monitor, and frequently by the master; . . . When a certain quota of sums are done, the class begins anew: and thus repetitions succeed each other, till practice secures improvement, and removes boys individually into other classes and superior rules, when each boy has a suitable prize, which our established plan appropriates to the occasion.

(J. Lancaster, The British System of Education, etc., 2nd ed., 1810, pp. 19-21)

With a staff-pupil ratio of about 1:500 discipline was inevitably a problem. Lancaster faced up to it with characteristic candour:

Instruments and Modes of Punishments

On a *repeated* or *frequent offence,* after *admonition* has failed, the lad to whom an offender presents the card, places a wooden log round his neck, which serves as a pillory, and with this he is sent to his seat. This log may weigh from four to six pounds, some more and some less. The neck is *not pinched* or *closely confined*—it is chiefly burthensome by the manner in which it incumbers the neck, when the delinquent turns to the right or left. While it rests on his shoulders, the equilibrium is preserved; but on the least motion one way or the other, it is lost, and the log operates as a dead weight. Thus he is *confined* to *sit* in his *proper position*, and go on with his work.

. . .

The Basket

Occasionally boys are put in a sack, or in a basket, suspended to the roof of the school, in sight of all the pupils, who frequently smile at the birds in the cage. This punishment is one of the most terrible that can be inflicted on boys of sense and abilities. Above all, it is dreaded by the monitors; the name of it is sufficient, and therefore it is but seldom resorted to on their account.

. . .

Confinement after School Hours
Few punishments are so effectual as confinement after school hours. It is, however, attended with one unpleasant circumstance. In order to confine the bad boys in the school-room after school-hours, it is often needful that the master, or some proper substitute for him, should confine himself in school, to keep them in order. This inconvenience may be avoided by tying them to the desks, or putting them in logs, etc. in such a manner that they cannot loose themselves.
(J. Lancaster, The British System of Education, etc., 2nd ed., 1810, pp. 34-35 passim)

It would be unfair to leave Lancaster on this note. As Francis Adams, writing in 1882 of the contribution which he and Bell had made to education, pointed out:

The true honour which attaches to Lancaster's name is not the doubtful one of inventing the Monitorial system, but that he conceived and tried to realise the idea that all children should be taught the elements of knowledge. The British and Foreign School Society was formed to continue his work, and indirectly he called the National Society into existence, as a rival institution.
(Francis Adams, History of the Elementary School Contest in England, 1882, p. 51)

Andrew Bell and the National Society
Francis Adams next considered the career of Dr. Andrew Bell, whom the Church of England advanced for the dubious distinction of founding the monitorial system of teaching:

. . . In India he had honorary charge of the Asylum for Children, at Madras, a position in which he made the important discovery that children can teach each other. In one of his letters home he speaks of the 'pleasing sight of a youth of eleven years of age, with his little assistants under him, teaching upwards of fifty boys'. In this school arrangement, nearly every boy was a master. 'He teaches one boy, while another boy teaches him.'

On his return to England Dr. Bell published an account of his experiences. On his own showing, his aims, as an educationist, were not extensive. 'It is not proposed,' he wrote, 'that the children of the poor should be educated in an expensive manner, or even taught to write and cipher.' 'It may suffice to teach the generality on an economical plan, to read their Bible and understand the doctrines of our holy religion.' To this curriculum he added manual labour and the useful arts. The schools he proposed to found were to be schools of industry. He had been appointed on coming home to the rectory of Swanage, where he opened schools on his own model, and it was here that he was visited by Lancaster. His pamphlet on education attracted little attention until it was made known by Lancaster's more widely circulated writings. Mrs. Trimmer, the editor of the *School Guardian,* also took pains to bring Dr. Bell prominently before the public. This was a lady of great and orthodox piety, who, as a Churchwoman, was very much alarmed at the growing influence and pretensions of Lancaster. She had compiled many books 'dear to mothers and aunts' for the Christian Knowledge Society, and had earned from the *Edinburgh Review* the title of 'voluminous female'. Sydney Smith had described her as 'a lady of respectable opinions, and very moderate talents, defending what is right

without judgment, and believing what is holy without charity'. *(Edinburgh Review,* 1806). In her eyes Lancaster was the 'Goliath of Schismatics', and she was anxious that he should have a check.
(Francis Adams, History of the Elementary School Contest in England, 1882, pp. 56-57)

The 'beautiful and efficient simplicity'[4] of the monitorial system, then, earned it the approval and protection of the rival religious societies. By 1816 there were over 274 British and Foreign Society schools; although the education which they were providing had not proved as cheap as Lancaster's sanguine estimates, a large school of 500 could nevertheless operate at a cost of twelve shillings per child a year.[5] The National Society, with the advantage of a unified church structure upon which to base its organization, already had about 710 schools; in some parts of the country at least, it was to develop a significantly more efficient system of finance, teacher training, and inspection than its rival.[6]

Robert Owen, with characteristic perception, already had grave misgivings about the monitorial system. He told Brougham's Select Committee:[7]

I consider the facility with which children acquire the common rudiments of learning, an unfortunate result of the new system . . .

I have found the children have derived very little benefit from being rapidly instructed in reading and writing, particularly when no attention has been given on the part of the superintendent to form their dispositions and their habits.

But, on his own admission, the improvements which he felt necessary in order to make the system acceptable for use in his school at New Lanark pushed up the expense for each child to as much as £1.

Time appeared to do little to moderate the defects of monitorial teaching, which indeed occasionally became stylized to an almost grotesque degree, as the following extracts from one inspector's report, printed in the *Minutes* of 1844 show:

Of the mechanical character of such teaching the following may serve as an illustration. On entering a large school, I requested that the instruction of the children might go on, according to its accustomed course – that I might judge of the means daily called into operation before I proceeded to inquire into the results. Astonished to find that some time elapsed before the machinery could be put in motion, I proceeded to inquire into the cause, and found that the monitors were in the act of placing the finger of each individual boy upon the first word of the lesson to be read. This accomplished, and the monitor having read one word of the lesson, and the boys simultaneously after him; each boy advanced his finger one word, and the process was repeated.
(Minutes of the Committee of Council on Education, 1844, Vol. II, p. 511, note)

I have visited schools in which a system of signals, communicated by the aid of a semaphore fixed to the master's desk, was substituted for the word of command.

The precision with which the boys interpreted and obeyed the instructions thus telegraphed to them was an interesting spectacle. Any person who might have been induced from it to form a favourable opinion of the efficiency of the instruction, would have been, I fear, in error.
(Minutes of the Committee of Council on Education, 1844, Volume II, p. 512, note)

A more explicit account of the educational limitations of the monitorial system was given by a witness before the Select Committee on Education of the Poorer Classes in 1838:

I will relate a circumstance which took place only a few days ago: A boy had been brought up in a school of this description, where monitors were employed; I asked him if he could read, to which he replied in the affirmative. I said, 'What can you read?' 'Such as God is love, and that like.' I said, 'How did you learn?' 'The monitor taught me.' 'What is God?' 'I do not know.' 'Who is he?' 'I do not know.' 'Where is he?' He looked at me; I said, 'Do you know where God is; did you ever see him?' 'No.' 'But can you tell me where he is?' 'At church.' 'Well, who is he like?' He looked up at me, and said, 'Like the parson.'
(Parl. Papers, 1837-1838, Vol. VII, Minutes of Evidence taken before the Select Committee on Education of the Poorer Classes in England and Wales, p. 123)

By the early 1840s Kay Shuttleworth, the secretary to the new Committee of Council on Education, was deeply embattled with the supporters of the monitorial system. The enraged reaction of the British and Foreign Society to a scathing report on their London schools by one of his first inspectors, Seymour Tremenheere, had led to the latter's resignation; when Kay Shuttleworth wrote the passage below, his pupil teachers were rapidly superseding monitors, but the bitterness obviously remained. The monitorial system, in his opinion, had

. . . not only utterly failed, but for the time ruined the confidence of the poor in elementary schools – exhausted the charity of the middle classes – and even dragged into the mire of its own dishonour, the public estimate of what was practicable and desirable in the education of the poor. It was, moreover, a consequence of the religious origin of Elementary Education, that the Day School should be little more than a less efficient edition of the Sunday School. . . . The religious formularies and the Bible itself, suffered therefore a painful desecration, as the hornbooks of ignorant scholars, in charge of almost as ignorant teachers, who were for the most part under twelve or thirteen years of age.
(Sir James Kay Shuttleworth, Public Education, etc., 1853, pp. 57-58)

The elementary schools of the mid-nineteenth century

Government inspection from 1840 onwards brought about an inevitable increase in the output of descriptive material dealing with elementary education. Seymour Tremenheere was one of the first two inspectors appointed (the other was the Rev. John Allen). His career was, in fact, to be a short one. The report which he submitted on the state of the British and Foreign Society's schools in the London area appeared in the *Minutes* of

1842-1843, and so strong was the indignation which it aroused that Tremenheere himself subsequently resigned and the Committee of Council was compelled to extend to the nonconformists the privileges which it had conceded to the Anglicans by the 'Concordat' of 1840. Tremenheere's criticisms had centred upon what he considered to be the inadequacy of school buildings and equipment together with the ineffectiveness of the instruction (generally based upon the monitorial system). Acute attendance problems served to aggravate these difficulties:[8]

Of 17 schools, in which the point could be accurately ascertained from their registers,

In 7 the total number had changed once in about   1 year
<pre>
  3   ,,   ,,   ,,   ,,   10 months
  1   ,,   ,,   ,,   ,,   9 months
  1   ,,   ,,   ,,   ,,   8 months
  2   ,,   ,,   ,,   ,,   6 months
  2   ,,   ,,   ,,   ,,   4 months
  1   ,,   ,,   ,,   ,,   3 months
 ───
 17
</pre>

(Minutes of the Committee of Council on Education, 1842-1843, p. 463)

Accommodation left a great deal to be desired:

The depressing effect of want of proper light and ventilation, both upon masters and children, must be sensibly felt in at least 17 out of the 35 boys' schools now under consideration; nine of these are under chapels, consequently below the level of the street, the only access to them being by means of the steps leading into a narrow area at the basement. In two of these localities the circulation of air and the access of light had been improved by the removal of a few boards of the floor of the chapel above.
(Minutes of the Committee of Council on Education, 1842-1843, p. 464)

It is interesting to note that the contention that the younger children – who of course were in the majority – were relatively neglected appears in Tremenheere's report. This was to be one of the ostensible reasons for the introduction of payment by results in 1863. Included also is the standard criticism of teaching under the monitorial system: lack of real comprehension on the part of pupils and monitors alike.

As regards their progress, the children of these schools may be classed in two divisions, which may be designated as upper and lower. The upper receives the greater share of the personal instruction of the master, the lower being chiefly intrusted to the monitors. The lower consists in general of about two-thirds of the whole, and comprises all ages, from four to five to about ten and eleven; these are taught to spell and read, to write and cipher. The rows of unconnected words upon the spelling-boards are supposed to be explained and illustrated by the monitors, aided sometimes by a list of analogous and explanatory sentences, printed, or written out by the master. It did not seem that a process, naturally irksome to a child's mind, was much facilitated by this method. Many of the words were quite alien to

the experience of children, and their attention seemed very soon fatigued by being called rapidly from one subject to another, without time to rest upon or follow out any idea suggested to them. Some very good-natured attempts to make spelling pleasant, by means of chanting, seemed to lead more directly to rote-like repetitions. The reading in the lower divisions consists generally of Scripture extracts, placed before the children, not with reference to any connected train of historical instruction, but according to the number of syllables composing the words of the sentence. I observed among them several instances of figurative language, together with words and forms of expression very difficult for a child to follow. I very rarely found that the monitors, when appealed to, could explain even the simpler expressions. The very slight degree of comprehension of meaning usually exhibited in these lower divisions, even by children who could pronounce the words fluently, seemed to indicate a habit of mere mechanical reading, without effort to associate the sense.
(Minutes of the Committee of Council on Education, 1842-1843, pp. 469-470)

As the number of inspectors and grants increased, more reports came in. For example, Mr. Bellairs reported on punishment from the Western District:

In many schools, from the course generally adopted, one would imagine that nothing but severity could induce children to do what is right, or that the master really found pleasure in punishing his scholars. On some occasions, I have observed him walking about the room, cane in hand, brandishing it over the heads of the children, who, trembling under the anticipated stroke, have lost all sense of the lesson in which they were engaged, and with eyes wandering from their book to the avenging rod, have brought upon themselves, as they caught the master's eye, the blow. At other times, I have witnessed a master step into a class where was some little inattention or disturbance, and deal out boxes on the ear, blows on the head, and cuffs on the back, promiscuously on all within his reach, and then, as though he had done all that duty required him, return to his seat.
(Minutes of the Committee of Council on Education, 1844, Vol. II, p. 234)

And Mr. Watkins expatiated from the north on such contrasting themes as parental indifference, regional variations in grubbiness and spontaneity, the condition of factory workers' children and the competence of their teachers:

We blame masters, and we blame monitors, and we punish children: we find fault with methods and systems, and rooms and situations; but we often leave untouched the tap-root of all the evil – the parent. . . . You find a group of children in the street playing at marbles, it may be, during school-hours. 'Why are you not at school to-day?' – 'Mother sent me for a bit of coal, Sir'; or, 'Mother's gone out, and I stayed to watch baby'; or 'Mother said I wo'rnt to go this morning'; or 'Please, Sir, mother wanted me'. It really seems that there is no errand so short nor business so trifling as not, in the mother's eyes, to be more important than for her child to be late or to be absent from school.
(Minutes of the Committee of Council on Education, 1884, Vol. II, p. 274)

. . .

Again, the characteristics of the Northumbrian schools are – intellectual activity, deficiency of discipline, and abundance of dirt. It is curious in this latter respect to compare the state of the schools at Leeds with those at Newcastle. At one school in the North, there were literally furrows of dust on the floor, in which the naked feet of the children seemed delighted to *burrow*. I pointed it out to the master, who assured me that the school was carefully swept twice a-week, and that it had undergone this process only two evenings before. In this school the intelligence and delight of the children in their lessons were very striking; but they had little or no discipline. Whilst in Yorkshire, in schools of the same class, where, according to the suspended notice, there was 'a place for everything, and everything in its place; a time for everything, and everything at its time' perfect order and silence prevailed; but it was difficult to obtain an answer from the children – not because they were more ignorant, but because they were less communicative than their more Northern contemporaries.

(Minutes of the Committee of Council on Education, 1844, Vol. II, pp. 249-250)

It may be allowed me to add here, that through all the manufacturing district I have looked anxiously for the sickly and starved and stunted children, which are so often described as the offspring of its inhabitants. I can thankfully say, that, with the exception of those children who came straight from the mill to the school, weary with their work, and, perhaps, in some cases dejected by its circumstances, I have looked in vain. They are not to be found in any number worthy of mention in our schools.

At Salford (St. Bartholomew's) infant-school – in an unpaved, and, I think, undrained, district, inhabited solely by operatives – I could not help remarking to the School Committee on the healthy looks and chubby cheeks of the little ones collected there, almost all of whom were the children of very poor parents. I observed the same satisfactory condition in the excellent infant-school at Middleton, near Manchester.

(Minutes of the Committee of Council on Education, 1844, Vol. II, p. 250)

At one school, in Yorkshire, I found that arithmetic was not taught. I asked the reason; 'Because I know nothing about it,' was the honest reply. At another, in Lancashire, where the children were very ignorant, and crowded together in classes made like solid sheep-pens, I begged the master to put some questions to them, as I could get no answer. He took a book out of a corner-cupboard (where it had not seen the light for many a day) and began: 'Who wrote the Bible?' and then qualified this strange question, 'that is, the greatest part of it?' 'Moses,' was the answer given, and allowed. 'Who collected the Scriptures into books?' Answer, 'Gomorrah!' The children had rarely been questioned before, and the mere form of a question was a difficulty to them. The greater part of them were poor mill children, 'short timers', – and a wilder set I have rarely seen.

(Minutes of the Committee of Council on Education, 1844, Vol. II, p. 289)

At the instance of Parliament the schools of Wales were subjected to a special enquiry in 1846-1847. The report of Ralph Lingen, Jelinger Symons, and Henry Vaughan Johnson on Welsh education, culture, and morals sometimes has a tone of superficiality and arrogance about it which contrasts sharply with the account of the country written a little later by George Borrow. The basic prejudices of the commissioners can perhaps be gauged from their comments upon the Welsh language:

The Welsh language is a vast drawback to Wales, and a manifold barrier to the moral progress and commercial prosperity of the people. It is not easy to over-estimate its

evil effects. . . . It dissevers the people from intercourse which would greatly advance their civilisation, and bars the access of improving knowledge to their minds. As a proof of this, there is no Welsh literature worthy of the name . . .
(Reports of the Commissioners of Inquiry into the State of Education in Wales, 1847, Part II, p. 66)

On the whole they and their assistants appear to have taken a deprecatory view of Welsh culture generally; certainly they seemed assiduous in singling out notable examples of squalor and depravity:

I shall never forget the hot, sickening smell, which struck me on opening the door of that low dark room, in which 30 girls and 20 boys were huddled together. It more nearly resembled the smell of the engine on board a steamer. Everything in the room . . . was hidden under and overlaid with children. One little creature, apparently about three years old, was placed in a child's chair in the midst, with its head back, fast asleep. I can conceive nothing more pernicious for a child to breathe than such a filthy atmosphere. The instruction consisted of the merest elements, and, as might be supposed, the children appeared riotous and ill-disciplined whenever the mistress's eye was removed. No school-books were kept . . .
(Reports of the Commissioners of Inquiry into the State of Education in Wales, 1847, Part I, p. 238)

Even when praise was given, it seldom went unmodified. The British and Foreign School at Ruthin (which 'in respect of the method of instruction, and the attainments of the scholars, is one of the best in North Wales') was described thus:

The master has inspired his pupils with a desire for knowledge, but has neglected to teach them proper discipline and good manners. When any movement was required, his pupils rushed pell-mell to their places, thwarting and tripping each other; then mounted the desks and sat upon them with their caps on, swinging their legs; some peeling sticks, others caning those near them with the master's cane, the rest struggling together, talking, or playing tricks with anything that happened to be at hand . . .
(Reports of the Commissioners of Inquiry into the State of Education in Wales, 1847, Part III, p. 25)

But it was the inexcusably lax (as it seemed to them) social and moral standards tolerated by the Welsh that really scandalized the Victorian susceptibilities of the commissioners. They cited the 'zealous clergyman of Builth' who

. . . was obliged to send for a constable to remove a drunken fiddler in the street, and he proved to be the schoolmaster of Aberedw, and some of the bystanders blamed the constable for doing it.

and made repeated allusion to the Celtic custom of 'bundling' – that is, courting in bed:

The system of bundling, or, at any rate, something analogous to it prevails extensively. The unmarried men-servants in the farms range the country at night, and it is a known and tolerated practice that they are admitted by the women-servants at the houses to which they come. I heard the most revolting anecdotes of the gross and almost bestial indelicacy with which sexual intercourse takes place on these occasions,

wrote one witness, while another despairingly complained that,

In England farmers' daughters are respectable; in Wales they are in the constant habit of being courted in bed. In the case of domestic servants the vice is universal. I have had the greatest difficulty in keeping my own servants from practising it. It became necessary to secure their chamber windows with bars to prevent them from admitting men. I am told by my parishioners that unless I allow the practice I shall very soon have no servants at all, and that it will be impossible to get any.
(Reports of the Commissioners of Inquiry into the State of Education in Wales, 1847, Part II, p. 32; Part I, p. 21; Part III, pp. 67-68)

The Newcastle Report

In 1858 the government appointed a commission under the Duke of Newcastle to 'inquire into the present state of Popular Education in England' and to recommend any changes it considered desirable 'for the extension of sound and cheap elementary instruction'. The Newcastle Commission's Report was fairly critical of the elementary schools though not perhaps so hostile as is sometimes implied. It did, however, repeatedly emphasize its conclusion that their overriding weakness lay in the relatively low standard of attainment in the younger classes:

It appears that even in the best schools, only about one-fourth of the boys attain the highest class, and are considered by the Inspectors to be 'successfully educated'.

The evidence indicates that there is a tendency in school-teachers to neglect both the more elementary subjects and the younger scholars, and these last appear to be capable of receiving a far better teaching in reading, writing, and arithmetic, than has hitherto been given to them.

As illustration of these inadequate standards the commissioners quoted the following answer (from a child 'of average intelligence of 11 years of age') to the catechismal question 'What is thy duty towards God?':

My duty toads God is to bleed in him, to fering and to loaf withold your arts, withold my mine, withold my sold, and with my sernth, to whirchp and to give thinks, to put my old trast in him, to call upon him, to onner his old name and his world, and to save him truly all the days of my life's end.

It is perhaps easier to understand than to condone the selection of such examples in the report. The assessments made by the HMI's of the time give a considerably more encouraging picture – a mere 0.7% of the 50,000 or so recorded in 1859-1860 were classified as bad.[9] Illiteracy, one recent writer claims, had ceased to be a problem years before 1870.[10] But the Newcastle commissioners, apparently satisfied that teachers too often exhibited unacceptable laxity of standards, duly recorded that

The children do not generally obtain the mastery over elementary subjects which the school ought to give. They neither read well nor write well. They work sums, but they learn their arithmetic in such a way as to be of little practical use in common life. Their religious instruction is unintelligent, and to a great extent confined to exercises of merely verbal memory.
(The Newcastle Report on the Present State of Popular Education in England, 1861, pp. 273, 256, and 154)

In their conclusion to the report's chapter on inspected and assisted schools, they mitigated their earlier strictures. The schools of the societies had, they conceded, accomplished much; what was needed was an extension of the benefits of their achievement to the younger pupils:

Even as to mere literary instruction, it would be a mistake to suppose that the existing system has failed because it has hitherto educated successfully only one-fourth of the pupils. The effort has been directed towards establishing a good type of education; towards the quality of the teaching more than to the number of the taught. In this point is has succeeded. In good schools the senior classes have turned out scholars really well taught; the pupil-teachers have been brought up in them, and even where the definite results in the junior classes might appear small in an examination, they have probably affected the whole school morally and intellectually. We think, however, that the time is come when a further attempt should be made to influence the instruction of the large body of inferior schools and of inferior pupils who have hitherto been little affected.
(The Newcastle Report on the Present State of Popular Educaton in England, 1861, p. 274)

Notes

1   T. W. Laqueur, *Religion and Respectability*, 1976, p. 94.

2   J. Lancaster, *The British System of Education, etc.*, 2nd ed., 1810, p. 23.

3   Monitors were usually taken from one class ahead. See J. Lancaster, op. cit., p. 43.

4   It is so described in the National Society's Report of 1814, p. 14.

5   Parl. Papers, 1816, Vol. IV, *Minutes of Evidence on Education of Lower Orders of the Metropolis*, pp. 28, 118, and 267.

6   See, for example, M. Sanderson in *Local Studies and the History of Education*, ed. T. G. Cook, 1972, pp. 29-30.

7   Parl. Papers, 1816, Vol. IV, *Minutes of Evidence on Education of Lower Orders of the Metropolis*, pp. 239-240.

8   The seriousness of the attendance problem appears to have varied considerably from school to school. Thus in 1840 the treasurer of the Kennington National Schools could write that 'The average weekly attendance of the children . . . is very satisfactory.' See P. and H. Silver *The Education of the Poor*, 1974, pp. 42-43; this work gives a detailed account of the history of a single school (St. Mark's voluntary aided primary school) in Kennington, London, from the mid-1820s onwards.

9   J. Hurt, *Education in Evolution*, 1971, pp. 64-65.

10   J. M. Goldstrom in *Popular Education and Socialization in the Nineteenth Century*, ed. by P. McCann, 1977, p. 140. Sir John Gorst (vice president of the Committee of Council) took a more reserved view. Speaking in the House of Commons about rural education in March, 1896, he claimed that of a number of youths tested by one

Wyckham Tozer (who ran a labour bureau in Ipswich) 'one-fourth could write fairly, one quarter could write moderately, and quite one-half could only write in a most disgraceful manner, both as to penmanship and spelling.' The question of nineteenth-century literacy is considered at some length in E. G. West, *Education and the Industrial Revolution*, 1975.

CHAPTER 3

TEACHING UNDER THE REVISED CODE: ELEMENTARY SCHOOL LIFE AND PROBLEMS IN THE LATER NINETEENTH CENTURY

Here lies the body of Robert Lowe,
Where he has gone to I don't know.
If he has gone to the realms above,
That's an end to peace and love.
If he has sought a lower level,
God have mercy on the Devil.[1]

Robert Lowe, it seems, inspired mixed feelings among his contemporaries no less than among subsequent educational historians. Endowed with a sharp mind and caustic wit, permanently afflicted with the irritating disability of albinism,[2] he was seldom disposed to suffer fools, or those he judged so, gladly. He was appointed vice-president of the Committee of Council in 1859; with R. R. W. Lingen he was largely responsible for transmuting the Newcastle Commission's recommendations of 1861 into the following year's Revised Code. The latter is popularly identified with the device of Payment by Results; this was the system by which central government aid was allocated direct to the managers of individual schools on the basis of an annual computation carried out on the spot by an H.M.I. Centred originally upon attendance and an examination of the three Rs, it lasted until the 1890s when it was phased out during the secretaryship of George Kekewich, who was later to stigmatize it, rather too emphatically perhaps, as 'that nefarious instrument for the stifling of education, which was apparently designed to torture the teachers and to minimise the instruction and intelligence of the children'. This verdict has tended to be endorsed by many twentieth-century commentators, though recent criticisms of attainment levels in schools and the movement towards a 'core curriculum' have induced some educationalists to modify their views: in 1971 the *Times Educational Supplement* actually featured an article entitled 'A place for payment by results'. Writing as early as 1937, however, G. A. N. Lowndes surmised that Lowe 'by this early measure of decentralisation saved English education once and for all from the pitfalls which have ensnared the systems of so many other countries' and further reassessments of the importance and implications of the Revised Code have recently been made by John Hurt and D. W. Sylvester.[3]

There was more to the Revised Code than Payment by Results, for it also constituted, as Lowndes pointed out, a rejection by the Committee of Council of the policy of creeping centralization which its first secretary, James Kay Shuttleworth, had initiated. The complicated and administratively untidy system of grants (for pupil teachers, certificated teachers, apparatus and so on) which had interposed a judiciously paternal committee between teacher and managers was swept away. No doubt this was done to the intense chagrin of Kay Shuttleworth himself, who had understandably repudiated this principle, though himself proposing that of payment by inspection, when giving evidence to the Duke of Newcastle.[4]

Robert Lowe, however, remained impervious to the adverse criticism which rained upon the Revised Code, maintaining later that the

... main object which I had in view, in the changes which I proposed on the part of the Government in the education system, was to benefit the working classes. Under the old system the poor children were not properly taught. The upper children, the children of richer parents, were examined, and the money was paid; but the lower and poorer children were neglected. The upper children had generally had some education at home; but the poor children had received no education at home, and they were not done justice to in the schools. The object of the Revised Code was to insure that education should be given to the poor just as much as to the rich.
(J. F. Hogan, Robert Lowe, Viscount Sherbrooke, 1893, p. 314)

Again, in a less idealistic vein, he wrote to Lingen:

As I understand the case, you and I viewed the three Rs not only or primarily as the exact amount of instruction which ought to be given, but as an amount of knowledge which could be ascertained thoroughly by examination, and upon which we could safely base the Parliamentary grant. It was more a financial than a literary preference. Had there been any other branch of useful knowledge, the possession of which could have been ascertained with equal precision, there was nothing to prevent its admission. But there was not ...
(A. Patchett Martin, Life and Letters of the Right Honourable Robert Lowe, Viscount Sherbrooke, 1893, Vol. II, p. 217)

These are interesting arguments;[5] the justification cited in the second passage – administrative convenience – is a familiar one. But the implication of the first passage – namely that the Revised Code was intended as an egalitarian measure – deserves attention, the more so as it seems to some extent to be corroborated by the inspectors themselves, whose approval tended to be focused on the evident ability of the new system to ensure a basic education for the average pupil in the lower standards. Under the old regulations, the latter had sometimes been given a raw deal compared with the older and necessarily better-off children of the top classes. Inspectors' reports at times appear to provide something of a consensus of opinion in favour of the Revised Code's working in this respect. H.M.I. Hernaman, for example, evidently considered it desirable to put the record straight when, in his General Report for 1869, he castigated a critic who

with a looseness and inexactitude which are characteristic of a certain class of minds, tried to make his audience believe that Her Majesty's inspectors generally spoke unfavourably of its operation and results; the fact being that out of the 17 inspectors who reported on National Schools in England last year only two spoke in any other but terms of commendation of the Revised Code.

Robert Lowe's resignation in 1864 resulted from a Commons resolution condemning the occasional censoring of inspectors' reports prior to their being printed in the annual Reports of the Committee of Council. He was later exonerated, but the validity of the reports published up to this date has naturally been questioned. The extracts given below, therefore, are taken from those written several years later under the vice-presidencies of Lord Robert Montagu and William E. Forster. First, then, the favourable conclusions of Mr. Temple, followed by the more qualified praise of Mr. Barry:

The truth is that the Revised Code did a most useful work in laying the foundation of an accurate knowledge of reading, writing and arithmetic (which did not previously exist), upon which the superstructure of wider instruction and cultivated intelligence might safely be built, but it never was intended to prevent the erection of that super-structure, to check knowledge, or to stunt intelligence.

So understood and worked, the Revised Code has done unmixed good, and every additional year convinces me more and more of the wisdom of its framers, and makes me more determined to protest and fight against misrepresentation or misconception of it, whether ignorant or wilful. Education before the Revised Code was showy, flashy, and unsubstantial; it had no backbone . . .

Education confined to the mere routine of the examination schedule (*i.e.* to unintelligent reading, writing, and arithmetic) is a skeleton of dry bones; but education under the Revised Code fairly worked has a strong and solid framework of accurate elementary instruction, clothed with a fair and healthy growth of knowledge and intelligence.
(Mr. Temple's General Report for 1869)

The common contrast between schools under the Old and the New Code is that under the former the upper classes were more advanced, but the lower classes neglected; under the latter the lower classes are carefully taught, while the upper classes have gone back in attainment. There is a great deal of general truth in this, except that in good schools under the Old Code all classes were attended to. Of the two it is undoubtedly more important that the mass of the school and the younger children should be carefully grounded in elementary points. But it is, I think, possible to have the lower classes as carefully taught as now, and yet to have upper classes as advanced as they were before, if sufficient inducements are held out by the Committee of Council. The New Code was introduced to remedy certain deficiences exposed in the Report of the Royal Commissioners. . . . The State insisted upon a certain progress in elementary subjects, but left the more advanced instruction to the option and control of local management. Proper discipline, and in Church of England schools a due progress in religious knowledge, were insisted on more stringently than before, but beyond these and the requirements of the standards nothing more was requisite to obtain the full grant. Now there is always a tendency both in teachers and pupils to confine themselves to the minimum of requirement. Attention is concentrated on the subject which pays to the exclusion of all others. This result took place under the New Code. The higher subjects, such as geography, grammar, and history, almost disappeared; no rules in arithmetic were taught except those required in Article 48. While, however, the upper classes suffered, the mass of the school undoubtedly gained.
(Mr. Barry's General Report for 1869)

The most sensitive critic of the Revised Code was Matthew Arnold. In his

1862 article he had cogently argued that 'The Twice-Revised Code' was a retrogressive step and that the education of the people would accordingly suffer. His General Report for 1869 reiterated his objections, but at the same time contained constructive suggestions for making it a more humane and genuine method of assessment:

... I have repeatedly said that it seems to me the great fault of the Revised Code, and of the famous plan of *payment by results,* that it fosters teaching by rote; I am of that opinion still. I think the great task for friends of education is, not to praise *payment by results,* which is just the sort of notion to catch of itself popular favour, but to devise remedies for the evils which are found to follow the application of this popular notion. The school examinations in view of *payment by results* are, as I have said, a game of mechanical contrivance in which the teachers will and must more and more learn how to beat us. It is found possible, by ingenious preparation, to get children through the Revised Code examination in reading, writing, and ciphering without their really knowing how to read, write, and cipher.

To take the commonest instance: a book is selected at the beginning of the year for the children of a certain standard; all the year the children read this book over and over again, and no other. When the inspector comes they are presented to read in this book; they can read their sentence or two fluently enough, but they cannot read any other book fluently.[6] Yet the letter of the law is satisfied, and the more we undertake to lay down to the very letter the requirements which shall be satisfied in order to earn grants, the more do managers and teachers conceive themselves to have the right to hold us to this letter ...
(Matthew Arnold's General Report for 1869)

Near the end of his life, looking back with more sorrow than anger, Matthew Arnold was able to write:

I knew the English Schools well in this period between 1850 and 1860, and at the end of it I was enabled to compare them with schools abroad. Some preventible neglect of the junior classes, some preventible shortcoming in the elementary instruction, there was; but not nearly so much as was imagined. What there was would have been sufficiently met by a capitation grant on individual examination, not for the whole school, but for the children between seven or eight years old and nine or ten, a grant which would then have been subsidiary, not principal. General 'payment by results' has been a remedy worse than the disease which it was meant to cure.
(T. H. Ward (ed.), The Reign of Queen Victoria, 1887, Vol. II, p. 260)

The impact of payment by results

Concocted, as Matthew Arnold acidly observed, in the recesses of the Privy Council Office, with no advice asked from those practically conversant with schools,[7] the Revised Code seemed both administratively tidy and educationally justifiable to its authors. Of the inspectors who had to enforce its provisions in the first decade of its operation, a significant number appears to have acquiesced to this opinion. But the advent of payment by results, coupled as it was with the withdrawal of government concern in the financial affairs of individual teachers, must have seemed little short of catastrophic to many of the schoolmasters and mistresses (not to mention the pupil teachers) who, from August 1863 onwards, were forced to endure a life of annually recurrent crisis. Financial stringency[8] and the tyranny of local interests combined with the yearly inspection to create a degree of personal and professional humiliation which must have darkened the careers of thousands of teachers. It is difficult, for example, not to appreciate the anguish of a schoolmaster forced by the code's regulations to inscribe the catalogue of his errors in the school logbook:

The writing and composition of the upper standards are creditable, and the Reading in most Standards has the merit of accuracy, but when I have said this, I have mentioned the only redeeming features in the thoroughly bad work of the School.

No epithet can be too severe to characterise the work of the first Standard, or the Arithmetic throughout the School, but with the exceptions mentioned above, the attainments in every class and in every subject are most unsatisfactory . . .

The annals of this School for the last six or seven years are merely records of failure and inefficiency, and unless steps are taken to raise it from its present unsatisfactory condition, it will soon be a question whether it can any longer be recognised as an efficient School.

(East Bergholt School Log Book, 1885)

Pathos (as well as courage) shows in the following entry:

Notwithstanding the unfavourable reports, year after year, of this school, the teachers seem to enter on their duties with renewed hopes, after the first feelings of disappointment have passed. The readers, if any, of these entries may have gathered the supposed causes of the ill success of our labours; they may however be summed up.

The children attending are inferior in social standing, in habits and manners, in regularity, in bringing up, to those usually attending our schools; they are admitted late and leave early, caring apparently only to earn a few shillings; the better-class of labourers, tradesmen and shopkeepers sending their children, for the most part, elsewhere. Many are manifestly deficient in intellect.

The teaching staff is unsuitable, and not nicely welded together; there being too many independent atoms.

There is no class room for needlework and noisy lessons, all are jumbled together and no class can be taken with comfort; the size of the room exhausting the powers of anyone not possessing lungs of leather and iron nerves. The school books and apparatus are not of the best description, and might be more plentifully supplied.

Lastly the master admits plenty of infirmities on his own part; and so we may as well make the best we can of matters and go on for another year.

(East Bergholt School Log Book, 17 June 1881)

Matthew Arnold protested that the relationship of schoolmaster and inspector tended under the Revised Code to degenerate into 'a game of mechanical contrivance'; James Runciman, a teachers' advocate if ever there was one, employed somewhat stronger terms:

. . . at present I can only declare that, sooner than teach in an elementary school, under any one of some score of inspectors whom I could name, I would go before the mast in a collier, or break stones in a casual ward – or, better than all, die. An inspector need not have any brains, but he is autocratic, whatever his disposition and ability may be, and, if he is stupid or malignant, he may make life a perfect hell for the scholastic drudges in his district.

(James Runciman, Schools and Scholars, 1887, p. 129)

. . .

A brilliant young friend of mine was dying of consumption. . . . He was stretched out – frail and hectic, but cheerful and sweet as usual. Someone brought in a report that the inspector was dead: the dying man started up, a wild light struck out of his eyes, like fire from steel, and he said, with a hideous broken scream, 'By God, I hope he's in hell!'[9]

(James Runciman, Schools and Scholars, 1887, p. 264)

Even the most efficient teachers occasionally suffered acutely, as the following somewhat melodramatic account of one of H.M.I. Swinburne's early inspections shows:

. . . The dignified figure of the mistress constituted our sole audience; and a grave silence was maintained by her.

In less than half an hour the children, like a mirror, had reflected the excellence of her work; scholar after scholar I waved aside with murmurs of satisfaction, and told myself that it was going to be one of those delightful mornings dear to the H.M.I. whose heart is in his work.

A sudden thud interrupted my absorption in Standard III, and, turning, I perceived a sea of small frightened faces eyeing me with startled horror and inquiry, while on the floor a pair of legs, encased in somewhat dirty white stockings, protruded from under the teacher's desk. Her fall had been more like the collapse of a tree than that of a human being, and there were no half measures about the way in which her head came in contact with the floor.

She had not only mistaken my grim relish for the Mephistolean *(sic)* smiles of an adverse critic, but had imagined that I was failing each of her pupils in turn.

Her last year's record of cent. per cent. of passes, and the recent three weeks of strain to reproduce it, had been too much for her. Would that I had perceived it sooner; as it was, I continued my work mechanically, as if to say, 'It is nothing,' for much depended on my keeping calm; but never did a man's inner consciousness more feebly support a counterfeit of external composure.

The pupil-teachers rushed to her assistance and half-lifted, half-dragged her from the room, but before anything approaching calm had descended on the children's ruffled minds, the door was thrown violently open and a diminutive man, in an ill-cut frock-coat with baggy trousers of a funereal hue, rushed into our midst. 'You have killed her! You have killed her!' he shouted; and, indeed, I began to wonder if I had. The children, their faces looking like rows of wind-cuffed flowers, turned a wide-eyed, terrified gaze on the ogre, who, in my person, stood before them.

(A. J. Swinburne, Memories of a School Inspector, 1912, pp. 41-42)

'. . . we may as well make the best we can of matters and go on for another year,' despondently remarked Charles Gedge, the schoolmaster at East Bergholt, after a particularly harrowing encounter with his H.M.I. in 1881. A fair enough comment, perhaps; but in point of fact the bleakness of payment by results seems not infrequently to have been mitigated by human ingenuity or benevolence.

A. J. Swinburne tells of the 'racy schoolmaster who said: "Pass – oh! they'll pass, all of them – certain – why (proudly), any one of them can copy three desks off",'[10] when assessing his pupils' chances at the coming examination. Likewise, W. P. Turnbull, after recounting how a Yorkshire schoolmaster once caned a class all round for leaving out the *d* in spelling *pigeon,* continued, 'In another Yorkshire school the children were taught to put up the hand when the Inspector questioned the class; those who knew the answer were to put the right hand up, while the others were to raise the left. The master would then select accordingly.'[11]

Nevertheless, the yearly inspection was inevitably a time of frayed nerves for all concerned. In the passages below two H.M.I.'s – A. J. Swinburne and E. M. Sneyd-Kynnersley – describe the preliminaries, the inspection itself, and one particular sequel in terms which invite the suspicion that there was more give-and-take in the process than might sometimes be supposed:

The Inspector gave notice of his approaching advent on a certain date, and for weeks beforehand the children were stuffed and almost roasted – (no wonder they resembled trussed fowls) – the mistress had sleepless nights, the parson and the squire of the village were in a flutter of anxiety, for so much depended at that time on the verdict of Her Majesty's Inspector.

Woe betide the official himself if he kept the school waiting, for each succeeding ten minutes made the mistress more hysterical, the children more nervous; and if the minutes extended to hours, the parson and the squire became likewise infected by the malaise which reigned on such occasions, while newspaper articles and complaints to headquarters would probably help to curtail H.M.I.'s career in consequence of such delays.

(A. J. Swinburne, Memories of a School Inspector, 1912, p. 37)

. . . The great aim of inspector, teacher, and children was to finish by 12.30 at the latest.

Our plan of campaign was delightfully simple. Most of the children were in the two lowest standards. These were supplied with slates, pencils, and a reading-book, and were drawn up in two long lines down the middle of the room. They stood back-to-back, to prevent copying, and did dictation, and arithmetic, sometimes dropping their slates, sometimes their pencils, sometimes their books, not infrequently all three, with a crash on the floor. When we had marked the results on the Examination Schedule, all these children were sent home, and the atmosphere was immensely improved. Then we proceeded to examine the rest, the aristocracy, who

worked their sums on paper. As a rule, if we began about 10 we finished about 11.45. If the master was a good fellow, and trustworthy, we looked over the few papers in dictation and arithmetic, marked the Examination Schedule, and showed him the whole result before he left. Then he calculated his 'percentage of passes', his grant, and his resulting income; and went to dinner with what appetite he might. But if the man were cross-grained, and likely to complain that the exercises were too hard, the standard of marking too high, and so on, he would be left in merciful ignorance of details. Half an hour in the evening sufficed for making up the Annual Report, and the incident was closed. Think of the simplicity of it!
(E. M. Sneyd-Kynnersley, H.M.I., Some passages in the life of one of H.M. Inspectors of Schools, 1908, p. 59)

Once the examination was under way there was no guarantee that initiative would remain with the inspector:

Mistress: 'What is the largest animal in the world?'
Chorus: An elephunt, teacher.
Mistress: Yes, quite right.

This heresy shocked me; but etiquette again forbade that I should contradict her. Yet – for *magis amica veritas* – I might, and did, interpose a question:
'Which is the bigger, an elephant or a whale?'
Chorus: A wheele.

The mistress looked scornfully at me, and returned the oblique shot:
'Is a whale an animal, children?'
Chorus: Noo, teacher.
Mistress: 'What is a whale, children?'
Chorus: A fish.

I was roused to more defence of truth, though tacitly accepting the fishhood of whales:
'Isn't a fish an animal, children?'
Chorus (sarcastically): Noo.
'Is a girl an animal?'
Chorus: Noo.

'Is a girl a vegetable? Do you grow them in a garden, like cabbages?'
Chorus: Noo.
'Is a girl a mineral? Do you dig them out of a mine, like coals?'
Chorus: Noo.

Now I seemed to have the landing-net ready:
'If a girl is not an animal, nor a vegetable, nor a mineral, what is a girl?'

The first and second classes felt the horns of the trilemma, and they were silent: but a boy aged four, or so, rose from his seat in the third class, and in strident tones supplied the crushing answer:

'Hoo's a WENCH.'

I fled into the next room.*

And finally, a note of sweetness and light:

From another country school after the inspection the mistress wrote to her former headmaster:

'Her Majesty's Inspector has been here. He was in a lovely temper. When he had done, he kissed all the boys, and all the girls: then he kissed the pupil-teachers; and last, but not least, he did not omit your humble servant.'

(E. M. Sneyd-Kynnersley, H.M.I., Some passages in the life of one of H.M. Inspectors of Schools, 1908, pp. 185-186 and 202)

Day-to-day problems

The system of annual inspections, the focus as it were of payment by results, sometimes tends to mask the other, more enduring, problems of school life: indiscipline, scarcity of money, lack of sympathy on the part of employers and parents. Here F. H. Spencer describes his feelings as he ineluctably sank towards failure in his first post. The passage has a certain timelessness about it:

I had to teach more than fifty boys and girls every subject of the curriculum, and a 'Higher Grade' curriculum at that: this I expected. But I was also condemned to hold them down by an iron discipline, with no backing from the head. Indiscipline of the pupil – an indiscipline measured by his standards – was in his eyes the fault of the teacher, and his only. There is enough truth in this doctrine to make it specially unpleasant to a lonely novice, friendless, and always too prone to self-criticism. I began to fear failure: certainly I lost self-confidence, and was much afflicted by the melancholy of youth, which I then thought was peculiar to me, though, of course, it is a very common complaint of people at my then age, thrown friendless into new and formidable surroundings.

This pessimistic melancholy was probably the root of my half failure. Two or three of the staff confided to me how they hated 'the old man'; how he was on the look-out for any sign of failure or weakness; how I could expect no support: the children and their parents would always be right, and these were chiefly, not the hardy artisan parents whom I had known, but the little bourgeoisie of a large town. I set my teeth and tried violently to master the situation. But my spiritual condition grew worse. I succeeded only in part. In many things I could interest the pupils. One or two boys, however, could torture me with silent insolence, and one or two girls could sail off with an indefinable impertinence; for they were by instinct past masters in the art of knowing how far they could go without being culpably and provably wrong.

. . .

Work in school, therefore, was one long, irritating grind. The boys and the girls played their respective tricks upon me. I could have managed either, I think. I could not manage both. I felt there was no justice in the situation, and little in the world.

(F. H. Spencer, An Inspector's Testament, 1938, pp. 158-160)

---

*Sneyd-Kynnersley was apparently not the only H.M.I. to be discomfited by the children he was examining. H.M.I. Codd (a less amiable person, it seems), while questioning a north Devon class in geography, 'asked which side of the house was the warmest: to which, after a pause for reflection, came the inspired reply "Inzoide, zur".' See Pamela Horn, *The Victorian Country Child*, 1974, p. 47.

One cause for constant concern was the school attendance figures which, apart from determining the size of the average grant, were a necessary qualification for the examination in the three Rs, the candidates for which were required to have at least two hundred attendances to their credit within the school year. These circumstances, coupled with the lack of really effective legislation before 1880, naturally gave great incentive to the teachers' efforts to ensure full registers. The simplest way to achieve this apparently laudable aim was, of course, to falsify the records. 'The temptation must be very strong, the chances of detection next to impossible,' wrote H.M.I. Blakiston in 1869. Next, attendance on the day of inspection had to be secured whatever the cost:

To hear paroxysms of whooping cough, to observe the pustules of small-pox, to see infants carefully wrapped up and held in their mothers' arms or seated on a stool by the fire because too ill to take their proper places, are events not so rare in an inspector's experiences as they ought to be. The risk of the infant's life and the danger of infection to others are preferred to the forfeiture of a grant of 6s. 6d.
(Mr. Stokes' General Report for 1866)

Lapses in attendance at other times could be tackled by haranguing the parents of the offenders or by sending them notes. Sometimes, however, direct and incisive action paid dividends:

Yesterday effected a very successful lateral movement . . . marching two pupil teachers up the coast – to surprise four truants bathing – posted myself between them and their clothes – cane in hand – and *waited*.
(A. J. Swinburne, Memories of a School Inspector, 1912, p. 219)

It would seem that the problem of poor attendance proved an intractable one; the 1870 Act enabled the school boards which it had created to draft and enforce by-laws making attendance compulsory, and six years later Lord Sandon's Act sounded a modern note by defining it as the duty of parents to ensure the competence of their children in the three Rs. It also made possible the formation of School Attendance Committees in areas where no school board existed and forbade the employment of children under the age of ten. Children between ten and fourteen seeking work were required to have a certificate of attendance or attainment. But in rural areas children could absent themselves for up to six weeks for agricultural work. The half-time system, based upon the 1844 Factory Act (which originally sought to compel children aged from eight to thirteen to attend school for three hours a day either before or after lunch), survived until the act of 1918[12]. Evasion of attendance regulations, however, remained common. According to Francis Adams:

Regularity has been very little improved since 1870. Irregular, convulsive attendance is still the great evil which managers, teachers, inspectors, and all who are engaged in the work have to struggle against.

Illegal employment is common. It is the rule and not the exception. Employers do not ask for certificates. The law is often unknown, or, when known, it is disregarded by employers, parents, and the local authorities. Members of school attendance committees frequently employ children who have not complied with the requirements of the Act.

. . .

The attendance officers are of the worst description. They are ill-paid for this special work, and are generally fully employed with other duties. In most cases the relieving officer is appointed to the post, and a small addition is made to his salary. As a rule his compliance with his duty is nominal. If he is energetic at the outset he soon discovers that his superiors are not in favour of too great a display of vigour, and he takes his cue accordingly.[13]

There is a general disinclination on the part of magistrates to convict. Sometimes they are afraid of unpopularity, often they are indifferent, they are generally disposed to accept frivolous excuses, and they inflict fines at which the parents laugh,* while the ratepayers grumble at having to pay the heavy costs. Their adminstration of the law has brought it into contempt.
(F. Adams, The History of the Elementary School Contest in England, 1882, pp. 335-336)

So none of these expedients proved particularly effective. The situation is clearly reflected in the contemporary logbook of a Suffolk village school:

As the children get into about standard 2 they seem imperceptibly to vanish from the school, or drag on an irregular school life for another year or two; with little advantage to themselves or the school.

. . .

A half timer soon merges into a quarter timer, thence by rapid degrees into a no timer.
(East Bergholt School Log Book, 16 June 1876 and 2 June 1882)

It would be facile to condemn unreservedly the lukewarm attitude of parents towards school. The scepticism of many regarding the value of the elementary education commonly available to their children is underwritten to some extent by the official and semiofficial criticisms which were periodically made of the system. Thus A. J. Balfour, introducing his Education Bill in 1902, gave a markedly reserved appraisal of the state of educational provision in the country:

To the educationalist I think I need make no apologies and offer no excuses. . . . He has long seen a vast expenditure of public money which has yet left this country behind all its Continental and American rivals in the matter of education. He has seen a huge average cost per child in our elementary schools, and yet at the same time many of these schools, half-starved, inadequately equipped, imperfectly staffed.

It is therefore against this background, and frequently also one of grinding parental poverty, that the problems of school attendance must be viewed.

---

*D. Rubinstein cites a case in London 'in which a parent had been summoned 53 times, paying a fine every two or three months from the earnings of his child during the period.'[14]

The letters quoted next illustrate how these considerations operated at grassroots levels; the faulty spelling and syntax should not be allowed to obscure the validity of the points which they make.

Sir, Please excuse the liberty I have taken in ritin to you if you dont no what is goin on at this hear school you ought bein as you are inspector my children dont lern nothin nor other peples nither, their is over 80 goes to school and only one man to tech them and he gets children out of the first class to tech mine as noes as much as they do, but not anough the masters wife have been confined and have not bin to school for three weeks and when shes well she only goes for a few ours at a time and what do she no who have never bin teched much herself and never did teach befor she come hear so she say herself she get paid as much as them as went before her and did the same work only better so I want to know how childen is to get on at all with such teechin as that and the master say there is to be no halftimers now how is poor fokes to live, there is alas such a nise in the school when any boddy go by they carnt lern like that, I havnt got a deal of lernin myself but I wants my childen to no somethin; so please excuse the ritin sir and be good anough to see into things. I remain Sir, Yours respeckfully, A Anxhious Mother.

P.S. I beg pardon sir for not putting my name as the master will be down on my childen and be a threshin of them if you speak about it and he do anough of that.

Sir, Will you kindly grant me a labour certificate for my boy age 13 the 10th day of last January as I am sorry to have to beg but I am in poor circumstances with 7 more below him to feed and find shoes for and he is not very strong we are always doctoring him and he have been sent to school ever since he was 3 ½ yrs old and I am sure he will be better from school as there insides are very poorly kept bread and butter is not enough for his age now and money will not allow more as there are 10 of us to 14 shillings a week 5 stone of flour and their clubs to pay so it is only starving there system. I am sorry if he did not pass as I have a little one ill with bronchutis for 9 weeks I have had to find new milk and am not strong myself as 3 youngest are from 3 yrs to 5 months so I think we need it and the next girl to him as a bad back we dont enjoy much only aflictions which pull us back very much indeed and I know of 2 places he can have 6d. a day which would help to his bread. I hope you will look through the case and grant him. The schoolmaster told me last year that I should have him from the 15 of May till September last year but it was never granted if not I shall have to try for a medical certificate from the doctor. If I were not so poor would not mind how long he come to school I am Yours truly and Obedient servant.

(A. J. Swinburne, Memories of a School Inspector, 1912, p. 76 and pp. 191-192)

Notes

1   There were several versions of this 'epitaph': A. Patchett Martin *(Life and Letters of Lord Sherbrooke*, 1893) claims that Lowe was highly amused. The variant given here is quoted in M. Sturt, *The Education of the People*, 1967, p. 240.

2   Hence his alleged witticism to Disraeli: 'My hair will be white as long as I live; yours will be black as long as you dye.'

3   See J. Hurt, *Education in Evolution*, 1971 and D. W. Sylvester, *Robert Lowe and Education*, 1974.

4   Parl. Papers, 1861, Vol. XXI, Part 6, pp. 372-373.

5   J. Hurt, op. cit., pp. 202-203, develops the further point that Lowe's policies over the Revised Code 'constituted a significant victory for the state in its struggle with the Churches for control over education' by asserting the state's right to define the nature and content of grant-earning subjects.

6   For a consideration of the books used by nineteenth-century schoolchildren see Valerie Chancellor, *History for their masters: Opinion in the English History Textbook*, 1970, J. M. Goldstrom, *The Social Content of Education 1808-1870*, 1972 and J. M. Goldstrom (ed.), *Education: Elementary Education 1780-1900*, 1972.

7   Matthew Arnold, 'The Twice-Revised Code,' 1862. See P. Smith and G. Summerfield, *Matthew Arnold and the Education of the New Order*, 1969, p. 182. J. Hurt, op. cit., pp. 66-67, points out that communication between the Inspectorate and the Education Department had been curtailed from 1859 onwards.

8   Mary Sturt, op. cit., p. 260: 'In 1862 the Education Grant was £840,000, by 1864 it had fallen by £135,000 to £705,000.'

9   A. J. Swinburne, *Memories of a School Inspector*, 1912, p. 39, tells of a pupil who actually believed that 'the inspector passed his night among the tombs, whence he issued in the daylight enveloped in a mist of blue schedules, on which her name would be engraved for her eternal weal or woe.'

10   Ibid., pp. 85-86.

11   H. W. Turnbull, *Some Memories of William Peveril Turnbull*, 1919, p. 153.

12   For the half-time system, see E. and R. Frow, *The Half Time System in Education*, 1970.

13   Marion Johnson, in *Derbyshire Village Schools in the Nineteenth Century*, 1970, p. 149, does record the dismissal of at least two attendance officers for failing to keep the attendance up to an adequate level in their areas. Francis Adams' observations about poor attendance, however, are corroborated by R. R. Sellman, *Devon Village Schools in the Nineteenth Century*, 1967, Chapter VIII. Nancy Ball's article in *History of Education*, Vol. 2, No. 1 (January 1973) refers to the prize schemes which were initiated in the mid-nineteeth century to provide an incentive to school attendance. An account of the central authority's attempts to combat the problem of poor attendance is given in Gillian Sutherland, *Policy-Making in Elementary Education, 1870-1895*, 1973, Chapter 5.

14   D. Rubinstein in *Popular Education and Socialization in the Nineteenth Century*, ed. by P. McCann, 1977, p. 247.

CHAPTER 4

'PARTNERSHIP FOR THE ACQUISITION OF
KNOWLEDGE': ELEMENTARY AND PRIMARY
EDUCATION IN THE TWENTIETH CENTURY

The intellectual climate of the so-called 'naughty nineties' and of the early years of the new century showed less stability and self-confidence than that of the Victorian age. In politics and industrial relations no less than in music, art, and literature, the established values were increasingly questioned and rejected. The *zeitgeist*, if it can be called that, predictably affected educational thought by shifting opinion towards the libertarian attitudes which had last been in vogue during the late eighteenth and early nineteenth centuries. The phasing-out of Payment by Results in the 1890s set the scene for this, while the 1902 Act, in substituting the relatively remote control of L.E.A. for that of parochially minded school board and voluntary management, gave further opportunity for curricular flexibility. The 1905 Handbook of Suggestions issued by the Board of Education seemingly endorsed a certain amount of revision and adaptation:

The only uniformity of practice that the Board of Education desire to see in the teaching of Public Elementary Schools is that each teacher shall think for himself, and work out for himself such methods of teaching as may use his powers to the best advantage and be best suited to the particular needs and conditions of the school.

and apparently redefined the pupil-teacher relationship:

The teacher, therefore, must know the children and must sympathize with them, for it is of the essence of teaching that the mind of the teacher should touch the mind of the pupil. He will seek at each stage to adjust his mind to theirs, to draw upon their experience as a supplement to his own, and so take them as it were into partnership for the acquisition of knowledge.
(Handbook of Suggestions for the Consideration of Teachers and others concerned in the work of Public Elementary Schools, 1905, pp. 6 and 15)

M. G. Llewelyn, taking up a teaching post in Wales after training, noticed the change at once:

'Is there a syllabus?' I asked.

'Yes,' (the headmaster) replied. 'Here it is, but you can use your own methods as long as the outlines of the syllabus are followed.'

. . . This was a long cry from the narrow syllabuses set out in the old codes in the days of payment by results. The elementary schools had, largely through the activity of the National Union of Teachers, achieved an independence of thought, of control of education and of method, which was unexampled in the world.
(M. G. Llewelyn, Sand in the Glass, 1943, pp. 211-212)

As might be expected, the trend towards greater curricular freedom in Wales was to result in an acceleration of the movement towards the revival of Welsh culture and language – a movement to which the central authority was to show itself responsive, having formed its own Welsh Department in 1907. The first Welsh-language school in an anglicized area (Ysgol Gymraeg) was set up in 1939; twenty years later there were almost 40

L.E.A.-run Ysgolion Cymraeg, and in 1967 the Gittins Report was strongly to recommend a policy of bilingualism throughout Wales.

In Britain as a whole, however, the last decades of the nineteenth century had witnessed the impact of the ill-defined and uncoordinated theories which have conveniently been lumped together under the umbrella title of 'the New Education':[1] the writings of Herbart and Froebel from Germany; those of Dewey from the U.S.A.; Sloyd and Ling's gymnastics from Scandinavia; new concepts of scientific and moral education from various sources; and, later of course, the methods of Maria Montessori.

It soon became evident that the more radical educationalists of the new century had the crosswires of their sights fair and square upon class teaching and all that it implied about the role of the teacher and the nature of the timetabled simultaneous lesson. In 1911 there appeared an influential and uncompromising endorsement of these views in the form of Edmond Holmes' book *What Is and What Might Be*.

What Is and What Might Be

Edmond Holmes, ex-H.M.C.I., intended his two-part book to be an indictment of attitudes prevailing towards elementary education and at the same time a signpost to a better, more enlightened approach to teaching. The 'What Is' section (subtitled 'The Path of Mechanical Obedience') was a sustained critique of the current teaching methods:

... the one end and aim of the teacher is to do everything for the child; – to feed him with semi-digested food; to hold him by the hand, or rather by both shoulders, when he tries to walk or run; to keep him under close and constant supervision; to tell him in precise detail what he is to think, to feel, to say, to wish, to do; to show him in precise detail how he is to do whatever may have to be done; to lay thin veneers of information on the surface of his mind; never to allow him a minute for independent study; never to trust him with a handbook, a note-book, or a sketch-book; in fine, to do all that lies in his power to prevent the child from doing anything whatever for himself. The result is that the various vital faculties which education might be supposed to train become irretrievably starved and stunted in the over-educated school child; till at last, when the time comes for him to leave school in which he has been so sedulously cared for, he is too often thrown out upon the world, helpless, listless, resourceless, without a single interest, without a single purpose in life.
(E. G. A. Holmes, What Is and What Might Be, 1911, pp. 4-5)

Holmes, like others before him, attributed this basic distrust of initiative to the old concept of original sin:

We tell the child that he is a criminal, and treat him as such, and then expect him to be perfect; and when our misguided education has begun to deprave him, we shake

our heads over his congential depravity, and thank God that we believe in 'original sin'.
(E. G. A. Holmes, What Is and What Might Be, 1911, pp. 46-47)

The 'What Might Be' half of the book (subtitled 'The Path of Self-Realisation') offered Holmes' solution to the problems which he had described – a solution which he claimed to have discovered in a rural school of 120 or so children deep in the green heart of England ('Utopia')* where 'Egeria', his ideal (and perhaps idealized) teacher, lived among her charges – 'the very symbol and embodiment of love, the centre whence all happy, harmonious, life-giving, peace-diffusing influences radiate . . .''[2] *What Is and What Might Be* is in some ways a Janus book, looking both forward and back. It is hardly conceivable, for example, that T. Percy Nunn, writing his classic *Education: its data and first principles* in the more egalitarian spirit of the post-1918 years, would have gone out of his way, as Holmes did, to observe how (their progressive education notwithstanding) 'the Utopian girls make excellent servants, and are well content "to go into service".'[3] But on the other hand it is hardly a strain on the imagination to see in the following passages model texts for Lady Plowden and her collaborators:

Two things will strike the stranger who pays his first visit to this school. One is the ceaseless activity of the children. The other is the bright and happy look on every face. In too many elementary schools the children are engaged either in laboriously doing nothing – in listening, for example, with ill-concealed yawns, to *lectures* on history, geography, nature-study, and the rest; or in doing what is only one degree removed from nothing, – working mechanical sums, transcribing lists of spellings or pieces of composition, drawing diagrams which have no meaning for them, and so forth. But in this school every child is, as a rule, actively employed. And bearing in mind that 'unimpeded energy' is a recognised source of happiness, the visitor will probably conjecture that there is close connection between the activity of the children and the brightness of their faces.

. . .

. . . The air of the school is electrical with energy. We are obviously in the presence of an active and vigorous life.

And the activity of the Utopian child is his own activity. It is a fountain which springs up in himself. Unlike the ordinary school-child, he can do things on his own account. He does not wait, in the helplessness of passive obedience, for his teacher to tell him what he is to do and how he is to do it. He does not even wait, in the bewilderment of self-distrust, for his teacher to give him a lead. If a new situation arises, he deals with it with promptitude and decision. His solution of the problem which it involves may be incorrect, but at any rate it will be a solution. He will have faced a difficulty and grappled with it, instead of having waited inertly for something to turn up. His initiative has evidently been developed *pari passu* with his

---

*The school was at Sompting, in Sussex; 'Egeria's' real name was Harriet Johnson.

intelligence; and the result of this is that he can think things out for himself, that he can devise ways and means, that he can purpose, that he can plan.
(E. G. A. Holmes, What Is and What Might Be, 1911, pp. 154-156 passim)

In one respect, however, Holmes remained responsive to the nineteenth-century discipline of Payment by Results: when Harriet Johnson's detractors pusillanimously claimed that she had faked the exercise books of her pupils because the real ones were so bad,* he was able to come to her help with a few figures† – a kind of evidence, it might be parenthetically remarked, which would possibly have assured certain parts of the Plowden Report itself a rather warmer reception in some quarters. Anyway, it would seem that such watchwords of modern progressive educational thought as individual development, activity methods, open-ended discovery, self-regulating discipline, and even noncompetitive family grouping were applicable in some degree to the school at Sompting.

In his book Holmes considered at some length the use made of drama; Harriet Johnson herself wrote about this in her *Dramatic Method of Teaching*. The idea must have caught on for it improbably provides the core of the plot in one of Saki's amoral short stories – 'The Schartz-Metterklume Method' – which was published as early as 1914. H. Caldwell Cook, whose book *The Play Way* appeared in 1917, also erected imaginative play into a system of education, determinedly scrapping classroom teaching *en route:* 'It would not be wise,' he maintained, 'to send a child innocent into the big world; and talking is of poor avail. But it is possible to hold rehearsals, to try our strength in a make-believe big world. And that is Play.'[3]

The sad condition of our schools is mainly owing to the teachers' unthinking compliance with a rotten tradition. The defence of those who *have* given thought to the matter of book-learning amounts to no more than this: 'The individual child cannot try over again for himself all the experience of the ages, and therefore he must study the record of the past.' But this study, to have any value, must persuade the child to live over again, briefly in his imagination, the ages gone by; and my simple contention is that the child be allowed to express his imaginings in the manner that most appeals to him, the way that is most natural. This will be the Play Way, with the high thoughts and noble endeavour of that super-reality which is make-believe.

It comes in the end to this: Why should we stop a game now going on in order to dictate the rules of another which we do not intend shall ever be played? Why call in Robin Hood and the Redskins and the Pirate Captain from the playground to read of Luther, or even of Coeur de Lion?
(H. Caldwell Cook, The Play Way, 1917, p. 11)

---

*She was also accused of not teaching the children to read properly and of being unable to control the older pupils. See E. G. A. Holmes, *In Defence of What Might Be*, 1914, pp. 334-341 passim.

†Holmes claimed that 21 compositions written in his presence by the first class averaged 336 words in length and contained on average 4 spelling mistakes; 25 compositions submitted by the second class averaged 150 words and 5 spelling mistakes. Ibid., p. 340.

The Play Way, as defined by Cook, was overtly directed towards preparation for the adult world: the children in the book are referred to as 'Littlemen'. Needless to say this scarcely tallied with the concept of 'readiness' advanced by Maria Montessori and later by Jean Piaget which, in its various forms was later to gain such wide acceptance in educational circles. But Cook was certainly at one with mainstream progressives in his cry, 'Why should there stretch such an abyss between the nursery and the classroom?'[4]

Montessori, Nunn, and Isaacs

Maria Montessori, T. Percy Nunn, and Susan Isaacs seem to be writing in a different age – and one more familiar to the modern reader – to that of the two previous authors. Their emphasis is upon scientific detachment; religious and metaphysical considerations are largely disregarded. The shift is not so much one of aims – for the right of the child as an individual had been implicit in the doctrines of such people as Charlotte Mason and Edmond Holmes – but of approach. Indeed, Holmes regarded the Montessori method as the apotheosis of individualism in teaching and was accordingly unstinting in his admiration:

The master-principle of the Montessori system is that of *self-education*. Dottoressa Montessori believes that childhood is the time when growth, under all its aspects, is most vigorous, most rapid, and most easily helped or hindered. She believes that the function of education is to help growth, to give it free play, to encourage it, to stimulate it, to lead the fountain of life into suitable channels, or rather to help it to shape suitable channels for itself. She realises that the business of growing must be done by the growing child, and cannot be delegated by him to his teacher or anyone else. And she infers from this that the teacher, instead of doing everything or nearly everything for the child, should do as little as possible, should stand aside, so to speak, and efface herself, giving the child such guidance and stimulus as he may need, and providing him with suitable materials, but leaving him free to exercise his own faculties, and relieving him of the pressure of vexatious interference and arbitrary constraint.
(E. G. A. Holmes, The Montessori System of Education, 1912, p. 4)

But Charlotte Mason, herself an eminent propagandist for 'masterly inactivity' on the part of parent and teacher, took a much cooler view: 'To make a cult of liberty in our schools would be to bring up a race of vagabonds,' she portentously cried. Then in a passage strikingly reminiscent of Robert Owen's criticism of the monitorial system[5] she censured what she regarded as the cultural deprivation inherent in Montessori's teaching:

. . . these children can read and write by the time they are four or five, while with us eight is the usual (and desirable) age at which these accomplishments are mastered. We run away with the fallacy that reading and writing are education, not as they truly are, mechanical arts, no more educative than the mastery of shorthand or the Morse Code . . .

She particularly disliked the Montessori system's apparent lack of religious or romantic content; speaking of a child thus educated, she maintained that:

. . . no fairies play about him, no heroes stir his soul; God and good angels form no part of his thoughts; the child and the person he will become are a scientific product, the result of much touching and some seeing and hearing; for what has science to do with those intangible, hardly imaginable entities called ideas? . . . song and picture, hymn and story are for the educational scrapheap.
(Charlotte Mason, The Basis of National Strength, 1913, pp. 49 and 51)

Between the initial impact of Montessori's ideas and the appearance of T. Percy Nunn's book *Education: its data and first principles* came the First World War. The latter caused a crisis of self-confidence which, in the educational world at least, had the effect of amplifying the trends of the prewar era. There was a widespread feeling that a civilization whose cultural values could lead to such insensate carnage, degradation, and sheer misery must be radically perverted in its institutions and wildly disorientated in its aims:

We stand (wrote Nunn) at an hour when the civilization that bred us is sick – some fear even to death. We cannot escape from the duty of seeking a cure for its distemper, any more from the responsibility that lies, in some measure, upon us all for having brought it to its present pass. But however good our will, however happy our inspiration, the problems we and those who came before us have created are problems we cannot hope ourselves to solve; they must be solved, if at all, by the generations that will take up our work when our place knows us no more.
(T. Percy Nunn, Education: its data and first principles, 1920, p. 219)

Nunn acknowledged man's need for a social framework in which to live; the purpose of his book was to suggest a means by which he might do so and yet at the same time avoid the price of war and suffering which society itself appeared to exact:

What is needed is . . . a doctrine which . . . reasserts the importance of the individual and safeguards his indefeasible rights.

Such a doctrine we seek to set out in these pages and to make the basis of a stable educational policy. We shall stand throughout on the position that nothing good enters into the human world except in and through the free activities of individual men and women, and that educational practice must be shaped to accord with that truth.
(T. Percy Nunn, Education: its data and first principles, 1920, p. 4)

Thus by the mid-1920s formal methods of class teaching had been under continuous and vocal attack for more than a decade. Edmond Holmes and H. Caldwell Cook (in their rather idiosyncratic ways), T. Percy Nunn and many others had argued against them from their own differing standpoints. In 1921 the New Education Fellowship had been founded, in the words of Beatrice Ensor, one of its moving spirits, to 'help forward the new era'. But it was Susan Isaacs who attempted to assess in terms of scientific detachment the effectiveness of an informal and individual approach to teaching. The results of observations made at the Malting House School near Cambridge between 1924 and 1927 were published in her books *Intellectual Growth in Young Children* and *Social Development in Young Children*. Susan Isaacs' own status as a psychologist assured the conclusions which followed from these two volumes a more favourable reception by the educationalists of the time than the subjective and sometimes impassioned writings of earlier supporters of progressive methods. In brief, although Susan Isaacs' ideas were not original, her presentation of them was; and this is what mattered.

At the Malting House School (which was founded, financed, and ultimately closed by the offbeat financial speculator Geoffrey Pyke), Susan Isaacs and her colleagues (the staff varied in number from two in the first two years to five in the last term) minutely recorded the actions and responses of the children (the school started with ten boys; eventually there were twenty children of both sexes):

A few days ago, Mrs. I. took a whole calf's head to school. Dan, Conrad, Priscilla and Jane interested themselves in it, looking closely at the eyes, ears, skin, inside of mouth, and so on. They tried to cut through the skin, but found it very tough. Today, (3.6.1927) as Jane had suggested cutting it open to see the brain, Mrs. I. took a hack-saw, and she and Jane bi-sected the head. It took a long time, and they had to rest occasionally, and go back to it; but Jane's interest did not flag, and the others kept coming to see how they were getting on, and sometimes took a helping hand. Jane was at first surprised at the 'smallness' of the brain, but then she said, 'Well, of course, cows are not very intelligent, are they? You wouldn't really expect them to have a big brain'. After a time, she volunteered, 'Then what about the *Diplodocus! That* couldn't have been very intelligent, could it, if you look at the size of its head!'
. . . She looked at the folds of the brain, and the blood-vessels on the surface, traced the ear-passage in the skull, and dissected the eye to get out the lens and see the retina.
(S. Isaacs, *Intellectual Growth in Young Children, 1930, pp. 200-201*)

The long-term significance of Susan Isaacs' work has seldom been questioned; its immediate relevance to the situation in the average state school was perhaps less obvious to contemporary teachers. Like Maria Montessori before her, Susan Isaacs was open to the charge of lacking practical experience in the harsh realities of state education. Although, as her admirers tend to stress, she was trained as an infant teacher as well as a psychologist, she went direct from postgraduate study to a training college lectureship. Her insistence that the Malting House School was a school, not a laboratory,[6] might also seem a little hollow. With a pupil-teacher ratio of about 5:1, children whose *average* I.Q. was 131, and a lavish provision of premises and equipment, it must have seemed to have had little in common with the relatively understaffed, underequipped and ill-housed state schools of the time.

In the book *The Children We Teach* Susan Isaacs summed up the results of her research :

. . . one is brought back to the fundamental conclusion that throughout the Primary School years, no less than in the years under seven, it is *the children's activity* that is the key to their full development. . . . Our part as teachers is to call out the childen's activity, and to meet it when it arises spontaneously. We can give them the means of solving problems in which they are actively concerned, but we cannot fruitfully foist problems upon them that do not arise from the development of their own interests . . .

There is little to be done with a large class of children, ranging in ability from the nearly defective to the very superior, but to keep them quiet and lecture to them. As we all know, the old conspiracy of silence and stillness arose from sheer necessity as much as from ignorance of child psychology. But when we make the groups smaller, and re-arrange them so that the members of any one group are roughly of the same level of general ability, it becomes more possible to let children have the free activity which is their breath of life.

(S. Isaacs, The Children We Teach, 1932, pp. 169-172 passim)

The progressives and Hadow

The progressive view was given friendly consideration by the Consultative Committee's report *The Primary School* (often referred to as the second Hadow Report) which appeared in 1931. It should be noted, however, that this did not amount to an unqualified endorsement of progressive methods; for example:

The well tried methods of corporate teaching have an indispensable place in the school economy, and should not be discarded wholesale in obedience to insufficiently tested theories.

(The Second Hadow Report, The Primary School, 1931, p. 122)

Nevertheless, it was recommendation 30 which was to become widely quoted as a snap summary of the whole report:

We are of opinion that the curriculum of the primary school is to be thought of in terms of activity and experience, rather than of knowledge to be acquired and facts to be stored.

Recommendations are one thing; implementation is another. The progressives demanded a radical rethink of educational practice no less than theory. The Consultative Committee seemed to agree – slightly equivocally perhaps in 1931 and more emphatically two years later, when, after consulting, among others, Susan Isaacs and Maria Montessori, it produced its report *Infant and Nursery Schools*. Ironically, however, these aims had already to some extent been proscribed by the committee's own previous policy. In 1926 it had recommended (in the first Hadow Report – *The Education of the Adolescent*) that an 11 + line be universally drawn between state primary and secondary education. At that age, children would be selected for grammar or for modern school. The entry to grammar school places was traditionally based upon examination in English and arithmetic, but by 1931 some authorities were including history, geography, and even other subjects.[7] Primary schools which appeared to jeopardize the 11 + success of their pupils by experiment with non-subject-based progressive methods of teaching were in consequence liable to come under intense criticism, particularly from articulate and worried middle-class parents.

The trend towards informality in junior education was, however, undoubtedly accelerated in the post-1945 period. Change appears to have come about largely on a local, grassroots basis in a number of fairly well-defined parts of the country. It seems far less to have been the result of any imposition from above of closely argued educational theory; as the Plowden Report later remarked: 'great advances appear to have been made without such theory, and research has still a long way to go before it can make a marked contribution.'[8] Better equipment and buildings (though Plowden was to reveal some disquieting facts on this count) undoubtedly made the process easier, as did the removal of the more formally taught 11 + classes to the new secondary modern schools. The increasing dependence of the 11 + examination itself upon intelligence tests (eventually to be used by 90 per cent of authorities) rather than upon formal written papers in basic subjects may well also have eased the doubts and fears of less enthusiastic teachers and parents.

The development of the trend towards progressive primary education in the postwar years appears to have been largely due to the individual efforts of a number of convinced educationalists in various parts of the country. Administrators such as J. H. Newsom in Hertfordshire and A. R. Clegg in the West Riding showed themselves actively prepared to encourage teachers working within their own L.E.A.s. The progressive methods of many of the latter probably owed far more to intuitive response and to experience at a purely personal level than to any theoretical considerations. During this period, too, child-centred and discovery methods of teaching were continuously publicized by a number of H.M.I.s. Prominent among these were Christian Schiller, L. C. Comber (who specialized in environmental studies), Edith Biggs (mathematics), Robin Tanner (art and design), and Alice Murton (infant teaching). On a more local basis, L.E.A. advisers (themselves mostly ex-teachers) did a great deal to break down the sense of isolation which had previously tended to restrict innovation within progressive junior schools, especially those in rural areas. By consciously acting as agents of communication for the exchange of ideas, L.E.A. advisers such as Peter Stone in the West Riding, Marian Parry in Bristol, and Edith Moorhouse in Oxfordshire were often able to give confidence to teachers whose own contact with other members of the profession tended to be limited or even nonexistent. But it is unlikely that such activities would have had any deep impact without the positive support of a significant number of the teachers themselves. The English tradition of down-to-earth progressive education has already been referred to; small rural schools on occasion found themselves endowed by natural circumstances with one or more of the Plowden hallmarks of progressive education. A lack, through small numbers, of formal classrooms or even classes; the fairly flexible grouping of children of different ages under a single teacher; these characteristics were inevitably more common in the country than in the large, more class-orientated and often streamed junior schools of the urban areas. *

Progressive attitudes towards education had, during the nineteenth and early twentieth centuries, been identified with individuals. The work of such people as Richard Dawes in the 1840s and Harriet Johnson in the early 1900s had not survived their departure from teaching nor, despite the support of the Inspectorate, had their example been followed by schools in their localities. A different situation prevailed in the post-1945 period as there emerged increasingly a resilient yet informal network of contacts between progressively minded teachers and the advisers, H.M.I.s, and education officers who supported them. Discussion groups, area conferences, exhibitions of work, and in-service courses all helped teachers to achieve a sense of identity and unity. Exchange schemes – for example, those operated during the 1960s between Oxfordshire on the one hand and the West Riding and Hertfordshire on the other – enabled teachers to coordinate their ideas and to feel their way towards the consensus of progressive approaches which the Plowden Report was to describe in 1967.[9]

The Plowden Report and after
The Plowden Report on English primary education (and its Welsh equivalent, the Gittins Report) were reasonably looked upon as an endorsement of progressive methods. They indisputably served to focus attention upon the primary scene – a double-edged benefit which was ultimately to have the effect of dissolving the general attitude of acquiescence (or sometimes apathy) towards primary education which had attended developments since 1931. In the years immediately after 1967, criticism of progressive methods was to become articulate and bitter. But at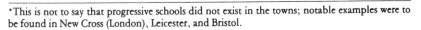

---

*This is not to say that progressive schools did not exist in the towns; notable examples were to be found in New Cross (London), Leicester, and Bristol.

the time, the report was to act as a powerful encouragement to progressive primary teachers for, like the second Hadow Report, it seemed to emphasize official approval of the distinctive nature of their work.

The main impression given by the Plowden Report is on the whole one of enlightened and humane change in the face of long-term financial neglect. On the latter count the committee recorded that 'there is a strong feeling that primary education, more than any other sector of education, is failing to secure its share of educational and of national expenditure. . . . We need only note that the staffing ratios, the condition of school building in many primary schools, and the treatment of primary schools in respect of equipment and capitation allowances all combine to provide for primary education less than it needs to do the job properly.'[10]

The committee made a grand gesture in their attempts to assess the actual quality of primary teaching, undertaking (with the help of the Inspectorate) what they described as 'a comprehensive survey' of the country's primary schools, each of which was placed by them into one of nine categories. The first of these comprised schools which were judged to be 'In most respects a school of outstanding quality'.[11] Category 9 – 'A bad school where children suffer from laziness, indifference, gross incompetence or unkindness on the part of the staff' – came at the bottom of the pile. The committee's overall estimate that 'One-third of the children in primary schools go to schools which are quite clearly good'[12] (categories 1-3) was perhaps hardly calculated to reassure the parents of the majority who apparently did not.

A key issue, of course, concerned the actual criteria employed by the Plowden Committee in making their judgements. These were subsequently to be questioned with some asperity. The committee's own preferences are revealed quite clearly in their composite descriptions of 'three schools, run successfully on modern lines, which might fall into any of the first three categories'.[13] In the first of these (an infant school) a hypothetical visitor would discover in the playground

. . . a group of children, with their teacher, clustered round a large square box full of earth. The excitement is all about an earthworm, which none of the children had ever seen before. Their classroom door opens on to the playground and inside are the rest of the class, seated at tables disposed informally about the room, some reading books that they have themselves chosen from the copious shelves along the side of the room and some measuring the quantities of water that different vessels will hold.

In the second school – a junior mixed one – fourth-year children were to be found broadcasting poems of their choice through a home-made microphone, while at the third school

. . . all the children in the first class were either on top of the church tower or standing in the churchyard and staring intently upwards. The headmaster appeared

in the porch and explained what was happening. The children were making a study of the trees in the private park which lay 100 yards beyond the church. The tower party had taken up with them the seeds of various trees and were releasing these on the leeward side, and were measuring the wind speed with a home-made anemometer.
(The Plowden Report, Children and their Primary Schools, 1967, paragraphs 279, 283, and 286)

The committee's principal recommendations on primary school organization were, in fact, notably moderate in tone:

96.   We recommend a combination of individual group and class work and welcome the trend towards individual learning.

. . .

100.   We welcome unstreaming in the infant school and hope that it will continue to spread through the age groups of the junior school.

Their attempt, however, to formulate what was termed 'a recognizable philosophy of education'[14] proved more controversial. This decision was apparently motivated by a reluctance on the part of primary teachers to advance one for themselves. 'It was interesting,' noted the report, 'that some of the head teachers who were considered by H.M. Inspectors to be most successful in practice were least able to formulate their aims clearly and convincingly.'[15]

Honestly, then, and perhaps incautiously, the Plowden Committee attempted their own definition:

A school is not merely a teaching shop, it must transmit values and attitudes. It is a community in which children learn to live first and foremost as children and not as future adults. In family life children learn to live with people of all ages. The school sets out deliberately to devise the right environment for children, to allow them to be themselves and to develop in the way and at the pace appropriate to them. It tries to equalise opportunities and to compensate for handicaps. It lays special stress on individual discovery, on first hand experience and on opportunities for creative work. It insists that knowledge does not fall into neatly separate compartments and that work and play are not opposite but complementary. A child brought up in such an atmosphere at all stages of his education has some hope of becoming a balanced and mature adult and of being able to live in, to contribute to, and to look critically at the society of which he forms a part. Not all primary schools correspond to this picture, but it does represent a general and quickening trend.
(The Plowden Report, Children and their Primary Schools, 1967, paragraph 505)

Six main points seem to crystallize out from this general statement: the primary school must be regarded 'as a community in which children learn to live . . . as children and not as future adults'; it is an institution which deliberately sets out to allow children 'to be themselves and to develop in the way and at the pace appropriate to them'; it 'tries to equalise opportunities and to compensate for handicaps'; it 'lays special stress on individual discovery'; it 'insists that knowledge does not fall into neatly separate compartments'; and it regards work and play as 'not opposite but complementary'.

Of these aims the third and the sixth aroused relatively little adverse comment. The concept of 'positive discrimination' and the committee's recommendations concerning the creation of Educational Priority Areas were initially welcomed as humane and imaginative; the insistence upon the value of play in learning had an acceptable and extended pedigree. But the remaining objectives, widely publicized by the enthusiastic reception which, in some quarters at least, had marked the appearance of the report, aroused considerable opposition. The latter was based as much upon fundamental considerations of principle as upon the committee's failure to produce incontrovertible proof that at least some of the approaches which they advocated offered (either singly or combined) a form of education superior to, or indeed even as good as, traditional and more directive classroom techniques. 'My contention,' wrote Professor R. S. Peters, who had himself been a witness to the committee, 'is that this summary of a "recognizable educational philosophy" proliferates in important half-truths that are paraded as educational panaceas.'[16] It would appear that he was by no means alone in this opinion.

Criticism of the first Plowden principle – insistence that children should be regarded as children and not as future adults – was no doubt amplified by the report's recommendation number 58 that the age limit for primary education be shifted upwards from 11 + to 12 + and by the committee's apparent rejection of the secondary ethos ('we do not want the middle school to be dominated by secondary influences').[17] As one commentator, Professor P. H. Taylor, put it: 'One wonders whether, unconsciously, the committee are arguing in fact for a longer period of childhood.'[18] He then proceeded to stress that

The goals of the social institutions called schools, whose main characteristic is that they cater for the young, are many. A major one is that they shall mould or shape the private person into a public person with all this entails in terms of initiating the young into the society into which they were born, into its language, culture and morality, into its economy and its modes of dealing with power, and to do all this in terms of the ideals which that society elaborates for itself as the best that man can strive for.
(P. H. Taylor, in 'The Middle Years of Schooling from 8 to 13', Schools Council Working Paper No. 22, 1969, p. 8)

Although Taylor stressed that 'intellectual self-determination' was a second important goal for schools to achieve in their pupils, he maintained that the social and preparatory role of the school could only be ignored by teachers at their own risk. 'Recall what happened to Socrates,'[19] he ominously reflected.

The Plowden requirement that children should 'be themselves' was also received with a fair amount of scepticism:

And what is one to make of this emphasis on being oneself?

demanded Professor Peters.

. . . Out of a context it is a vacuous recommendation which is consistent with any form of development; for presumably the Marquis de Sade was being himself as much as St. Francis. They just had different selves to develop.
(R. S. Peters, in Perspectives on Plowden, 1969, p. 6)

Intimations of a growing polarization of opinions in education became painfully apparent with the publication in 1969 of the first two 'Black Papers' on education. In the second of these, Professor G. H. Bantock cast a cold eye upon the Plowden-approved methods of individual discovery. His article cited the work of the American psychologist, Dr. D. P. Ausubel, concerning 'the crucially important role which "reception"* can play even in the education of young children' and emphasized possible dangers of an assumption that superficial 'discovery' can in any way be equated with genuine understanding:

I am technically quite inept, and I rely on the good services of mechanics if anything goes wrong with my car, for indeed I know practically nothing about its functioning. Let us say I suffer a breakdown in a wild and desolate spot. I raise the bonnet and face the engine; I see it, I touch it, I even listen to it; but because I have no idea of the meaning of what I see, my 'experience' is null and void; and the car remains stationary.
(G. H. Bantock, in Black Paper Two, 1969, p. 113)

Neither Peters nor Bantock was impressed by Plowden's contention that 'knowledge does not fall into neatly separate compartments'. The latter complained that a wilful refusal to acknowledge the separateness of individual academic disciplines would lead to the adoption of a 'magpie curriculum' in which

History, biology, anatomy jostle side by side, and children are persuaded to start after any hare that crosses their path, or that can arouse a temporary ebullition of 'interest' – and children's interests are often very temporary.
(G. H. Bantock, in Black Paper Two, 1969, p. 115)

R. S. Peters took a similar view and shrewdly drew the reader's attention to the Plowden chapter on curriculum, which, true to a general precedent set by previous reports, scarcely reflected the progressive tone of the more theoretical sections; he continued

It took acute thinkers such as Hume and Kant a considerable time to establish that mathematics is different from empirical science in important respects and that

*i.e., the *presentation* of knowledge to pupils as opposed to their discovery of it on their own initiative.

morals is not really much like either of them. Are we suggesting that philosophers since the seventeenth century have been wrong in such matters? Are we to go back and maintain that religion is indistinguishable from science and that morals is similar to geometrical demonstration? Surely one of the great achievements of our civilization is to have gradually separated out and got clearer about the types of concepts and truth-criteria involved in different forms of thought.
(R. S. Peters, in Perspectives on Plowden, 1969, pp. 13-14)

Perhaps the implication that the Plowden Committee was attempting to subvert the whole structure of modern Western thought was not a wholly serious one. But there seems to be little doubt that the report itself, and the reaction to it, finally dissipated the mist of *laissez faire* acquiescence which had for some time enveloped primary education. This, as has been mentioned, was to prove a mixed blessing. Primary teachers were no doubt gratified by the Labour government's quick response to the report's E.P.A. recommendations (£16 million was voted and a research programme promptly initiated) and by Mrs. Thatcher's subsequent allocation of £44 million (beginning in 1973-74) towards primary school building. The Plowden suggestion that the teachers themselves should consider seeking out and visiting reluctant parents[20] was possibly less welcome to an already overworked profession. Less welcome, too, has been the edginess occasionally shown by parents and government alike towards certain aspects of the primary curriculum. In 1972 an alarmist N.F.E.R. report, 'The Trend of Reading Standards', caused Mrs. Thatcher to appoint (somewhat precipitately, as events were later to show) a committee of enquiry chaired by Sir Alan Bullock into 'all aspects of teaching the use of English'. Meanwhile the Black Papers and their adherents continued to snipe at progressive schooling, the E.P.A. programme began to flag, and in November 1974 the Inner London Teachers' Association published a survey of *primary* schools in Southwark (a tough area, admittedly) which claimed, among other rather worrying things, that 23 percent of the teachers had 'personally been hurt or injured attempting to control children'.[21] In late 1975 trouble erupted at the William Tyndale junior school in Islington, North London, when a long drawn-out quarrel between managers, parents, and staff resulted in the temporary withdrawal of the headmaster and six of his teachers to their own alternative establishment nearby. The subsequent enquiry by Robin Auld, Q.C. concluded that, 'The formidable weight of evidence . . . suggests strongly that the quality of education that the children were receiving was bad . . .''[22] The William Tyndale incident was an isolated one. Potentially more damaging to the general cause of informalism was the study of 37 primary teachers and their 950 pupils in Northwest England by Neville Bennett and his colleagues. The children 'were tested on a wide range of attainment and personality tests' in September 1973 and again, to assess their progress, in June 1974. Bennett claimed that the ensuing results were not only 'very similar' to those obtained by the most recent American research, but also that they were 'in line' with what *all* the teachers themselves had expected:[23]

The results form a coherent pattern. The effect of teaching style is statistically and educationally significant in all attainment areas tested. In reading, pupils of formal and mixed teachers progress more than those of informal teachers, the difference being equivalent to some three to five months' difference in performance. In mathematics formal pupils are superior to both mixed and informal pupils, the difference in progress being some four to five months. In English formal pupils again out-perform both mixed and informal pupils, the discrepancy in progress between formal and informal being approximately three to five months.
(N. Bennett et al., Teaching Styles and Pupil Progress, 1976, p. 152)

The validity of Bennett's work was immediately questioned, but the publicity which it attracted was some indication of a widely felt concern about methods of teaching which, however enlightened and humane in spirit, continued to lack the support of decisive proof of superiority over the more traditional ways. The government discussion document 'Education in Schools' (1977) made a determined attempt to make a judicious view of the question; while abstaining from any overt criticism of the principle of progressive teaching, it nevertheless conceded that in some cases certain mistakes had been made. 'The primary curriculum,' it stated, 'has been enriched by a feeling for colour, design and music, and by the introduction of simple scientific ideas' – and then continued:

While only a tiny minority of schools adopted the child-centred approach to the exclusion of other teaching methods, its influence has been widespread.

It has proved to be a trap for some less able or less experienced teachers who applied the freer methods uncritically or failed to recognise that they require careful planning of the opportunities offered to children and systematic monitoring of the progress of individuals.

While the majority of primary teachers, whatever approach they use, recognise the importance of performance in basic skills such as reading, spelling and arithmetic, some have failed to achieve satisfactory results in them. In some classes, or even some schools, the use of the child-centred approach has deteriorated into lack of order and application.

The challenge now is to restore the rigour without damaging the real benefits of the child-centred developments . . .

Notes

1   R. J. W. Selleck, *The New Education*, 1968.
2   E. G. A. Holmes, *What Is and What Might Be*, 1911, p. 210.
3   H. Caldwell Cook, *The Play Way*, 1917, p. 1.
4   Ibid, p. 2.
5   See above, p. 18.

6   S. Isaacs, *Intellectual Growth in Young Children*, 1930, p. 1.

7   Second Hadow Report *(The Primary School)*, 1931, p. 101.

8   Plowden Report, paragraph 550.

9   Much of the information in the preceding paragraphs was kindly supplied by Miss Edith Moorhouse.

10   Plowden Report, paragraph 1170.

11   Ibid, paragraphs 269-276. The report placed primary schools in the following categories:
     1 'In most respects a school of outstanding quality' (containing about 1% of the children);
     2 'A good school with some outstanding features' (containing about 9% of the children);
     3 'A good school in most respects without any special distinction' (containing about 23% of the children);
     4 'A school without many good features, but showing signs of life with seeds of growth in it' (16% of the children);
     5 'A school with too many weaknesses to go in Category 2 or 3, but distinguished by specially good personal relationships' (6% of the children);
     6 'A decent school without enough merit to go in Category 3 and yet too solid for Category 8' (28% of the children);
     7 'Curate's egg school, with good and bad features' (9% of the children);
     8 'A school markedly out of touch with current practice and knowledge and with few compensating features' (5% of the children); and
     9 'A bad school where children suffer from laziness, indifference, gross incompetence or unkindness on the part of the staff' (0.1% of the children).

12   Ibid, paragraph 270.

13   Ibid, paragraph 277.

14   Ibid, paragraph 504.

15   Ibid, paragraph 497.

16   R. S. Peters, in *Perspectives on Plowden*, 1969, p. 3.

17   Plowden Report, paragraph 383.

18   P. H. Taylor, in 'The Middle Years of Schooling from 8 to 13', (Schools Council Working Paper No. 22), 1969, p. 7.

19   Ibid, p. 9.

20   Plowden Report, paragraph 113.

21   See Marie Maxwell's article 'Stress in Schools' in *Centre Point*, 3 November 1974, p. 6.

22   *Times Educational Supplement*, 23 July 1976, p. 24.

23   N. Bennett et al., *Teaching Styles and Pupil Progress*, 1976, pp. 152-154.

CHAPTER 5

'WHAT THE COUNTRY HAS A RIGHT TO
DEMAND': MIDDLE-CLASS SECONDARY
EDUCATION AND 'THE LADDER OF
OPPORTUNITY' IN THE LATER NINETEENTH
CENTURY

Contemporary accounts of nineteenth-century education sometimes give the impression that elementary school life was often overshadowed by interference on the part of central and local authority. The same claim cannot be justifiably made of secondary education. Nevertheless, superficially at least, the position of many secondary schools resembled that of the elementary: they were, of course, subject to government enquiry, they were eligible for government aid (from the Department of Science and Art) in return for the successful pursuit of specific examination courses; under the provisions of the Endowed Schools Act of 1869 the government (in the form of the Endowed Schools and later the Charity Commissioners) was vested with wide powers to determine the regulations controlling individual schools; and finally, in the last decade of the century, the secondary schools became increasingly dependent upon financial subsidy from local authorities.

Indeed, control by the agencies of central or local government existed in a not insignificant number of cases: the Schools Inquiry Commission, which reported under Lord Taunton in 1868, listed twenty grammar schools as being controlled by local corporations;[1] by the time of the Bryce Report on Secondary Education in 1895 a further seventeen secondary schools had been founded by the newly formed county councils, usually in conjunction with the Charity Commission.[2] Then there were the controversial higher grade schools, owing a precarious existence from the mid-1870s onwards to the semantic ambiguities of Forster's Act. Essentially extensions of the elementary school system, there were sixty-three of these in England by the time of the Bryce Report; a further seventy-four board elementary schools contained post-elementary forms. Like the pupil teacher centres[3] (themselves part of the ill-defined but wide-ranging area of secondary and further education included under the general heading of teacher training), the higher grade classes were mostly run by school boards, and, like the school boards, they inspired mixed feelings. As Michael Sadler pointed out:

The name Higher Grade was . . . ambiguous from the first. To the ambitious School Board men, it meant intellectually superior; to the affronted ratepayer it meant a higher fee; to the poor struggling clerk it meant a socially higher grade of school; to the Department in 1879 it seemed at once to harmonize two things:
(a) Grading of schools according to the Schools Inquiry Commission;
(b) Keeping the ordinary elementary school cheap and nasty.
. . . 'Conceived in iniquity' is the thing I am inclined to quote on it all.
(Lynda Grier, Achievement in Education, 1952, pp. 71-72)

Sadler's view was by no means universally endorsed. Representing a relatively unselective form of secondary education and one conveniently arranged 'end on' to the elementary schools, the higher grade concept was to attract considerable support both in the late nineteenth and twentieth centuries. By the mid-1890s the higher grade schools were in some areas posing a genuine threat to neighbouring endowed schools: John Massie, investigating the situation for the Bryce Commission, observed a particularly hard-line instance in Birmingham, where 'the Albert Road higher grade school professedly and indifferently overlaps the adjoining King Edward's Schools, preparing for the "College of Preceptors, Oxford Local, and London Matriculation Examinations,"[4] and placarding the walls of Aston with bills to that effect.'[5] But the development of the higher grade schools was to be irreparably blighted by the Cockerton Judgement of 1900, which reemphasized that money raised by school boards from the rates under the 1870 Act could not legally be devoted to postelementary schooling.

Most secondary schools, however, fell broadly into three categories – endowed, proprietary, and private – and it was upon this basis that, with the exclusion of the nine most prominent endowed schools,* they were investigated by the Schools Inquiry Commission, which found that there were 572 endowed schools offering education of a postelementary nature, nearly 37,000 scholars being in attendance.[6] All boys' and girls' proprietary schools known to the commission (about 120, with a total of more than 14,000 pupils)[7] were also considered, as were some of the estimated 10,000 private secondary schools.

What type of school constituted each of these general categories? The term 'endowed school' was applied to a whole range of establishments from the wealthy and exclusive university-orientated 'public' schools to such citadels of bucolic latitude as Ottery St. Mary, where

. . . Six day boys, all very young and paying fees, composed the school. The boarders' dining room was occupied as a coach-house by two of the master's carriages, the night study was a laundry, and the large dormitory a billiard room.

or Netherbury, where

. . . the master has other business, and at one time carried on continuously with the school the business of a flour and spinning mill.
(The Taunton Report, Schools Inquiry Commission, 1868, Vol. I, pp. 224 and 226)

Faced with such variety and originality the commissioners felt constrained to divide secondary schools into three grades according to the leaving age of the pupils, which tended in some to be eighteen or nineteen, in others about

---

*Whose affairs had been considered in the Clarendon Report of 1864.

sixteen, and in the least ambitious schools about fourteen.[8] Grade-one schools, they discovered, were patronized by the offspring of

. . . men with considerable incomes independent of their own exertions, or professional men, and men in business, whose profits put them on the same level.

together with those of

. . . the great majority of professional men, especially the clergy, medical men, and lawyers; the poorer gentry; all in fact, who, having received a cultivated education themselves, are very anxious that their sons should not fall below them.

Some of this class also sent their children to grade-two schools, where they mingled with those of

. . . the larger shopkeepers, rising men of business, and the larger tenant farmers.

Grade-three establishments, however, relied upon the fees* paid by

. . . smaller tenant farmers, the small tradesmen, the superior artisans;

the requirements of whose children were confined to

. . . very good reading, very good writing, very good arithmetic.
(The Taunton Report, Schools Inquiry Commission, 1868, Vol. I, pp. 16-20 passim)

These schools had no classical pretensions and consequently little connection with the universities or professions.

The same triple grading was applied to private and proprietary schools. The latter comprised a largely transient class of institution, mostly of fairly recent foundation, which in the course of time was expected either to decline to a purely private status or to make the grade and transfer to the rank of endowed school.

. . . all are alike private property, either of one or more individuals or of a corporate body; the buildings and funds are not permanently dedicated to educational uses. Yet they do not depend on the will of the schoolmaster . . . the school has a life beyond his, and he is only a chief officer for the time being.

Such places as Radley, Haileybury, Clifton, Malvern, and Rossall came under this heading, as did the Ladies' College at Cheltenham, which was singled out for particular praise. In the words of the commissioners

The educational character of proprietary schools stands very high. Some of them rank with the most famous of the Grammar schools, as places of preparation for the Universities . . .
(The Taunton Report, Schools Inquiry Commission, 1868, Vol. I, pp. 310 and 318)

---

*The cost . . . of first-rate instruction is about 20 l.; in a second-grade school . . . is 8 l. to 10 l.; of a third-grade school, from 3 l. to 5 l.
(The Taunton Report, Schools Inquiry Commission, 1868, Vol. I, pp. 147-8)

The estimated 10,000 private schools, mostly owned by their own head teachers, constituted, so to speak, the submerged mass of the nineteenth-century secondary education iceberg. As the report pointed out,

Private schools exist on their own merits; they owe no account to any one, they are subject to no inspection or control; any man or woman may start one tomorrow if persons can be found willing to send their children to it. The profession of private schoolmaster is absolutely unrestricted. . . . The one practical condition of his success is his satisfying the parents of his pupils. . .

From the tone of the foregoing passage it is not perhaps surprising that the generality of private schools received a rather jaundiced verdict:

In particular it seems to be clear, that, excellent as are many of the private schools of the more expensive sort, we find a rapid deterioration as we descend the scale in price, and most of those, which we should reckon as belonging to the third grade, are quite unequal to the task that they have undertaken.
(The Taunton Report, Schools Inquiry Commission, 1868, Vol. I, pp. 104 and 284-285)

The endowed schools

The demand for secondary places in proprietary and private schools, no less than the governmental concern evidenced by the calling of the Schools Inquiry and Bryce Commissions, indicates that the efficiency of the traditional source of secondary education – the endowed schools – was becoming increasingly open to question. Such suspicion was well founded. The Schools Inquiry (or Taunton) Report revealed two extensive and fundamental flaws in the position of the endowed schools. Either of these alone would have been cause for alarm and despondency; in combination they seemed to add up to something approaching a breakdown in the secondary area of education.

First (and most easily understandable) was the irregular geographical distribution of endowed secondary schools. Here the increase and redistribution of population, together with the vagaries of private munificence and of its guardians, had left 228 towns of 2000 inhabitants or more unprovided for.[9] Unless, consequently, a mid-nineteenth-century parent was wealthy and at the same time prepared to commit his offspring to the not-so-tender mercies of a boarding school, he might well have found it impossible to obtain a secondary education for them.

But such difficulties were by no means at an end even if an endowed school did exist in the proximity. For the academic standards of these schools were apparently being subjected to a pernicious erosion, the cumulative effects of which constituted the core of a paradox that seemed to dominate secondary education for much of the nineteenth century. This was the apparent failure of so many of the endowed schools in the face of an increase in the wealth and numbers of their potential clientele and at a time when there was a widespread acknowledgement of a national need for the services for which their original purpose seemed to fit them. But, as the Schools Inquiry Commission concluded:

> . . . the instruction given in the endowed schools is often very far removed from what their founders could have anticipated, or from what the country has a right to demand.
> *(The Taunton Report, Schools Inquiry Commission, 1868, Vol. I, p. 138)*

The Taunton commissioners (who, unlike their successors under Bryce, carried out their investigations upon a nationwide basis) discovered the disquieting fact that of the 820 schools or separate departments controlled by foundations* intended to provide secondary education in England and Wales, no fewer than 50 were in abeyance and 198 had regressed to elementary status.[10] Many of the remainder were sinking into a parlous condition:

> The classical education of the highest order is every day to a greater degree quitting the small grammar schools for the great public schools, and others of the same kind. Those who want such education can no longer find it, as they could in the last century, close to their doors, all over the country. They are compelled to seek it in boarding schools, and generally in boarding schools of a very expensive kind.
> *(The Taunton Report, Schools Inquiry Commission, 1868, Vol. I, p. 18)*

How could this anomalous situation be explained? Here again there appeared to be two principal reasons – the inadequacy of charitable funds and the steady refusal of the government to involve itself in the finance or administration of the endowed schools. The Taunton commissioners were quite explicit upon the first of these points:

> It will be at once seen that very few of the grammar school endowments can, unassisted by fees, educate more than a very limited number of scholars, at least of the first or second grade. . . . It is only, therefore, by reducing the education to what is suited only to boys leaving school at 14 years of age that the grammar school endowment can (except in a comparatively few cases) hold out; and by this reduction (it cannot be too often repeated) the school is rendered nearly useless to many whom the founders distinctly intended to benefit, and it fails to give the poor boy, who is apt to learn, the means of putting out his talents to the best advantage.
>
> The facts abundantly confirm this conclusion. The only schools giving a really high education gratuitously to a large number of scholars are Birmingham, Bedford, and Manchester.
> *(The Taunton Report, Schools Inquiry Commission, 1868, Vol. I, p. 148)*

The implications were inescapable. In an age when even the rudiments of

---

*Of which there were 782.

elementary education had to be at least partly paid for by an indigent working class, the centuries-old concept of gratuitous or generously subsidized grammar school education had little chance of survival. Children from poor homes were at a double disadvantage for, as the commissioners remarked, free places tended to be appropriated by the well-to-do classes. Aware, no doubt, of the possible consequences of these harsh facts, they recorded their concern for the bright working-class child:

We cannot but consider, that it is a matter of national interest, that boys of real ability, in whatever rank of life they may be found, should receive every aid and encouragement, that can be rightly given, to enable them to rise to a position suitable to their talents. We cannot but look on it as one of the glories of this country, that so many men should have risen to eminence from humble stations, and should have found so much in our institutions to aid them so to rise. And we think, that it would be a serious defect in our means of education, if any obstacles were thrown in the way of what is so excellent in itself and so useful to the country.
(The Taunton Report, Schools Inquiry Commission, 1868, Vol. I, p. 309)

But if endowments, even when efficiently administered, were inadequate, and the cost of efficient secondary instruction remained too high for many parents, state aid alone could provide a meaningful alternative to a system based squarely (if not unashamedly) upon the qualification of parental wealth. The validity of this argument, however, conflicting as it did with the sturdy Victorian ideals of independence, self-help, and the limitation of governmental interference in civil life, was not officially conceded until the last years of the century. Indeed, the whole issue of free versus tax-subsidized schooling was an emotive one, fraught with moral implications of an elemental nature. Illustrative of the passion which it could arouse is the highly charged reaction of Edward Thring, regarded by many of his contemporaries as one of the leading Christian educationalists of the age:

No law has any right when a man has been industrious, thrifty, restrained in his passions, and married late, to take his money in order to pay for the support of the children of his idle, thriftless, dissolute neighbour, who seduced, or married some unhappy woman because of his lust, and now demands that his self-denying neighbour should pay, by maintaining the children, for his gratifying his passions.
(George R. Parkin, Edward Thring, 1898, Vol. II, p. 215)

Not everyone, however, shared the prevailing attitude. Matthew Arnold, for one, had vehemently rejected it:

How vain, then, and how meaningless, to tell a man who, for the instruction of his offspring, receives aid from the State, that he is humiliated! Humiliated by receiving help from himself as an individual from himself in his corporate and associated capacity! help to which his own money, as a taxpayer, contributes, and for which, as a result of the joint energy and intelligence of the whole community in employing its power, he himself deserves some of the praise! He is no more humiliated by being on

the foundation of the Charterhouse or of Winchester, or by holding a scholarship or fellowship at Oxford, or Cambridge.
(Matthew Arnold, A French Eton; or, Middle Class Education and the State, 1864, p. 76)

And he had characteristically put forward his own scheme, which was to some extent (but abortively) endorsed by the Schools Inquiry Commission.

Over twenty years later, near the end of his life, Arnold could still analyse the situation in terms which amounted to a damaging indictment of contemporary secondary education: 'our provision of secondary schools,' he wrote in 1887, 'is utterly incoherent and inadequate'.

Here, as illustration of secondary schools in the Taunton era, is a description of a bad third-grade school, which, in the words of H.M.I. Fearon, 'though *one* of the worst endowed schools which I visited . . . was not a solitary case':

Having given the usual notice of my coming I arrived at the school at about 10 o'clock in the morning, and found the boys not yet all assembled. In the course of about 20 minutes, however, all that appeared that morning had come in, that is to say rather more than two-thirds of those whose names were on the register.

Having spoken to a few of the boys, and made the master's acquaintance, I requested him to conduct the school as usual, and sat down at one side of the room. The master had to conduct the school quite single-handed, having no assistance. After watching for about half an hour, there being no time-table in the room, and being quite unable to make out what the classification of the school was, I entered into conversation with the master. In reply to my questions he said there were 'about five classes, more or less'; but in fact there was no regular classification, as he found it necessary to shift boys every day for arithmetic or for reading or for some separate subject. He had not much opinion of classification, but preferred individual teaching as much as possible. He had no system, and no method; he just took them as they came. The teaching then proceeded.

The order was very bad. The floor as well as the desks being occupied by boys, those quarters of the room towards which from time to time the master's back happened to be turned were the scenes of regular rows. Boys were kicking, clawing, spitting, crawling, prompting, copying, and occasionally yelling. Having seen enough of this, I asked the master whether the governors would permit me to examine some of the boys. . . . He seemed to be very unwilling to do so, remarking that he was not used to be visited in this way, and that "he and his boys could precious soon turn anyone out if they chose". I quite admitted the truth of this sentiment, and then proceeded to examine. The master being unable to tell me of any definite classification of the boys, I was obliged to classify them by inquiring the attainments of each individual scholar. In about 20 minutes I had them classified for reading and writing. The reading was passable only among the first 16 boys, who were over 12 years old. As one went down lower in the school, and came among the boys eight, nine, and 10 years old, it became exceedingly bad. Indeed I was convinced that the younger boys got no teaching in it at all. The writing in copybooks of those first 16 boys was exceedingly bad. I really think it had almost every possible fault. . . . The copybookds were dog's-eared, very dirty, and blotted, and did not show any signs of correction. The transcribing of the younger boys upon slates was also very bad.

. . .

Only one (of the top 40 boys) would have passed the inspector's examination in writing and dictation at a National school. At 12 o'clock we dismissed, appointing 2 o'clock for our reassembly. The master, who lived some way from the school, was 15 minutes late. Some boys were an hour late; and these were placed in a corner for the remainder of the day, where they had capital fun together.

(The Taunton Report, Schools Inquiry Commission, 1868, Vol. VII, pp. 309-310)

Next, by contrast, Fearon's account of an exceptionally efficient second-grade school. The Whitechapel Foundation Commercial School was, at the time of the Taunton Report, a recent creation which had originated in 1854 from the consolidation of a number of local charities. In a sense, therefore, Fearon was reporting upon a prototype of the secondary schools which were to be established in consequence of the Endowed Schools Act. Certainly the efficiency with which the school appears to have been run markedly contrasts with the degraded and broken-down condition of the majority of the schools the endowments of which had remained unreformed:

The trustees are the rector, churchwardens, and overseers of the poor of the parish, *ex officio;* but associated with them are 12 lay trustees, who at the present time are respectable tradesmen, such as iron-mongers, sugar bakers, grocers, linendrapers, italian warehousemen, etc. The trustees do not seem to interfere unduly. They have elected a good master, and they give him rope, and indeed, seem to put considerable confidence in him. . . . There is a tendency on the part of the shopkeepers among the trustees to decry the instruction in Latin, Euclid, and other scientific branches of study; but this has been counteracted by the influence of the rector; and there is *salt* even in these utilitarian views. After all, the school is for the benefit of these shopkeepers. It is their children who are being taught there; and their influence ought to be felt in shaping the curriculum.
. . .
The school is strictly a day school. It is intended to give education, as the trustees express it, 'without the necessity of removing the children from the care and control of their parents'. The boys attending it are chiefly the sons of tradesmen. There are also, not unfrequently, sons of superior mechanics, men who make delicate and intricate parts of machines or instruments, and whose business requires intelligence, and fineness of touch and sight; such as watchmakers, opticians, and the like. The head boy in the school at the time of my visit was of this class. Almost all of them live quite close to the school. . . . (The curriculum's) main feature, according to the scheme, is the omission of Greek at the same time that Latin is retained. This was, no doubt, a most necessary and proper regulation; but all my experience shows that it would not have been sufficient of itself to satisfy the wants of the parents. The mere omission of Greek would have removed objections to the curriculum but would not have caused it to be so thoroughly satisfactory as it now seems to be to all the thoughtful and intelligent among the parents. The cause of this satisfaction appears to be *that the master puts the modern languages and mathematics upon exactly the same footing as that on which Latin stands . . .*
. . .
On the whole the school has been decidedly successful. It was opened in March 1858 with 50 scholars. In 12 months the attendance has risen to 152. In March 1860 it was 188; in March 1861 it was 201; in March 1862 it was 192; in March 1863 it was 214; in March 1864 it was 280; in March 1865 it was 221. There are no doubt some defects

voidable and unavoidable in the arrangements or constitution of the school, but they are of minor importance. The school has on the whole been judiciously planned and efficiently worked.
(The Taunton Report, Schools Inquiry Commission, 1868, Vol. VII, pp. 461-464 passim)

The endowed schools after the Taunton Report

'But the saddest part of the experience of the Commissioners,' stated Joshua Fitch in 1888 of Lord Taunton and his collaborators, 'appears to have been the discovery that four-fifths of the endowed schools were fulfilling neither the one purpose nor the other; and that the whole machinery, while in some cases producing positive mischief . . . was even in the best cases yielding results sadly inadequate to its costliness, and unsuited to the educational wants of the community for whose benefit it was designed. These evils have been to a large extent remedied.'[11]

The important sentence, of course, is the last one: it shows a point of view apparently irreconcilable to that of Matthew Arnold quoted earlier.[12] But then Fitch, himself an ex-inspectorate colleague of Arnold, had been closely identified with the workings of the Endowed Schools Act since his appointment as assistant commissioner at Exeter in 1870.[13] His claim therefore deserves attention.

It is not infrequently assumed that endowed grammar schools remained largely unregenerate until the era of Robert Morant when the post-1902 local authority funds combined with the free-place legislation of 1907 to create the instantly recognizable image of the twentieth-century grammar school. This view tends to overlook the effects of the Endowed Schools Act of 1869; hence the significance of Fitch's appraisal.

There is some indication that before the end of the nineteenth century several hundred endowed schools already had a number of the characteristics generally attributed to the post-1902 grammar school. They consequently provided a conscious or unconscious precedent for the administrators of the early 1900s. Thus the Return of 1897[14] could list 619 endowed secondary schools with 76,671 pupils: in the boys' schools 64.7 percent of the full-time male staff were graduates and in the girls' 23.8 percent of the mistresses; on average about 10 percent to 15 percent of the places for children of eleven or over appear to have been filled on a scholarship basis and frequently restricted to local public elementary school children (of whom most of the successful candidates tended to be of middle-class origin). Descriptions of such schools in the Bryce Report arguably seem to give a preview of twentieth-century grammar school life.

The Endowed Schools Act gave the commission which it created wide powers to manipulate charities and endowments. Although the commissioners shared the Taunton conviction that endowed schools should derive a substantial part of their income from fees, they also seem from the beginning to have been at pains to heed the injunction that 'boys of real ability, in whatever rank of life they may be found, should receive every aid and encouragement, that can be rightly given, to enable them to rise to a position suitable to their talents'.[15] By 1894 the amalgamation and reallocation of bequests by the Endowed Schools and Charity Commissions[16] had produced 851 new schemes in England. These together accounted for no less than five-sevenths of the available funds.[17] From 1889 the working of the Endowed Schools Act in Wales was supplemented by that of the Welsh Intermediate Education Act. The latter created local education authorities (on which the Charity Commission was represented) for 'intermediate' (i.e., postelementary) and 'technical' schooling; by the end of the century just under 100 Welsh schools had been reorganized or founded under its provisions.

Concern for the outstanding working-class child had been evident from the first. Endowed Schools commissioner H. J. Roby, speaking in 1873, explained how in regulating the award of free secondary places, 'we frequently add a . . . safeguard by restricting the competition to boys from the public elementary schools, or boys who are orphans, or boys from a lower grade school'.[18] One of the earliest schemes, that for Palmer's Endowed School at Grays Thurrock in Essex, stipulated that a maximum of 10 percent of the places should be totally exempt from fees, up to a further 10 percent partially exempt and that half the exhibitions thus awarded should be open in the first instance only to boys from the local public elementary schools.[19] In those schemes (initiated under Section 30 of the act) which dealt with minor charities, the restriction of scholarships whenever possible to boys and girls from public elementary schools seems to have become a fairly standard procedure. An example of the increasing availability of scholarships to elementary school children is evident in the records of St. Mark's School at Kennington, where from 1881 to 1888 the boys successfully competed for 39 places in the neighbouring secondary schools.[20]

It must be admitted, however, that this policy of reserving places for the deserving poor failed to be wholly effective. The problem was that elementary school children from working-class families predictably had difficulty in competing for scholarship places with their socially advantaged classmates. By the time of the Bryce Report this had become recognized as one of the facts of school life; but in 1885 the commissioners felt concerned enough to go to the trouble of finding out from 101 of the reformed secondary endowed schools exactly how many children of parents employed in manual labour had actually been awarded scholarships during the previous three years. The total appears to have been between 700 and 750.[21]

The evidence given before the Bryce Commission by Miss M. M. Blackmore, the headmistress of the Roan School for Girls at Greenwich, is especially illuminating about the way in which the system worked in one of the girls' grammar schools of the post-Taunton era. The commissioners themselves had shown considerable solicitude for the problem of girls' secondary education and were obviously impressed by the testimony of such witnesses as Dorothea Beale, Frances Buss and Emily Davies[22] (who had tartly observed that the 'ideal presented to a young girl is to be amiable, inoffensive, always ready to give pleasure and to be pleased').[23] Their report regretfully conceded that 'on the whole the evidence is clear that . . . the Girls' Schools are inferior . . . to the Boys' Schools',[24] and while they were unable to allow Emily Davies' claim that half the grammar school places should be open to girls[25] the commissioners nevertheless recommended that 'in any enactment . . . brought into operation on this question the principle of the full participation of girls in Endowments should be broadly laid down.'[26] The Endowed Schools Act had subsequently contained a requirement that 'provision shall be made, as far as conveniently may be, for extending to girls the benefits of endowments', and by 1890 approximately 80 endowed schools for girls existed around the country.[27]

In the period following the Endowed Schools Act, the Charity Commission had been instrumental in reformulating John Roan's charity. As Miss Blackmore was to explain, the principal aim had been to ensure that the children of the poor would benefit:

3628-9. . . . There are three special clauses of the scheme of the Charity Commissioners under which our schools are worked, and they have direct reference to the advancement of children who have been educated in public elementary schools. . . . When the scheme was first made, in 1873, it was probably considered that children of the poorer classes only would avail themselves of the public elementary schools, and these clauses were inserted to benefit the poor. In the first year after our opening, 28 children entered at half fees; the number increased each year until it is now 140; and more than 600 children thus privileged have passed through some parts of the school; the larger proportion of them are not of poor parentage, in many cases the elder sisters have been full paying scholars; the children are well dressed, well fed, their fees are paid mostly by cheques, they live in good houses and their general appearance is prosperous; the parents have sent them to the elementary schools for three years on purpose to qualify for entrance into our school.

. . .

3633. . . . A certain proportion, however, come from homes where the parents are evidently making great efforts to give their children the benefit of higher education; many are poor, little, undersized, pallid creatures, very deficient in physique, often with brain power abnormally developed. Their mid-day meal is meagre and not nutritious; they do not care for play, are anxious to learn, but their stay in the school is short – and they gain little real benefit from their new knowledge, as it is very superficial.

. . .

3707. . . . If the scholars come to you at 12 years do you not find it difficult to fit in their work with the work of the other children? – No, I do not. . . . With specially selected girls who enter with scholarships, there is little or no effect on the tone of a class; they rapidly acquire the manners of their schoolfellows; their earnest efforts to take and keep a good position are most praiseworthy, and they prove a credit to the schools. I can find no evidence of exclusiveness on the part of the other girls. I have very rarely had a failure in one of our own Roan scholars. The present captain of the school is one of them: she has been with us five years; has passed both junior and senior Cambridge Locals in First Class Honours; has gained the Roan Leaving Exhibition of 45 l. per annum for three years, and won the Reid Scholarship tenable at Bedford College, value 46 l. 10s. 0d. She will study for the London degree of B.A. This is one instance of a complete ladder. Five girls only, out of over 600 from elementary schools have passed from us to a university career, and from inquiries I have made, one in a hundred is about the average. Probably a larger proportion of boys are able to benefit more fully by Secondary Education, as they are more considered in their homes, and are not called upon for the many duties that lower middle-class girls are expected to perform after school hours.

3708. . . . (Dean of Manchester) You have a considerable mixture of what we might call social classes in your schools, have not you? – Yes.

3709. . . . Do you find that works comfortably? – We have very little trouble in our school. We have so many elementary scholars in the middle part of the school that they work well together, and in the upper part of the school a girl holding a scholarship is usually so bright and intelligent that she is looked up to for her ability. The teachers are watchful, and we are all careful to check anything in the way of class prejudice, so I have little trouble.

. . .

3713. . . . What proportion of the girls in your school come from elementary schools? – We have at the present time about 140. This is about two-fifths. There are 338 in the school. We began with 28 only; we increase every year, and I suppose we shall go on in the same way.
(The Bryce Report on Secondary Education in England, 1895, Minutes of Evidence, Vol. II, pp. 345-354 passim)

Several points emerge from Miss Blackmore's evidence regarding entry to and opportunity in the new kind of reformed endowed school. There did indeed (at least at the Roan Girls' School) exist a significant proportion of free places which were reserved for bright pupils from public elementary schools; these, however, appear to have been dominated by children with fairly elevated social backgrounds; at the same time, the 'ladder of opportunity' was a reality, though only for the truly exceptional child. This pattern was confirmed by the Rev. A. R. Vardy, the headmaster of King Edward's School, Birmingham, which had been remodelled in 1878:[28]

1932. Have you many scholars who have worked their way upwards from the elementary schools to the university? – In the 10 years to which my statistics refer we have had seven boys take leaving exhibitions to Oxford or Cambridge, who at some time previously were at public elementary schools. They either came to us direct from public elementary schools or they passed through our own grammar schools after leaving the public elementary school. That, I imagine, is the full number of boys who have gone to Oxford or Cambridge from public elementary schools. I do not imagine that any boy has come to us from the public elementary school and has managed to get to the university unless he had obtained one of our leaving exhibitions.*

. . .

1934. Then you have not found difficulties arise of what are called a social nature? – No, not at all. But I think this is an important point, and one that ought to be made clear to the Commission. I am bound to say that most of those who have previously been in public elementary schools are to some extent picked boys. Many of them, for instance, are the sons of public elementary schoolmasters; others, one or two, the sons of men who are connected with public elementary education, sub-inspectors or assistant examiners. There are a few who are the sons of artisans, but I think most of them come from homes where education is more thought of, and where there has been from the first a good deal of thought expended and judgment brought to bear upon the training of the boys.

1935. So that they would be even at starting boys of probably a somewhat exceptional degree of culture? – Yes, I think so. They come from better homes. But of those who have gone to universities, and done exceedingly well, some have come quite in the ordinary way. I remember one son of an artisan, a man in receipt of a weekly wage which I should think probably have never exceeded 40 shillings, even if it has been as much as that. One boy came to us direct from a public elementary school; he passed through our classes, obtained a school exhibition and an open scholarship at Oxford; he took a first in Moderations, and I think a second in Classical Greats, but he has since obtained a first in Jurisprudence, and has a very promising career before him.

1936. (Mrs. Sidgwick) Is it a fact that to any great extent children are sent to the public elementary schools in order to get the scholarships at King Edward's School? – Yes, I think these restricted scholarships in our grammar schools have led the parents to send their children to our public elementary schools, in order that they may have a better chance of getting foundation scholarships.

1937. (Chairman) You mean children who otherwise would have gone to what class of schools? – Private schools perhaps.

. . .

1939. (Mr. Llewellyn Smith) Do you consider that the proportion of a third of the places free is the ideal proportion? Would you like to increase it if you had the funds? – I think as matters stand we are giving a sufficient number of foundation scholarships.
(The Bryce Report on Secondary Education in England, 1895, Minutes of Evidence, Vol. II, pp. 195-196 passim)

Meaningful statistics concerning the absolute and proportional number of scholarship places in endowed secondary schools during the post-1869 era are rather elusive. The 'Fortescue Returns' of 1882-1883[29] indicate that 219 of the schools regulated by schemes under the Endowed Schools Act were

---

*A few of the scholarships and exhibitions at King Edward's School were intended to help towards maintenance at school or university.

awarding scholarships. Just under 3000 of the latter were then valid and, of these, 1145 were held by children from public elementary schools.* It can be calculated roughly that in 1882-1883 an average of something over 10 percent of scholarship places were offered in those endowed schools which provided them.

By the mid-1890s the number of scholarship places was being significantly augmented by contributions from the newly formed county and borough councils using the powers conferred by the Local Taxation Act (1890)† and the Technical Instruction Acts of 1889 and 1891. At the time of the Bryce Commission there were approximately 2500[30] extra free places thus provided and by the end of the century the provision of local authority places had increased to 5500.[31]

The act of 1902 facilitated investment by local authorities in secondary education. Though the Board of Education was unable to give direct financial incentive towards the provision of free places until 1907, the preface to the Regulations for the Instruction and Training of Pupil-Teachers (1903)[32] made official sentiment clear by stating that '. . . a well-organized scholarship system, open to the cleverest pupils from all the schools in the area, without distinction, should be the first care of every Local Education Authority.'

An increasing number of free grammar school places was made available to intending teachers, and by May 1907 (before the 25 percent free place regulations of that year became effective) a survey[33] of 600 out of the 676 schools on the grant list revealed that the total of free places stood at no less than 29,440 (28 percent) out of 104,938; of these 25,269 (24 percent) of the pupils had previously attended a public elementary school. In the light of these figures the Regulations of 1907 seem to be as much a confirmation of the existing pattern of grammar school evolution as a visionary directive for the nature of future development.

Private secondary schools
The private secondary schools of the nineteenth century appear to have resembled the little girl with a little curl – when they were good they were very very good, but when they were bad they were horrid.

The estimate of 10,000 or so private schools quoted in the report of the Schools Inquiry Commission seems staggeringly large; it works out at one

---

*The same returns give a secondary school population (1883) of 27,912 for a total of 265 establishments; not all of these gave scholarship details.

†This legislation enabled funds (originally raised to compensate publicans whose licences had been withdrawn) to be used for technical education – hence the term 'Whisky Money'.

school per 2000 or so of the all-age population. So the figure only begins to make sense when it is realized that many establishments included in this figure would hardly be considered by modern definition to be schools at all; the term 'educational homes' was perhaps nearer the mark, though still by no means accurate, as the following extract from Mr. Bryce's report for the Schools Inquiry Commission shows. First, however, an introduction by Matthew Arnold:

The great mass of middling people, with middling incomes, not having for their children's future establishment in life plans which make a public school training indispensable . . . will not pay for their children's schooling a price quite disproportionate to their means. They demand a lower school-charge – a school-charge like that of Toulouse or Sorèze.*

And they find it. They have only to open the *Times*. There they will find advertisement upon advertisement offering them, 'conscientiously offering' them, in almost any part of England which suits their convenience, 'Education, 20 l. per annum, no extras. Diet unlimited, and of the best description. The education comprises Greek, Latin, and German, French by a resident native, mathematics, algebra, mapping, globes, and all the essentials of a first-rate commercial education'. Physical, moral, mental, and spiritual – all the wants of their children will be sedulously cared for.
(Matthew Arnold, A French Eton; or, Middle Class Education and the State, 1864, pp. 40-41)

James Bryce (who, of course, was later to chair the Secondary Education Commission of the mid-eighteen-nineties) acted as an assistant commissioner for Lancashire under Lord Taunton. His general description of the cheap boarding schools which he visited has a tone of hostility tempered with a measure of snide humour; this kind of establishment, he wrote,

. . . is not primarily a place of teaching, but a place of lodging and feeding. Boys are sent there to get them out of the way at home; boys, it may be, who have lost their mothers, or whose father is gone to America, or who are found unmanageable at home, or who have been lazy and neglected for several years, so that some desperate measure is needed to prepare them for an office in nine months time. Or perhaps some self-made man, conscious that his boy will not learn manners at home, and having heard of the virtues of boarding schools, is caught, as he runs his eye down the advertising columns of the Manchester Guardian or the Examiner, by the advertisement of Mr. So-and-so's establishment, where the comforts of a well-regulated home are combined with a sound commercial education on moral and Christian principles, for the low charge of 25 guineas per annum, washing included. In this he thinks he has cheapness and elegance both together, forgetting the commercial shrewdness which would not let him buy any other article below its value without a careful scrutiny of its quality.

That it is quite impossible for a private schoolmaster to give good food, good accommodation, and a thorough plain education at such a charge it needs no minute

---

*These were two schools – one a lycee and the other run by the Dominicans – which Arnold had visited in France.

calculation to prove. . . . The cheap private school must give something bad, in order to leave a profit; either the lodging, or the food, or the instruction, sometimes all three.

As respects food, there does not seem reason to believe that boys are positively ill-treated; at least, one hears of no well-authenticated cases of starvation. One master admitted to me that the staple nutriment of his boys was bread, which, he said, he was careful to procure unadulterated. He took me down to the kitchen, and showed me some of his loaves to be admired, pressing them with his thumb to show their elasticity, which, it seems, is a good sign. They certainly looked very solid, and, to use a familiar expression, filling at the price. Asking him how he managed to take boys so cheap at the present price of butchers' meat (his charges were for boys under 12, 20 l. to 24 l.; over 12, 26 l. to 30 l.), he explained that he always carved the joints himself, proportioning the quantity put on the plate to the size of the boy, and that no boy was permitted to have a second help. If he had been well plied with the incompressible bread, he would hardly have asked for one. Whether such a practice is general I could not discover.*

In the matter of lodging there is far more ground for complaint. If even the more expensive schools are not wholly free from blame, much less these. Occasionally, in looking through the rooms, I marked down their dimensions with as much accuracy as was attainable under the circumstances. Once in a bedroom 24 feet by 20, and as nearly as I could judge, 9 or 9½ feet high, there were 13 boys, that is, about 350 cubic feet per boy. In another room in the same house the allowance was about 280 cubic feet per boy. A third room had a roof somewhat higher but the floor was covered with beds so thick that one could scarcely get in among them, and the boys must have had to dress and undress standing on their beds. Miserable, dirty-looking beds they were, with half-ragged discoloured counterpanes, yet it was only the elder boys who had each one to himself; the younger were packed two together. It need hardly be added that the provision for washing was of the roughest character. The 'lavatory' was a small dark room, or rather passage, in which were placed a number of pewter basins. This school is an extreme but not a solitary case; other instances occur to me in which the overcrowding was quite as reckless.

It is in the teaching and officering of these schools that the head-master's economy is chiefly seen. He is himself as often as not quite incompetent to teach, and, curiously enough, it is the illiterate men who are sometimes, by dint of their business qualities, the most successful. The stuff of which his assistants are made, on whom, while he is occupied with the domestic management, the work of instruction mainly devolves, may be judged from the salaries they receive.†

. . .

It would have been very desirable to ascertain what was the moral tone of these schools, and how discipline was maintained there. There were, however, no means of doing so. The boys did not seem to be beaten or otherwise ill-treated – from the vice of cruelty at least one may believe the cheap private schools to be free – but discipline would be easy enough over such feeble, dejected-looking boys as most of them are. Whether it is the want of good air that makes them pale, or the want of a fresh vigorous life in this isolation, where they are kept always pretending to learn, yet feeling, if they have any sense, that the whole thing is a sham; or whether they

---

*This schoolmaster announced in his prospectus that he gave his pupils 'an unlimited supply of the best provisions'.

†These varied between £25 and £50 p.a.

are naturally poor specimens of boyhood, sent away from home on that very account, certain it is that there is something almost painful about the aspect of boys in these places – no colour in their cheeks, no animation in their answers, no glee in their sports.* I would, more than once, have given a great deal for ten minutes in private with them or with some discontented usher who might have revealed the secrets of the prison-house. But with a vigilant headmaster showing the visitor about, this was not to be thought of.

These remarks are not to be taken as applying to all the cheap private boarding-schools, for I visited one or two whose fees would place them in that class, but who, there was reason to believe, were doing the best they could for their pupils in an honest way. . . . In a bad form I believe the cheap boarding-schools to be not uncommon; in their worst form they are perhaps rare. But this is not enough. That schools should be rare in which children have no air and little decency in their sleeping rooms, a scanty dole of flesh meat at their meals, no instruction worth the name, nothing free, cheerful, honest in their life at any time, that these schools should be rare is not enough – they should be impossible.
(The Taunton Report, Schools Inquiry Commission, 1868, Vol. IX, pp. 568-572 passim)

Bruce Castle School, at Tottenham, was a very different place to those just described. In many ways its apparent virtues seem to constitute a direct contrast to the defects which so angered James Bryce when he considered the cheap boarding schools of Lancashire. But then Bruce Castle was a unique and celebrated establishment. It was the last of three private schools – the others being Hill Top and Hazelwood at Birmingham – founded and run by the Hill family, whose best-known member, Rowland, introduced the penny post in 1840. Prominent among the select radical *chic* of the early and mid-nineteenth century, the brothers Arthur, Rowland, and Matthew Davenport Hill were able, by means of a critical and adaptive eclecticism, to create an educational climate in which academic and cultural attainment could be combined with advanced ideas of pupil responsibility and freedom. Incentive was provided by an overtly competitive atmosphere, moral conduct as well as intellectual prowess counting towards material rewards such as prizes, holidays, and privileges.

Some impression of the efficacy of the Hills' methods can be seen in the following account of the *mental* computations with which the upper classes at Hazelwood were wont to exercise their minds and, on occasion, entertain the local gentry:

The following questions, with their answers, are extracted from the minutes of the public Exhibitions . . .
What is the value of 25,231 articles, at 16s. 8d. each?

---

*As a specimen of the aesthetic influences which are brought to bear on the pupils of some of these schools, I may mention that in the dining hall (which was also the sitting room) of one of them I saw over the chimney-piece three pictures. On the one side was a highly coloured representation of the heart and lungs, on the other a corresponding one of the stomach and intestines, and in the middle, a picture of the Crucifixion.

Tell the discount on £864 6s. 8d. at 15 per cent.

What is the square of 952?

What is the square of 54¼?

On what day will Easter Sunday fall in the year 1827?

A rectangular garden, of which the breadth is two-thirds of the length, contains in area 661½ square yards; what are the length and breadth respectively?

What was the time of high-water at London Bridge on the 17th of September, 1820?

Gay Lussac rose in a balloon from Paris to the height of four miles and three furlongs. What was the distance of his horizon when looking towards the sea?

. . . At one of our public Exhibitions, a class of ten or twelve boys stood prepared to extract the cube roots, (disregarding fractions) of any numbers, whether exact cubes or surds, which did not exceed two thousand millions. Many gentlemen present were furnished with tables of cubes, and their roots; several questions were proposed, and answered, with a rapidity which astonished the audience.

(M. D. and R. Hill, Public Education, 1825, pp. 118-120)

Hazelwood School closed in 1833; Bruce Castle, however, founded in 1827, continued until 1891. Among its admirers was Charles Dickens, who stated in 1845 that he considered the system there 'a perfectly admirable one; the only recognition of education as a broad system of moral and intellectual philosophy, that I have ever seen in practice'[34] – the very antithesis, in fact, of the obnoxious Dotheboys Hall. Seven years later a description of Bruce Castle School[35] actually appeared in his magazine *Household Words:*

The porch, overgrown with honeysuckle and creepers, looked as unforbidding a school-house entrance as one would wish to see; and the servant-maid who opened the door seemed to be cut out of the same pattern of neatness as the white bedroom curtains. We speedily found ourselves in the presence of the matron. . . . She was a good-tempered, well-spoken, bunch-of-keys-at-her-waist sort of personage, who never seemed at a loss about anything. On producing my card, she seemed fully prepared for my visit, and requested me to wait in the library until tea was prepared for me after my journey.

. . . here was something calculated really and truly to develop and foster the mind of a boy, enough to furnish and expand ideas, without being enough to drive the imagination riot, or to deprive the reasoning faculties of a definite stand-point. Good sound histories and gazetteers, the best encyclopaedias, a few practical and comprehensive works on arts and sciences, were blended with a complete collection of such classics as, without coming within the limits of a regular course of school study, might yet be available for reference. Nor were the more fascinating studies excluded. Poetry and the drama found their best and purest representatives, and the whole collection gave me the idea of a good private library, purchased without ostentation or affectation of rarity, and arranged with a sole view to utility and improvement.

. . .

The bedroom story was evidently the favourite hobby of the matron, whose life might have been well-nigh spent in looking after clean towels, seeing that the filters (there was one in every room) were filled, and the windows kept open. But she was a great favourite with the boys, the confidante of all their sorrows, and they did all in their power to save her trouble. The plain, cheap, deal furniture of these little chambers was faultlessly clean; everything was uniform and compact, yet of the simplest, plainest, and most substantial make. A beautiful incentive to holy thoughts on beginning or ending the toil or sports of the day, was the number of little prints of scriptural subjects which adorned the wall that faced the bedstead – silent and unobtrusive, yet pleasing and impressive companions to the Bible and Prayer Book that graced every table.

. . .

Everything in the school-room was neat and orderly; the communication with the library was direct; so that if a doubt or discussion was raised during lesson time (an event which the master never sought to discourage), information was readily to be had. The walls were decorated with specimens of the pupils' talents, less artistic than those in the library, but more rigidly useful. Maps, carefully copied, on a large scale; comparative charts of history and chronology – all the work of boys, some of whom were still hovering about the head class – were sufficient stimuli to a healthy emulation.

The diary, or daily plan of study, was especially worthy of notice. While every boy was bound to observe the same hours as the rest of his class, in spelling, writing, and other too-often neglected items of English education, the residue of his time was divided in a manner calculated to develop the peculiar bent, and to furnish means of attaining the object, of each. Those who were pursuing classics devoted their time to them, and were not compelled to fritter away time in vain attempts to study mathematics, or other sciences, for which they had no taste. Above all, everything seemed done with reference to an end; as though education were really the means of gaining a living, instead of a mere concession to a conventional custom of society.

. . .

. . . returning through the kitchen (which in educational establishments is always a sight worth seeing), I joined the master of the Model School, having first gazed in intense admiration upon six huge urns of tea, and some leviathan piles of bread and butter and water-cresses, that were just starting out to the refectory. The bread and butter were thoroughly home-made – and I should have guessed so, even if the matron, with a slight air of pride on her good-natured countenance, had not told me so.

(Household Words, No. 101, 28th February 1852, pp. 548-550 passim)

Notes

1   Taunton Report, Schools Inquiry Commission, 1868, Vol. I, pp. 255-6.

2   Bryce Report (on Secondary Education in England), 1895, Vol. I, p. 34.

3   See pp. 167-169.

4   For an explanation of some of the pressures leading to the adoption of examinations in the secondary schools of the later nineteenth century, see D. Allsobrook, 'The Reform of the Endowed Schools', in *History of Education*, Vol. 2, No. 1 (January 1973), and J. P. Roach, 'History Teaching and Examining in Secondary Schools 1850-1900', in *History of Education*, Vol. 5, No. 2 (June 1976).
    A concise account of the development of examinations in nineteenth-century secondary schools is given in the Beloe Report ('Secondary School Examinations other than G.C.E.'), 1960, pp. 3-4:
    At this time (the mid-nineteenth century) the middle classes were increasing fast, and the endowed and private schools increased in size and number to provide for

them. Examinations came into being to meet the needs of these schools for standards. First came the College of Preceptors, whose examination was set up in the early 1850's. This was replaced at the instance of the schools by the Local Examinations of Oxford and of Cambridge Universities which were started in 1858. The University of Durham first instituted examinations of this kind in the same year. . . . In its origin an examination for entrance to London University, unrelated to the courses of study in individual schools, (the London Matriculation Examination) came in practice to be used as a leaving examination by many pupils who did not intend to go on to University.

Already in 1868 the Report of the Schools Inquiry Commission was drawing attention to the dangers for the schools of an uncontrolled proliferation of examinations. 'When a school has to prepare boys for several different examinations,' they wrote 'an adaptation of the school course to suit them becomes impossible. . . . It is easy if the examinations are very stringent to push . . . divergence so far as to make effective organisation of the school impossible.' The remedy proposed by the Commission was the establishment of a statutory council for examinations in secondary schools. But this was successfully opposed at that time by the headmasters of public schools, who regarded the idea as a dangerous form of state intervention. This was the origin of the Oxford and Cambridge Schools Examination Board, which came into being in 1873 (girls were admitted in 1879). The Central Welsh Board came into being in 1896.

A general account of the development of examinations is given in J. P. Roach, *Public Examinations in England 1850-1900,* 1971.

5   Parl. Papers 1895, Vol. XLVIII, Mr. John Massie's report on Warwickshire, p. 59.

6   Schools Inquiry Commission, 1868, Volume I, Appendix V, pp. 150-151.

7   Ibid, p. 322 and Appendix VI.

8   Ibid, Volume I, p. 15.

9   Ibid, p. 111.

10   Ibid, Appendix V, pp. 150-151.

11   J. G. Fitch, *Endowments: An Address,* 1888, p. 17.

12   See above, p. 66.

13   A. L. Lilley, *Sir Joshua Fitch,* 1906, p. 86.

14   Parl. Papers 1897, Volume LXX, *Return of the Pupils in Secondary and Other Schools, etc.,* p. 577 seq.

15   See above, p. 65.

16   The work of the Endowed Schools Commission had subsequently been taken over by the Charity Commission.

17   Bryce Report (on Secondary Education in England), 1895, Vol. I, pp. 24-25.

18   Parl. Papers 1873, Volume VIII, *Report from the Select Committee on Endowed Schools Act* (1869), p. 22.

19   Parl. Papers 1871, Volume LVI, *Copy of a Scheme for the Management of Palmer's Endowed School at Grays Thurrock,* p. 6.

20   Parl. Papers 1886, Volume IX, *Report from the Select Committee on Endowed Schools Acts,* Appendix 7, pp. 488-494.

21   Ibid, pp. 525-562. Between 30 and 40 working-class boys appear to have gained entry to schools of the first grade.

22   Dorothea Beale (1831-1906): appointed Lady Principal of Cheltenham Ladies' College in 1858.
Frances Mary Buss (1827-1894): opened North London Collegiate School (1850) and Camden School (1871).

Emily Davies (1830-1921): described as 'the incisive, sharp-tongued prophetess of higher education for women'. See J. Kamm, *Hope Deferred*, 1965, for an account of the careers of these women.

23   Schools Inquiry Commission, 1868, Vol. I, p. 547; the commission also noted the statement by one endowed schoolmistress 'that she never heard a wish expressed by a parent for any branch of instruction to be taught except music'. (p. 570).

24   Ibid., p. 549.

25   Ibid., p. 566.

26   Ibid., p. 568.

27   J. Kamm, op. cit., pp. 212-213.

28   Bryce Report (on Secondary Education in England), 1895, *Minutes of Evidence*, Volume II, p. 195.

29   Parl. Papers 1886, Volume IX, *Report from the Select Committee on Endowed Schools Acts*, Appendix 4, p. 476.

30   Parl. Papers 1913, Volume XX, *Report of the Board of Education (1911-12)*, p. 15.

31   Ibid. For an account of the work of the local authorities in establishing scholarships, see P. R. Sharp, 'The Origin and Early Development of Local Authority Scholarships', in *History of Education*, Vol. 3, No. 1 (January 1974).

32   Ibid., Volume XX, pp. 10-11.

33   Ibid., p. 13.

34   P. A. W. Collins, 'Bruce Castle: A School Dickens Admired', *Dickensian*, Volume LI., No. 316 (September 1955), p. 175.

35   Referred to in the article as 'Gable College'. See W. A. C. Stewart and W. P. McCann, *The Educational Innovators*, Volume I, p. 121.

CHAPTER 6

STATE SECONDARY EDUCATION IN THE TWENTIETH CENTURY

The grammar schools of the early twentieth century

According to the Education Department's return of 1897[1] there were 619 endowed secondary schools in England. Initial response on the part of the new L.E.A.s to the rather offhand instructions of the 1902 Act 'to supply or aid the supply of education other than elementary' was, however, hardly precipitate:

The Local Authorities are now considering what they ought to do about secondary education. Their interest in the subject is on the whole rather languid and perfunctory, but they have an uneasy feeling that they must do something and that it will cost them a great deal to do anything worthwhile.

wrote Michael Sadler in 1904;[2] and two years later the Board of Education was still complaining about the 'very limited' provision of secondary schools by the L.E.A.s.[3] Nevertheless, within the first quarter of the twentieth century the number of L.E.A. secondary grammar schools in England and Wales was to rise to about 650,[4] giving an overall total of 1284 state-aided secondary schools. Grammar schools as a whole dominated the secondary sector, outstripping both in numbers and prestige other types of schools providing postelementary education. The 31 higher elementary schools of the prewar period had already been superseded by the provisions of the 1918 Education Act. Central schools, to be praised in due course by the 1926 Hadow Report and (in a backhanded way) by Lord Eustace Percy[5] were not recognized as secondary schools by the central authority until 1944. In fact, the only genuine rivals to the grammar schools during the interwar period were the 13 + junior technical schools. About 220 existed in 1937, when the Spens Committee commented upon their 'atmosphere of vitality, keenness and happiness'[6] and singled them out to be the prototypes of the technical high schools which, with the secondary moderns and the grammar schools, were to provide the three legs of the tripartite system.

The development of the secondary school curriculum

By the end of the nineteenth century the curriculum of many secondary schools had diverged significantly from the traditional classics-orientated timetable. The Clarendon and Taunton commissioners alike had advocated a greater emphasis upon the teaching of science, the latter stating:

We cannot consider any scheme of education complete which omits a subject of such high importance.

We think it established that the study of natural science develops better than any other studies the observing faculties, disciplines the intellect by teaching induction as well as deduction, supplies a useful balance to the studies of language and

mathematics, and provides much instruction of great value for the occupations of after life.
(The Taunton Report, Schools Inquiry Commission, 1868, Vol. I, p. 34)

These opinions were in tune with the views of such popular scientific writers as Herbert Spencer and Thomas Huxley and were further underlined by the conclusions of the Devonshire and Samuelson Reports of the 1870s and 1880s. Material incentive to teach science and its allied subjects at secondary level was provided by the grants made available by the Science and Art Department. By 1900, 183 institutions had received official designation as schools of science; each offered systematic instruction in science, though not, in the words of the department's instructions, to the exclusion of 'those literary subjects which were essential for a good general education'.[7] There were in addition 3562 day science classes in receipt of grants.[8]

Relatively well-endowed or otherwise prosperous schools were apparently less inclined to concede pride of place to the teaching of science. The lessons taught in seven[9] second-grade endowed schools were analysed by the Bryce Commission and a breakdown of the IVth form timetables of the boys' schools give the following average time allocations:

English, History and Geography (total) : 5.92 hours per week
Mathematics   : 6.33 hours per week
Science   : 1.83 hours per week
French   : 4.00 hours per week
Latin   : 3.67 hours per week

German (2 boys' schools only)   : 2.25 hours per week
Greek: not taught in any IVth form
R.I., P.E. and Drawing were also generally taught.

In the opening years of the twentieth century the Board of Education issued two successive sets of regulations for state-aided secondary schools. By those of 1901-1902 maximum grants would be earned by schools which offered thirteen hours of mathematics, science, and art each week. But the Board's report of 1902-1903 contained an alarmist account by J. W. Headlam about the teaching (or rather lack of it) of literary subjects in some boys' secondary schools. Headlam admitted that in the past too much time had been spent in grammar schools upon classical studies, but argued

This time has gone by. One almost fears that the reaction has gone too far. It is becoming increasingly difficult for a professional man who cannot afford to send his son to an expensive Boarding School to procure in the Grammar School of his district an education which will prepare him for a professional career. Greek has practically disappeared from nearly all these Schools. In many of the Endowed Schools an extra fee is charged to those who learn it – this at the same time that large grants are made by the Board of Education and the Local Authorities for those who devote their time to the study of Natural Sciences! In many Schools Latin is also disappearing . . .

He concluded with a stern warning:

It must be remembered that those who are educated in these Schools are those in whose hands will rest the greater part of the local government of this country. From them come the greater number of the teachers and the writers for the Press. They are allowed to leave School without any adequate training in some of the most important parts of mental activity. While fully recognizing that the Natural Sciences and Mathematics must in very many Schools have the predominant place, I submit that the neglect of and indifference to other sides of education must have a most harmful influence on the intellect and character of the nation.
(Report of the Board of Education, 1902-1903; General Reports on Higher Education, pp. 62-63 and 66)

The views of Headlam and others of like mind were suggestive of changing attitudes within the board. The controversial and definitive secondary school regulations of 1904 shifted curricular emphasis towards the humanities. It has been argued that the change was due to the influence of Robert Morant, the ambitious and intransigent secretary to the Board of Education. If this was the case, it would at least appear that precedents for the 1904 regulations existed in the timetables of the second-grade schools published in the Bryce Report. Indeed, it is possible that the regulations were basically an endorsement of the curriculum which had evolved in such schools during the late nineteenth century:

The Course should provide for instruction in the English Language and Literature, at least one Language other than English, Geography, History, Mathematics, Science and Drawing, with due provision for Manual Work and Physical Exercises, and, in a girls' school, for Housewifery.

Not less than 4½ hours per week must be allotted to English, Geography and History; not less than 3½ hours to the Language where only one is taken or less than 6 hours where two are taken; and not less than 7½ hours to Science and Mathematics, of which at least 3 must be for Science. The instruction in Science must be both theoretical and practical. Where two Languages other than English are taken, and Latin is not one of them, the Board will require to be satisfied that the omission of Latin is for the advantage of the school.
(Regulations for Secondary Schools, 1904-1905, p. 18)

The original 1904 regulations were soon modified: in 1907 the minimum subject time quotas were withdrawn, and from 1911 onwards work of 'a practical and vocational character'[10] was officially encouraged. In its report for 1912-13 the board conceded that 'the school course may be given a certain bias throughout with the object of developing interest in a capacity for the occupations, whether rural, industrial, or commercial, which the majority of the pupils are likely to take up.'

One feature of grammar school organization which was later to obtain universal currency within the state system was the principle of entry at about the age of eleven to twelve. The 1904 regulations had stipulated a minimum average age of twelve for pupils in a class starting the secondary course. Evidence had been given to the Bryce Commission by Miss Blackmore and the Reverend A. R. Vardy that, in their schools at least, the age of entry was commonly 11 + to 12 + . By 1905-1906 the board itself appeared to be basing its secondary policy upon the assumption that

The age of 12 is that about which transference from the primary to the Secondary School normally occurs; and the required course of Secondary Schools certified or aided by the State in England is fixed with reference to this fact. It is the age . . . at which statutory exemption from school attendance begins . . .
(Report of Board of Education, 1905-1906, p. 62)

And in 1920 the Departmental Committee on Scholarships and Free Places stated unequivocally that:

On no point perhaps have we had greater unanimity of evidence than on the question of the right age of transfer from the elementary to the secondary school. Witnesses are agreed that the best age is 11 plus.
(Parl. Papers 1920, Vol. XV, Report of the Departmental Committee on Scholarships and Free Places, p. 17)

Five years later Circular 1350 announced the board's intention to enforce (if necessary) a clean break at about 11 + across *all* state-aided education, elementary as well as secondary. Final confirmation of 11 + as the standard age of entry to state-aided secondary schools was forthcoming in recommendation 3 of the Hadow Report of 1926; eventually it was to be given the force of law by the 1944 Education Act.

The grammar school image

In one important respect at least the secondary grammar school of the earlier years of the twentieth century differed significantly from that of the post-1944 era. For whereas the grammar school was characterized from the mid-1940s onwards by intellectual élitism, that of the earlier period tended to be intellectually inclusive, if not comprehensive. The 'microcosmic' aspect of grammar school education tended repeatedly to be stressed by the staff associations during the interwar period and entry was often indeed more dependent upon the ability of parents to pay fees than upon the academic ability of the candidates. The Board of Education's report for 1905-1906, lamenting the apparent lack of entrance requirements, recorded that 'it is only in exceptional cases that there is at present any effective test, graduated according to age, imposed upon scholars at entrance. Until, however, such a test has come into general use classification cannot be satisfactory.'[11] The low intellectual calibre of some secondary school pupils was remarked upon by Mark Grossek, himself a free placeholder of humble origins:

Besides about a dozen scholarship boys, most of whom still smacked heavily of the

Board School, but showed signs of intelligence, there was a majority representing a more genteel element, the sons of dentists, tradesmen, bank clerks, and so on, who could afford to pay school fees. On the whole they were a dull, stolid lot, without any distinguishing features. But among them was a handful (and they *were* a handful) for whom the word dunce seemed almost a too flattering description. Not even at Gibraltar Street* had I come across so close an approach to mental deficiency . . .

(Mark Grossek, First Movement, 1937, p. 83)

The disparity between the intellectual attainment of the scholarship pupils in secondary grammar schools and the ones who paid fees remained; of those who left school in 1926-1927, for example, 48.1 percent of the former and only 19.8 percent of the latter obtained the School Certificate.[12]

A personal view (and one not untinged with irony) of the secondary grammar school at the turn of the century is given by Mark Grossek. In April 1900 he received instructions to attend the examination for junior county scholarships at the Whitaker Foundation School in London. His seat was to be number 684: 'how many candidates would there be in all?' he reflected. 'As the whole lot were grabbing at one hundred and fifty scholarships, the scramble would, without a doubt, be ruthless and unseemly.'

The examination, when it came, was, however, less awe-inspiring than the school in which it was held:

My performance, as far as I could judge, combined possible gains with probable losses, but I soon became too bewildered to surmise where the balance lay, and too jaded to care. During what was styled, rather grandly, the lunch interval, . . . I soon wandered off on my own to inspect the premises of the Whitaker Foundation School, as far as they were accessible to the profane outsider. . . . as I prowled round the corridors . . . my feelings resembled those of a traveller who, for the first time, sets foot on the soil of some classic land which hitherto he has known only from the pages of guide-books. The true atmosphere of 'The Willoughby Captains' and 'The Fifth Form at St. Dominic's' was now fully brought home to me. This process was assisted by the gowns of the gentlemen who collected our papers, investigated demands for extra writing materials, made sure that we didn't cheat, and, in general, imparted to the examination a certain austerity and pomp. . . . My imagination was kindled also by a sprinkling of young Whitakerians whose presence at school on Saturday morning was, I thought, due most likely to some advanced line of research which they were pursuing. This conjecture seemed to be confirmed when I perceived that one youth was carrying under his arm a small azure-coloured book, the title of which, by craning my neck, I discovered to be 'Vergil'. Some of these young patricians, too, all of whom bore themselves with hauteur and sported gaudy school-caps at the back of their heads, were dressed in Eton suits, and actually had stiff white cuffs. This exquisite stylishness left no doubt in my mind that I had set foot in the authentic world of prefect and fag, as portrayed in the masterpieces of Talbot Baines Reed. With a pang I reminded myself that my stay in this lofty domain was to be brief.

---

*Grossek's elementary school.

Of course, I didn't communicate any of these thoughts to my compeers from Gibraltar Street. On the contrary, I pretended that, in my opinion, Whitaker Foundation School was an uppish and mouldy sort of show, for which any Board School boy worthy of the name could feel only a hearty scorn. This idea met with approval, and as we straggled homewards I pandered to the sons of the sons of toil by mimicking to the point of burlesque the lardy-dardy voice of the gowned gentlemen who had been in charge of the day's proceedings. *'Don't forget,'* I bleated, *'to wrate your names and numbahs in the top rate-hand cornah of your papah.'* And my audience guffawed with class-conscious zest.
(Mark Grossek, First Movement, 1937, pp. 66-67 passim)

Success attended Mark Grossek's efforts; he was in due course offered a scholarship at the Whitaker Foundation School. This is his description of the place:

The ground-plan of Whitaker Foundation School had originally been very simple. Its centre was the big hall, in which the scholarship examination had been held, but which was normally used as a place of worship twice a day at 10 a.m. and 4.30 p.m. On each side of the hall there were four doors. The end one led to a holy of holies, where the Headmaster received visitors, hatched plans, or interviewed wrong-doers, while the door immediately opposite was the entrance to a less holy, but still quite awesome spot – the masters' common-room, where I once caught a glimpse of a billiard table. This left six class-rooms, which formed the nucleus of the school, but which soon proved inadequate for its growing needs. New buildings had already been added when I arrived, and newer buildings were in progress for many months after my arrival. Indeed, now I come to think of it, extensions or improvements of some sort or another, science laboratories, a gymnasium, lecture-rooms, and so forth, were continually under construction throughout my stay. The vision and enterprise of the Rev. G. A. Jones seemed endless. After I left, the old boy went in for an engineering workshop and a swimming bath. He must have aimed at making Whitaker Foundation School bigger, brighter, and more modern than any similar establishment in London, or, possibly, in Great Britain . . .

. . .

. . . Whitaker Foundation School could fairly be considered a cut above Gibraltar Street. The buildings themselves, with their outer lapses into stucco and interior hints at sham Gothic, were no masterpiece of architecture, but at least they were free from the leading features of the Gibraltar Street pile, which suggested that the place had been built, with slight modifications, from a plan originally intended for a jail. The gowns of the masters, too, suggested the presence of a profounder learning than could ever exist at Gibraltar Street. And the pupils all wore collars, clean white collars, while some of them actually sported cuffs. These refinements were in keeping with certain niceties in the use of words. Whitaker Foundation School was divided, not into *standards,* like vulgar Gibraltar Street, but into *forms;* its wrong-doers were not *kept in,* but *detained;* the year there consisted not of two nondescript periods, but of three *terms;* pupils didn't crudely go up from one class to another, but were *promoted.* And, as I have remarked, plebeian *dinner* was replaced by classy *lunch.* Also, one spoke in general with the kind of accent which was regarded as a touchstone of niceness by the occupiers of semi-detached villas in Dulwich, Herne Hill, Honor Oak, and such-like select areas. This differed notably from the patois of them who dwelt in tenements at Deptford.

And I observed certain other signs that I was now moving in a far tonier atmosphere than before. Or rather, the absence of certain signs made me realize it. Things that happened regularly at Gibraltar Street never happened at all at Whitaker Foundation School. Thus, one of the features of the daily round at Gibraltar Street had been a search for dirty ears and unwashed necks. . . . Whitaker Foundation School knew naught of such indelicacies. Nor was it ever the scene of brawls between parent and teacher which sometimes ended in the police court. . . . And any such disagreements that may have arisen at Whitaker Foundation School were settled in the Headmaster's study, and if a rumpus ever did occur, no signs of it reached us.

Yes, undoubtedly, by entering Whitaker Foundation School I had made a distinct advance in the social scale. And I lived up to it by wearing my Sunday suit on weekdays. What, however, from my own point of view really clinched my rise in the world was my school-cap with the ornate Whitakerian badge. I soon learned to wear it slightly tilted, and with much the same degree of swagger as is displayed by the middle-aged nonentity with the sash of the Order of the Bath athwart his dickey, or the rosette of the Legion of Honour in his button-hole.
(Mark Grossek, First Movement, 1937, p. 82 and pp. 89-90)

The 'exquisite stylishness' (to use Mark Grossek's words) of the grammar schools was to be assiduously fostered by both Board of Education and the L.E.A.s. In 1917 the secondary grammar schools were provided with a range of standardized and university-supervised examinations[13] (School Certificate and Higher School Certificate); in the same year a system of special grants for specific VIth form courses was initiated by the Board.[14] The Burnham pay scales of the interwar period emphasized the special status of the grammar school teacher; classes, too, were comparatively small. The average size on the 1938 census day was 24.6 pupils.[15]

Under such circumstances the grammar-schools were more or less bound to be relatively successful. They accommodated without undue strain pupils of a relatively broad spectrum of academic ability but nevertheless appear indisputably to have carried out the limited role of working class betterment implicit in the 'ladder' doctrine of the late nineteenth and early twentieth centuries. Thus, for example, it could be claimed that the proportion of boys from unskilled and semiskilled families almost doubled in grammar schools between 1909 and 1926,[16] while in 1938 the Board of Education could note with some pride that of the 798 open scholarships and exhibitions to Oxford and Cambridge, 437 had been won by pupils of grant-aided secondary schools.[17] More importantly, over two-thirds of these went to students whose parents' income was low enough to gain exemption from the payment of fees. The process could have gone further; Lord Eustace Percy (president of the Board of Education from 1924 to 1929) had, in a memorable speech, criticized the grammar schools for failing in their élitist role:

The main function of the secondary school as we know it to-day is not in any sense selective of the highest talent. I do not deny that it does send up very good talent to the universities and to higher technical studies but the main function of the secondary schools in our social system is not, as it should be, that of a lift or a stairway to the higher storeys of the social structure.

It is an intermediate school devoted to giving education up to the age of 16, an education, in turn, mainly devoted to cramming for a leaving certificate, and that function it performs no better but rather worse, in many instances, than the ordinary central school.

(HON. MEMBERS: Rubbish.) . . . It is, so to speak, a social factory for turning the sons of clerks and shopkeepers into clerks and shopkeepers.

(Lord Eustace Percy, in Hansard, Fifth Series, Vol. 280, pp. 1120-1121, 12 July 1933)

Some of Lord Eustace's strictures were to be repeated by postwar critics of the grammar school. But, nevertheless, by 1939 the grammar school had become clearly segregated in both official and public thinking from other, less prestigious, 11 + schools: the view of the honourable members remained in the ascendant.

The tripartite involvement
In 1924 the Consultative Committee under the chairmanship of Sir W. H. Hadow began a consideration of ways in which non-grammar school children up to the age of fifteen might be given a valid and socially acceptable form of education. Two years later its report, entitled *The Education of the Adolescent,* recommended the adoption of a structural pattern which, refined and extended by the Spens Report of 1938 and the Norwood Report of 1943, was to dominate English administrative and political policy on secondary education for almost forty years.

The aim of the 1926 Hadow Report was to provide a blueprint for a scheme of 'secondary education for all'. This phrase had been widely publicized by the economist R. H. Tawney, whose book of that name also supplied the report's own title.[18]

Much of Tawney's book is sincere, punchy left-wing stuff:

The Labour party is convinced that the only policy which is at once educationally sound and suited to a democratic community is one under which primary education and secondary education are organised as two stages in a single and continuous process; secondary education being the education of the adolescent and primary education being education preparatory thereto.

. . .

The organisation of education on lines of class, which, though qualified in the last twenty years, has characterised the English system of public education since its very inception, has been at once a symptom, an effect, and a cause of the control of the mass of men and women by a privileged minority. The very assumption on which it is based, that all the child of the workers needs is 'elementary education' – as though

the mass of the people, like anthropoid apes, had fewer convolutions in their brains than the rich – is in itself a piece of insolence.
(R. H. Tawney, Secondary Education for All, 1922, pp. 7 and 33)

Tawney was unspecific about the actual *form* his advocated system of secondary education should assume. But as a member of the committee which composed the report of 1926 he presumably participated in the far-reaching decisions which were to orientate English secondary education upon its subsequent course.

What, then, did the 1926 Hadow Report suggest? The principal recommendations may be summarized as follows:

Eleven plus transfer:
There should be an 11 + line between primary and secondary education. (Recommendation 3).
'All normal children should go forward to some form of post-primary education.' (Recommendation 4).

Types of secondary school:
There should be two main types of secondary school, designated 'Grammar' and 'Modern'. Post-primary departments in elementary schools should be known as 'Senior Classes'. (Recommendation 8).

Curriculum:
'Though the subjects included in the curriculum of Modern Schools and Senior Classes will be much the same as those in Grammar Schools, more time and attention will be devoted to handwork and similar pursuits in the former.' (Recommendation 9(ii)).

Relative status:
'The qualifications of the teachers and the standard of staffing in proportion to the number of pupils in the (Modern) school should approximate to those required in the corresponding forms of Grammar Schools.' (Recommendation 18).
'The education of children over the age of 11 in Modern Schools and Senior Classes is one species of the genus "secondary education". It is not an inferior species, and it ought not to be hampered by conditions of accommodation and equipment inferior to those of Grammar Schools. We attach great importance, therefore, to ensuring that, so far as possible . . . the construction and equipment of Modern Schools should approximate to the standard from time to time required by the Board in schools working under the Regulations for Secondary Schools. At the same time, we fully recognise that finance is a limiting factor. . . .' (Recommendation 19).

Selection procedure:
'While we think that all children should enter some type of post-primary

school at the age of 11 + , it will be necessary to discover in each case the type most suitable to a child's abilities and interests. For this purpose a written examination should be held, and also, wherever possible, an oral examination. A written psychological test might also be specially employed in dealing with border-line cases.' (Recommendation 20).

'Adequate arrangements should be made for transferring children, who shew ability to profit . . . from Modern to Grammar Schools at the age of 12 or 13. Conversely, similar arrangements should be made for transferring pupils from Grammar Schools to Modern Schools or to Junior Technical Schools, as need may be.' (Recommendation 17).

According to one contemporary writer at least,[19] the 1926 Hadow Report met with 'instantaneous success in all quarters'. If this was indeed the case, second, less euphoric thoughts soon began to emerge. For example, *Education,* the influential journal of the Association of Education Committees, displayed an acerbity of tone in its appraisal of the report, maintaining that

The report is grievously mis-titled . . . apart from certain administrative recommendations, the Report does little or nothing beyond laying down a new nomenclature for schools hitherto described as elementary or secondary and making recommendations as to the organisation, objective and curriculum of courses of study for children from the age of eleven to the verge of adolescence. *(Education, 1 April 1927, p. 371)*

Such criticisms may be placed under three general headings. The first is that the report's title *(The Education of the Adolescent)* was inaccurate because it did not deal with all the children in the age group concerned, many of whom were in the grammar schools expressly excluded from its terms of reference. Secondly, the title itself seemed to indicate, if nothing else, a certain ignorance of the facts of life. Adolescence is usually defined as 'the period between puberty and maturity': puberty in England at this time was usually attained two to four years *after* the 11 + line. Hence *Education's* careful reference to 'the verge of adolescence' as the *upper* age limit of the report.* It was arguable, therefore, that at least half of the four-year courses proposed in Hadow would not concern adolescents at all, and that the basic assumption of the report's celebrated Shakespearean introduction.

There is a tide which begins to rise in the veins of youth at the age of eleven or twelve. It is called by the name of adolescence. If that tide can be taken at the flood, and a new voyage begun in the strength and along the flow of its current, we think that it will 'move on to fortune'

---

*A detailed consideration of the Hadow Report's attitudes on this and other matters can be found in R. J. W. Selleck, *The Hadow Report: a Study in Ambiguity*, Melbourne Studies in Education, 1972.

was itself open to question, the general adoption of the 11+ transfer possibly being more attributable to existing grammar school usage than to the physical or psychological needs of children. The third point made in the *Education* critique is one which has echoed through the ensuing years: were things really going to change, or was reorganization to be principally confined to repainting the school name-boards?

The Spens Report and the Norwood Report
The Spens Report of 1938 *(Secondary Education)*[*] contained a certain amount of debate about the pros and cons of multilateral education; it nevertheless further advanced the selective line by formulating a true tripartism. Its principal innovatory recommendations in this direction were:

Types of secondary school:
There should be *three* kinds of secondary school: grammar, modern and 'a new type of higher school of technical character' to be called technical high schools. (Recommendation 109).

Selection and fees:
No fees should be payable in secondary schools. (Recommendation 138).

'We recommend the adoption of the system of 100 percent Special Places.'[†] (Recommendation 139).

About half the special places should be allotted by examination alone. The remaining half should be distributed to candidates 'on the result of a method of selection, including an interview, in which facts other than their relative place as determined by the examination are brought into account'. (Recommendations 140 and 141).

'We recommend that there should be a further review, at about the age of 13, of the distribution of children among all schools in the secondary stage.' (Recommendation 144).

Curriculum:
The curriculum for pupils between the age of 11+ and 13+ should be broadly the same in different types of secondary school of equal status. (Recommendation 111).

Next, in 1943, came the Norwood Report on Curriculum and Examinations in Secondary Schools. A product not of the Consultative Committee but of the Secondary School Examinations Council, it assumed a significant inversion of emphasis. Whereas the earlier reports had attempted to rationalize three types of secondary school for 11+ children, Norwood

---

[*]To the exclusion, however, of modern and central schools and senior classes.
[†]i.e., scholarship places. See below, pp. 216-217.

defined three types of children for the schools. Meaningly prefaced by a quotation *in Greek** from Plato (hardly an advocate of democratic egalitarianism, whatever his virtues) it confidently maintained that the nation's children, like Caesar's Gaul and like, too, the citizens of Plato's own *Republic,* were divided into three parts '. . . each of which can and must be treated in a way appropriate to itself.'[20]

Types of child and their schools:
For example, English education has in practice recognised the pupil who is interested in learning for its own sake, who can grasp an argument or follow a piece of connected reasoning, who is interested in causes, whether on the level of human volition or in the material world, who cares to know how things came to be as well as how they are, who is sensitive to language as expression of thought, to a proof as a precise demonstration, to a series of experiments justifying a principle: he is interested in the relatedness of related things, in development, in structure, in a coherent body of knowledge.

The remainder of the children – presumably those less capable of grasping arguments or following a piece of reasoning – fell, according to the Norwood Report, into two brackets. There was

. . . the pupil whose interests and abilities lie markedly in the field of applied science or applied art. . . . He often has an uncanny insight into the intricacies of mechanism whereas the subtleties of language construction are too delicate for him.

The final Norwood category was apparently typified by the potential navvy, who

deals more easily with concrete things than with ideas. He may have much ability, but it will be in the realm of facts. He is interested in things as they are; he finds little attraction in the past or in the slow disentanglement of causes or movements. His mind must turn its knowledge or its curiosity to immediate test; and his test is essentially practical.
(The Norwood Report, Curriculum and Examinations in Secondary Schools, 1943, pp. 2-3)

It is almost superfluous to add that the three kinds of school destined for the children thus defined were grammar, technical high, and secondary modern respectively.

Selection:
The Norwood Report recommended that 11 + selection 'should be made upon the basis of (a) the judgement of the teachers of the primary school, supplemented if desired by (b) "intelligence" and "performance" and other tests. Due consideration should be given to the choice of the parent and the pupil.' (Recommendation 5).

---

*A translation was provided (in smaller print).

Relative status:
The report took a rather hard though perhaps realistic attitude on this critical point: '. . . each type of school should have such parity as amenities and conditions can bestow; parity of esteem in our view cannot be conferred by administrative decree nor by equality of cost per pupil; it can only be won by the school itself.' (p. 14).

By 1943, therefore, official policy on secondary education appeared to have attained a coherent and inclusive form. Final government approval was to be provided by the 1944 Act and by subsequent statements of ministerial policy. Realistic implementation was able to begin with the final victory of the Allies in 1945.

The 1944 Act and *The Nation's Schools*

The 1944 Education Act finally gave legal sanction (in a curiously circumlocutory way) to that long-standing feature of the educational scene, the 11 + transfer; it also confirmed the hopes of the 1920 departmental committee (reiterated and amplified in Spens) that no fees should be payable in maintained schools. But it contained no mention at all of the form which secondary education should take, tripartite or otherwise. The omission was noticed; one Labour M.P. (Mr. L. Silkin) rather sceptically commented that

. . . we may find that things go on very much the same and that we have merely changed the names of the schools and increased the age to 15 and that is all.[21]

There could be little doubt about governmental preferences: the Hadow, Spens and Norwood Reports, together with the 1943 White Paper on Educational Reconstruction, all pointed towards a segregated system of secondary education. The very first pamphlet issued by the new Ministry of Education, entitled *The Nation's Schools*, once it had dispensed with the customary deferential protestations ('Nor is any claim made of finality for any of the suggestions here discussed'), put forward a *diktat* of tripartism. Referring to modern, technical, and grammar schools, it stated that:

These three broad types, now at very different stages of development, are intended to meet the differing needs of different pupils. These differing needs will still require to be satisfied, and it may be assumed that these broad types furnish the point of departure for further development.

. . .

The most urgent reform to which the development plan must be addressed is the completion of 'Hadow' reorganisation.
(The Nation's Schools, Their Plan and Purpose, 1945, pp. 13-14)

In 1945 the Socialists took office with a large majority in the House of Commons and Ellen Wilkinson became Minister of Education. Since 1942 the Labour Party had been committed (albeit in rather vague terms) to a comprehensive form of secondary education. When, therefore, the new minister endorsed *The Nation's Schools,* her action was received with unconcealed indignation by some members of her party:

. . . the right hon. Lady is a danger to the whole Labour movement so far as educational policy is concerned. She is not true to the policies which we have adumbrated over a series of years. She does not believe in the capacity of the ordinary child, in the provision of educational facilities for the ordinary child, nor does she believe in an equalitarian system of education.
(Mr. W. G. Cove [Aberavon][22] in Hansard, Fifth Series, Vol. 424, p. 1834 (1 July 1946))

The Nation's Schools was withdrawn but not scrapped. Indeed, the tripartite theme was reemphasized in 1947 by the publication of the pamphlet entitled *The New Secondary Education.* Tripartism was to be the general policy for England's first system of universal secondary education.

The years of tripartism
Thus from 1945 onwards the tripartite system grew and took shape. By 1956 there were 3636 secondary modern schools (as opposed to 1357 maintained and direct grant grammar schools). Secondary technical high schools remained rather thin on the ground; there were 303 of them in 1956, a deficiency which led the members of the Crowther Committee three years later to question the very applicability of the term 'tripartite' to English secondary education.

By the late 1940s the grammar school had, as an institution, attained a formidably high status. The secondary modern, starting more or less from scratch, still had to do so. Yet it was to be upon its success in establishing itself in Hadow terms as a genuinely acceptable alternative to the grammar school that the whole credibility of the tripartite system was to depend.

The secondary modern ethic
The Nation's Schools and the *New Secondary Education* both stressed that the secondary modern school was to have a character of its own. The central authority, however, was perhaps less specific than it might have been in explaining how this end might be achieved in the economic austerity of postwar Britain:

Something noble and grand and good,
Won by merely wishing we could.

were lines which soon began to seem to have a certain appositeness to the developing secondary modern situation.

Both pamphlets emphasized that the curriculum of the new schools was not to be a mere downgraded facsimile of that of the grammar school (with its stress on academic study), nor yet was it to be simply an improved version of that of the superseded but traditional elementary schools. As *The Nation's Schools* put it:

> The possibilities that the modern schools offer are generally too little understood and too little appreciated: they have their own contribution, and a vital contribution, to make to the development of secondary education. Free from the pressures of any external examination, these schools can work out the best and liveliest forms of secondary education suited to their pupils. It is essential that they should retain this invaluable freedom which the best of their predecessors have used to such advantage, and should be enabled to advance along the lines they themselves feel to be right.
> *(The Nation's Schools, Their Plan and Purpose, 1945, p. 21)*

Thus teaching in the new secondary moderns was to be free from the restraints of external examination work, concentrating upon lively, pupil-centred approaches dealing with topics closely related to the interests of the students. *The New Secondary Education,* indeed, dwelt expansively upon the curricular aspects of secondary modern schooling and anticipated relatively few obstacles to the attainment of a full equality:

> As the modern schools develop, parents will see that they are good; it will become increasingly common for them to keep their children at school beyond the compulsory age, and to select a modern school as the one best suited to their children's requirements on grounds unhampered by considerations of 'prestige'. Moreover, as the organisation of industry continues to become more flexible, it will offer the product of the modern school the same hope of promotion to the more responsible and better-paid jobs as is now in practice largely confined to the products of the grammar and technical schools.
> *(The New Secondary Education, 1947, p. 47)*

The secondary modern image

The Nation's Schools came out in 1945; in 1963 the Newsom Report *(Half Our Future)* assessed the achievements of the intervening years. By this time enthusiasm for tripartism was waning. There existed a fairly wide consensus of opinion that, as Edward Boyle later put it, 'separate schools at eleven over the next four years would be increasingly on the way out'.[23]

Half Our Future is, by and large, a dispiriting report. It begins with a series of comments by secondary modern students and teachers. The first of these reads:

> A boy who had just left school was asked by his former headmaster what he thought of the new buildings. 'It could all be marble, sir,' he replied, 'but it would still be a bloody school.'

And it ends with the following assessment of the provision of facilities:

The overall picture is that one-fifth of the modern schools are generally up to standard, but two-fifths are seriously deficient in many respects.

What, then, had become of those bright new ideas, that 'freedom and flexibility', that 'generous expenditure', and – crucially – that 'parity of conditions with other types of secondary school' so confidently predicted in *The Nation's Schools* and *The New Secondary Education?* Newsom and his colleagues recorded that, of the children in the secondary moderns,

Too many at present seem to sit through lessons with information and exhortation washing over them and leaving very little deposit. Too many appear to be bored and apathetic in school, as some will be in their jobs also. Others are openly impatient. They 'don't see the point' of what they are asked to do, they are conscious of making little progress: 'The reason why I left at fifteen is because I felt that by staying on I should be wasting two years learning nothing. I could have worked harder, but what's the use if you don't get any encouragement?' argues one girl. A headmaster acknowledges, 'There are far too many of our slow and average children who long ago reached saturation point doing tedious and hateful work year after year.'
The Newsom Report, Half Our Future, 1963, pp. 14-15)

Something, it would seem, had gone wrong.

The secondary modern, like the nineteenth-century public school, managed to produce a literary *genre* of its own. Edward Blishen's two books – *Roaring Boys* (1955) and *This Right Soft Lot* (1969), E. R. Braithwaite's *To Sir, With Love* (1959) and Michael Croft's *Spare the Rod* (1954), all give fictionalized but fundamentally autobiographical accounts of the experiences of young teachers caught up in what has with some perception been termed the 'Passchendaele policy' of the ministry: the despatch of inexperienced, ill-prepared and, one suspects, expendable teachers into the maintained schools of postwar Britain.[24]

Conditions such as those I have described, although not universal in reality, are nevertheless sufficiently prevalent in certain districts to justify the picture I have given,

wrote Michael Croft, while Edward Blishen gave the following account of how he came to write his second Stonehill Street book:

I have taken all my experiences and put them on the chopping board; and from the fragments that resulted I have composed this fictitious school and these supposititious people.

This is Blishen's account of his first lesson at Stonehill Street:

'You'll have to keep Class 2 under your thumb,' said the headmaster. To make this clear, he showed me his thumb; a huge thing, like a pocket cudgel. I felt very pale. I had reason enough to distrust my thumb.

Class 2. They were top-year boys. Their own teacher had been sick for a long time; a succession of startled substitutes had stood before them, ducked, winced and fled. I was the seventh that term. No one quite knew where the class had got to in any subject. It was plain that the headmaster thought they had got nowhere. But I was to take them for nearly everything; and first, that awful afternoon, for history.

I trembled down to Room H. In the hall I was nearly knocked over by a boy illegally running. I should have told him off; instead, I apologised. It was all wrong; my mood was all placatory; I was, inwardly, all white flag.

The room was easily traced by the noise that was coming from it. It didn't sound a studious noise. I crept through the door. Enormous boys were everywhere, doing indefensible things. I can't recall much in particular that they were doing; indeed, that was the worst of it – that these improprieties couldn't be nailed down.

I managed to make out that mixed up with these young giants was a certain amount of furniture. This consisted, I found, of individual desks; doll's-house things that rested on mountainous knees and swayed from side to side. Too negligently or maliciously treated, one would, from time to time, crash on the floor. There were certainly fights going on; and I believe one desk was chasing another. The air was full of pieces of chalk, a strange rain of it.

Feeling invisible, I walked towards the teacher's desk. Not an eye was turned in my direction. I just stood there and looked at them and the awful pointless indignation mounted in me. Was I not a teacher! Had I not been approved by the Ministry itself! Was I really so puny, so ineffective?

. . .

I shouted for a while, but it was beyond me. I hadn't the manner, was a plain imposter. My blushing and bawling were a joy to them. There was, for a time, pandemonium, like the big scene in an opera being played backwards on a gramophone.
(Edward Blishen, Roaring Boys, 1955, pp.2-4)

In Michael Croft's school, staff solidarity was regarded as an essential prerequisite for professional survival: in the words of the disillusioned headmaster:

You know what this School is like. You know it's a suicidal battle every day, every lesson, just getting through, just keeping nerve and brain intact. You know that education – what we understand by education – doesn't even get a chance. You've been here one term and you must have realised that if we once allow a weakening of control, a crack in the front of authority, or any sign of disunity among ourselves then we're building a gallows for the pupils to hang us on. Give them the slightest sign and they'll get the rope ready and spit in our faces.
(Michael Croft, Spare the Rod, 1954, pp. 248-249)

What struck Edward Blishen was the absolute cultural alienation of staff and students:

The staff in their neat suiting, even in their old sports jackets and flannels, looked like visitors from another world. And, in fact, in Stonehill Street two worlds clashed. You couldn't help seeing it that way. The masters and the boys had very different backgrounds. And even though a teacher managed in the end to master the manners of his charges, it was always an act of mastery and never an act of intimacy. Even the most experienced members of the staff would discuss the boys as barbarous celts might have been discussed by a Roman garrison.

I was paralysingly aware that most of the boys hated school with a coarse sullen hatred; that a kind of teaching both much more skilled and much more arresting than I could provide was needed to make their schooling more than a sulky mockery. *(Edward Blishen, Roaring Boys, 1955, p. 42)*

The problems of teaching recalcitrant children were not made easier by the widely held assumption that a qualified teacher ought to be able to control any class and that failure to do so could be construed as infallible proof of professional incompetence. The preparation in form organization given to students in training colleges and university departments of education tended to be less than adequate; but it is uncertain whether *any* training (within, that is, the usual framework of class organization) could have enabled teachers to overcome problems of the magnitude described by the authors dealt with here. E. R. Braithwaite tried all the usual, hackneyed solutions:

. . . but somehow, as day followed day in painful procession, I realised that I was not making the grade. I bought and read books on the psychology of teaching in an effort to discover some way of providing the children with the sort of intellectual challenge to which they would respond, but the suggested methods somehow did not meet my particular need, and just did not work. It was as if I were trying to reach the children through a thick pane of glass, so remote and uninterested they seemed.

Looking back, I realise that in fact I passed through three phases in my relationship with them. The first was the silent treatment, and during that time, for my first few weeks, they would do any task I set them without question or protest, but equally without interest or enthusiasm; and if their interest was not required on the task in front of them they would sit and stare at me with the same careful, patient attention a birdwatcher devotes to the rare feathered visitor. I would sit at my desk busily correcting some of their written work and feel their eyes on me, then look up to see them sitting there, watchful, waiting. It made me nervous and irritable, but I kept a grip on myself.
. . .
Gradually they moved on to the second and more annoying phase of their campaign, the 'noisy' treatment. It is true to say that all of them did not actively join in this, but those who did not were obviously in some sympathy with those who did. During a lesson, especially one in which it was necessary for me to read or speak to them, someone would lift the lid of a desk and then let it fall with a loud bang; the culprit would merely sit and look at me with wide innocent eyes as if it were an accident. They knew as well as I did that there was nothing I could do about it, and I bore it with as much show of aplomb as I could manage. One or two such interruptions during a lesson were usually enough to destroy its planned continuity, and I was often driven to the expedient of bringing the reading to an abrupt halt and substituting some form of written work; they could not write and bang their desks at the same time.
. . .
Then, finally, came the third or bawdy stage of their conduct:

. . . the words 'bloody' or 'bleedin'' were hardly ever absent from any remark they made to one another, especially in the classroom. They would call out to each other on any silly pretext and refer to the 'bleedin'' this or that, and always in a voice loud enough for my ears. One day, during an arithmetic period, Jane Purcell called out to me: 'Can't do this sum, Mr. Braithwaite, it's too bleedin' hard,' and sat there looking coolly up at me, her large breasts greasily outlined beneath the thin jumper, her eyes innocently blue in appeal.

'Tell me,' I replied, my voice chill and cutting with repressed anger: 'Do you use such words when speaking to your father?'

'You're not my bleedin' father.' Her voice was flat and vicious. I was answered, and I shut up. You nasty little slut, I thought, I played right into your hand.
(E. R. Braithwaite, To Sir, With Love, 1959, pp. 67-69 passim) *

One commentator who took a radically different view of secondary modern schools was H. C. Dent. In his judgement, many of them were by the late 1950s successfully translating the secondary modern concept into sound education practice. The schools so explicitly criticized by Blishen, Braithwaite, and Croft had all been located in dreary, rundown urban environments; so here, by contrast, is Dent's account of one rural secondary modern:

The buildings are new, and very attractive, having been designed by an architect with imagination who was given space and freedom. The plan is simple; a long main block consisting of an assembly hall and classrooms which look south across broad playing fields, with, north of this, on the other side of a wide entrance court bright with flowers, a block containing dining-hall, gymnasium, and workshops.

Standing in the courtyard, admiring its rosebeds, the brightly painted coats of arms over the main entrance, the murals just inside it, and, over the way, the daintily laid dining-hall, I was driven to reflect: what will be the effect upon these children of this gracious modernity? They were the school's first generation; it opened only in September 1953. They came from something like a score of schools, most of these until the opening of the new secondary school small 'all-age' schools, scattered round the countryside within a radius of roughly a dozen miles. What will result from the move out of the secluded antiquity of those little schools into this far larger society housed in the best the present has to offer?

Only the future can say. Meanwhile the children loved it, and the Modern School idea was popular with the parents. One imagined that this particular school would before long be something more than popular, for it was in very good hands: an experienced Head with original ideas who had shown elsewhere what can be made of a rural school, supported by a young, able and enthusiastic staff.
(H. C. Dent, Secondary Modern Schools, An Interim Report, 1958, pp. 84-85)

The material deficiences of the secondary modern schools described by Blishen, Braithwaite, Croft, and even by Dent himself, were exacerbated by the twin issues of assessment for capitation allowances and 'points' for graded teaching posts. The methods adopted tended to discriminate sharply in favour of the older, 16 + students who, almost by definition, went either

---

*From the book, *To Sir, With Love* by E. R. Braithwaite. © 1959 by E. R. Braithwaite. Published in USA by Prentice-Hall, Inc., Englewood Cliffs, New Jersey.

to grammar school or college of further education. For example, the figures issued by Huntingdon and Peterborough L.E.A. for 1972/3 show that the capitation allowance in the area was £17.90 for each pupil under sixteen and £28.25 for each pupil over that age.[25] Similarly, at least from 1951, a pupil over seventeen would bring in ten points to count towards the number of graded posts in his school, whereas a pupil aged up to thirteen would only count as one.[26]

Despite, therefore, the specific assurances of the authors of *The Nation's Schools* and *The New Secondary Education*, the situation regarding parity of conditions came to assume a thoroughly Orwellian appearance. All pupils were equal, but some (the older ones) were more equal than the others. And they were mostly in the grammar schools.

In financial terms this all meant that, in the oft-quoted estimate of John Vaizey, 'it is likely that the average grammar school child receives 170 percent more per year, in terms of resources, than the average modern school child.'[27] Vaizey also estimated that the 29 percent of children attending grammar schools preempted no less than 49 percent of the available financial resources.

These differentials affected the whole maintained secondary school scene: there were more special allowances to be earned in grammar schools, so they tended to attract abler staff; equipment in secondary moderns was frequently inferior in quality and quantity. The headmaster of one new, relatively well-equipped fourth-form entry secondary modern school, (singled out by H. C. Dent as having a particularly good library)[28] actually recorded in his own book that his school had received no initial capital grant for library books and that originally his annual library allowance had amounted to the inconsiderable sum of £15.[29] One of the unofficial hallmarks of the secondary modern school became the distribution and collection of textbooks which opened and closed each lesson. John Partridge, who taught in one of the new, spotless, purpose-built secondary moderns (and wrote a saddening account of his experiences there) considered that

One could write a separate section on books alone; suffice it here to say that Middle School is short of good text books. This is, of course, because there just is not the money to provide every school in the area with a sufficiency of books. In a Grammar school each boy is loaned a copy of any book being used as a basic text by the teacher with the particular class, and is allowed to keep it until it is no longer required; but in our School, as undoubtedly in other Secondary Modern schools, there is one set of twenty, thirty, or forty books, as the case may be, and these are used for at least two, and sometimes all the year groups. Text books are distributed at the beginning of a lesson and collected up at the end; such a set may be passed on to another colleague, who will use it for one of his classes and then return it, or the same teacher may use the set with different classes. As well as the waste of time involved – this is worth a

'Time and Motion' study by itself – there is an inevitable bias against 'C' and 'D' streams. In some sets of books there are only twenty or twenty-five copies, so that some of the boys in a class have to share; with a 'D' or 'C' class the disruption so caused is worse than with other classes.
(John Partridge, Middle School, 1966, pp. 85-86)

An insufficiency of basic equipment could hardly have been conducive to the introduction of the kind of courses anticipated in *The Nation's Schools* and *The New Secondary Education*. The cost of reference books needed for project work, for example, has always tended to be very high. Perhaps, however, in some schools at least they were never needed. For Dent claimed by 1958 to have discerned a drift away from 'freedom and flexibility' in the curriculum, while William Taylor, whose book *The Secondary Modern School* was published in the same year as the Newsom Report, was moved to make the comment that

One interesting feature of this basic curriculum is the extent to which it has withstood the onslaughts of educational ideas which at one time might have seemed likely to alter substantially the 'subject-centred' timetable in favour of projects, centres of interest, individual assignments, and subject groups. Schools in which the work is based on such approaches are objects of comment and clearly exceptional in the general run of Modern schools.
(William Taylor, The Secondary Modern School, 1963, p. 84)

'Freedom and flexibility' had wilted, or so it seems. So, crucially, did parity of esteem. Perhaps it never had a chance. It had originally been presented as an educationally valid counterpoise to that less acceptable feature of the Hadow package, pupil segregation at 11 + . From the mid-1950s onward it became increasingly regarded as a confidence trick, and a pretty shabby one at that. There is doubt as to whether the concept had ever carried much conviction with those who were best placed to judge its worth – the teachers themselves. As John Partridge wrote:

It's always education for someone else's children. One senior colleague said bluntly, 'Well, you wouldn't send your kid here, would you?' Indeed, no! But nor would any of the teachers if they could possibly help it, certainly some of the staff had growing children, but none of them were known by me to be sending them to any local Secondary Modern. There were no teachers' sons attending Middle School during the past year. Teachers' children in this City typically seem to pass the eleven plus or to attend a local Preparatory or Public school. Teachers, in fact, want their children to enjoy better educational and hence occupational opportunities than the boys in Middle School do.
(John Partridge, Middle School, 1966, pp. 145-146)

The external examination issue
The exclusion of external examinations from the secondary modern school had been one of the keynotes of the policy outlined in *The Nation's Schools*.

By the late 1950s, the idea was beginning to take on a rather jaded aspect. Even as early as 1955 pressure for the provision of some form of external examination for secondary modern schools had led the minister to issue Circular 289 which, although it welcomed school-based experiments, reiterated official disapproval of 'general examinations of national standing'[30] and stood firm on the grant regulations requirement that school authorities should refrain from entering any pupil under sixteen for external examination.* The minister did nevertheless refer the issue to the Crowther Committee which duly reported in 1959 that about 'one-third or rather more of the pupils in modern schools over the age of fifteen' might reasonably be entered for 'external examinations below the level of the G.C.E.'.[31]

Meanwhile the Secondary School Examinations Council had set up its own group – the Beloe Committee – to look into the question. Its report, published in 1960, indicated that ministerial policy concerning the entry of pupils under sixteen for external examinations was being widely flouted:

In effect what has happened, on an increasing scale, has been that parents have, at their own expense, with or without encouragement from the teachers and from the Examining Bodies, been acting in a manner contrary to the spirit if not to the letter of the Minister's policy.
(*The Beloe Report, Secondary School Examinations other than the G.C.E.*, 1960 p. 16)

In 1959 the committee had taken a random sample of English and Welsh secondary moderns: 51 per cent (in England) and 71 per cent (in Wales) entered pupils for some form of external examination. Non-G.C.E. examinations were taken by 46 per cent and 64 per cent respectively of the secondary modern schools sampled in England and Wales.[32] They were provided by a variety of agencies: London-based organizations such as the Royal Society of Arts and the College of Preceptors; 'regional' examining bodies like the Union of Lancashire and Cheshire Institutes and the East Midland Educational Union; the further education regional examining bodies; and specialist examining institutions – for example, the Pitman Examinations Institute and the General Nursing Council.[33]

In the committee's opinion, the time had come to bow to *force majeure*, and it unanimously recommended that 'the Minister should take the initiative at an early date in stimulating and if necessary assisting the formation of Examining Bodies to provide suitable examinations'. As a result, the first C.S.E.examinations made their appearance in the mid-1960's.

But by 1965 the fate of the secondary modern concept of education had

---

*Head teachers could, however, recommend specific pupils under sixteen for entry to G.C.E. alone.

virtually ceased to be an emotive issue. During its long period in opposition, the Labour Party had come round increasingly to favour a policy of comprehensive reorganization.[34] Successive statements of intention – for example, 'Challenge to Britain' in 1953 and 'Learning to Live' in 1958 – seemed to indicate that reorganization, when it came, would be flexible: 'It would be nearer the truth to describe our proposals as a grammar school education for all,' argued Hugh Gaitskell in 1958; but his successor, Harold Wilson, emphasized that 11 + differentiation would have to go. When it assumed office in 1964 the Labour Party was unequivocally committed to the dismemberment of the tripartite system:

. . . as a nation we cannot afford to force segregation on our children at the 11-plus stage . . .

Harold Wilson had said at the 1963 Labour Party Conference.[35]

We cannot afford to cut off three-quarters or more of our children from virtually any chance of higher education. The Russians do not, the Germans do not, the Americans do not, and the Japanese do not, and we cannot afford to either.

Implicit in this statement was an assumption that the very principles of examination at 11 + and of tripartism were no longer socially acceptable. The failure of the concept of parity of esteem had of course contributed to this conclusion. But it was the simultaneous erosion of confidence in the effectiveness of the 11 + examination itself which made a reassessment of the whole system of state secondary education imperative in the early 1960s and compelled one Labour government to undertake the task of dismantling the system of tripartism which another had done so much to create twenty years earlier.

The credibility of the 11 + examination (i)

Parity of conditions and an effective 11 + segregation were, by Hadow's definition, the twin buttresses of the tripartite system. The long-term failure of the former was to shift a critical proportion of the supportive function onto the credibility of the 11 + selection procedure. For as long as it could be reasonably presented as objective, accurate, and based upon acceptable 'scientific' criteria, the 11 + exam was likely to remain a fairly reliable prop. The task of selection was not an easy one. The Departmental Committee on Scholarships and Free Places had regretted in 1920 that under the existing examination procedures 'a great many excellent fish slip past the net'.[36] There was an evident demand for alternative, more reliable selection tests: tests that would, for example, automatically discount at one and the same time the effects of the cramming sometimes given to pupils from relatively well-off homes and the cultural disadvantages which were frequently the lot of the bright child of working-class origins. Intelligence tests, it was claimed, fulfilled both these conditions. They had been used to supplement the traditional grammar school scholarship examination since 1921 in Northumberland,[37] where Godfrey Thomson,* their instigator, regarded them as a powerful instrument for social equality, maintaining that 'these psychological tests favour the gifted boy with poor advantages, rather than the rich boy with gifted tutors, and are therefore essentially a democratic method of selection.'[38]

The Hadow Report, reasonably, was cautious in its assessment of this novel method of selection; but Spens appeared to accept the claims made for it with rather less reserve. The two witnesses from the National Institute of Industrial Psychology (Dr. C. S. Myers and Mr. Angus Macrae) certainly put their case in confident terms:

The witnesses said that the group intelligence test afforded a trustworthy instrument for the selection of pupils at the age of 11 + , and they held that it was quite unnecessary to postpone the final selection of pupils for post-primary school from the age of 11 + to that of 13 + , except for entrants to Junior Technical and Junior Commercial Schools.

They stressed that '"intelligence" remained constant throughout life' and suggested a three-part 11 + filtering procedure:

English and Arithmetic should be regarded as a qualifying test in the selection of pupils for post-primary schools, and 'character' should be assessed on the Headmaster's Report. The actual selection of pupils, however, should be on the basis of a group intelligence test. The witnesses would be prepared to reject a candidate if the results of the group tests were poor, even though the candidate had secured high marks in the test of English and Arithmetic.
(Spens Committee documents: PRO Ed 10.152)

One apparent advantage of intelligence testing was that it could be presented (to the layman at least) as giving a mathematically precise and clear-cut statement of the ability of each child. As such, it could be used not only to silence the protests of doubting parents, but to narrow or even eliminate the number of 'border-zone' candidates. By the mid-1950s intelligence testing had become an integral part of 11 + selection procedures throughout the country: 90 per cent of the authorities used intelligence tests and over 70 per cent used objective attainment tests in English and arithmetic.[39]

---

*It is perhaps ironic that Godfrey Thomson, who was an ardent supporter of the multilateral school (see below, p. 111) should have been a key figure in the evolution of intelligence testing in Britain, thus contributing in no small way to the general adoption of the tripartite system.

The credibility of the 11 + examination (ii)

It has already been noted that the concept of parity of esteem was sagging visibly by the mid-1950s. The validity of 11 + segregation was also becoming increasingly open to question. As early as 1953, Brian Simon (a strong opponent of tripartism) summarized the position in these terms:

Some directors of education do not understand what exactly tests are, and how results are worked out; nor do members of education committees, though they assure parents, in perfect good faith, that the particular system adopted in their area is the fairest and most objective that can be devised, adding, no doubt with truth, that an enormous amount of time and money has been spent to ensure that this is so.

The real truth of the matter is that there is no fair or objective method of selection at ten, and that the present system results not only in individual heartbreak but also in a disastrous wastage of ability from the social point of view.
(Brian Simon, Intelligence Testing and the Comprehensive School, 1953, pp. 110-111)

The principal complaints against testing came generally under two headings: that the methods used discriminated against working-class children and that individual attainment scores were, in the normal run of things, subject to significant variation. The latter might be caused by age, by a changing environment, or by a combination of both.

Research published in the mid- and late-1950s seemed to confirm criticisms of the 11 + selection procedures. In 1956 the results of a series of investigations carried out under the auspices of the Department of Sociological and Demographic Research of the London School of Economics led to the disturbing conclusion that:

. . . the probability that a working-class boy will get to a grammar school is not strikingly different from what it was before 1945, and there are still marked differences in the chances which boys of different social origins have of obtaining a place.[40]

In the following year the results of an inquiry by the British Psychological Society (initiated originally 'in view of the natural concern of many parents and the spate of misleading and often emotionally-toned writing on the topic'),[41] indicated that many educational psychologists had already adopted a judiciously modified view of the long-term accuracy of intelligence testing. The cautious approach to the border-zone question was particularly noteworthy:

Psychologists should frankly acknowledge that completely accurate classification of children, either by level or type of ability, is not possible at 11 years, still less on entry to the junior school at 7 . . .

. . .

Only among the top 5 % or so and the bottom 50 % (with a 20 % acceptance rate) do we consider that allocation to grammar, technical and modern schools can be made

automatically from test scores and scaled estimates. All intermediate pupils should be regarded as border-zone, and given special consideration by a panel of teachers, an Education Officer and/or an educational psychologist.
(P. E. Vernon, ed., Secondary School Selection, 1957, pp. 169 and 177)

In 1957 also the N.F.E.R. Third Interim Report on the allocation of primary school leavers to courses of secondary education stressed that although 'a verbal intelligence test was the best single predictor among the tests and examinations used',[42] it was nevertheless

. . . clear that, if children are to be segregated into courses of secondary education which are sharply differentiated for those who just secure entrance to a grammar school and those who fail by a narrow margin to do so – as is the case in most tripartite or bipartite systems, then even the use of the most efficient procedure that can, in the light of our present knowledge, be devised, results in a considerably greater number of wrong allocations than can be viewed with equanimity.

Our estimates suggest that this number is likely to amount to 10% of the children in any age-group, or about 60,000 children per year at present.
(Alfred Yates and D. A. Pidgeon, Admission to Grammar Schools, 1957, p. 192)

So the critics were justified: within two years the message had got through to the Central Advisory Council. *15 to 18* (the Crowther Report) noted in measured terms that

The longer the period for which a system of selection is asked to predict, the greater the subsequent need for redistribution. Much careful research work has shown pretty clearly that a fresh classification after four years, i.e. about the age of 15, would have redistributed between selective and non-selective schools about 14% of the pupils. By the time they join up for National Service this 14% has become 22% among Army recruits and 29% among the more homogeneous group of R.A.F. recruits, according to the evidence of the National Service Survey. This is what we would expect from the changes and chances of mortal life, and it seems increasingly clear that we cannot hope to avoid error by further refinements in the process of selection. . . . With human beings, no selection can be regarded as final.
(The Crowther Report, 15 to 18, 1959, p. 72)

This conclusion has the definitive tone of a Last Judgement. *Vis inertiae* would delay immediate action; but unless a new support could be found the tripartite concept appeared doomed. The ever-prolonged absence of parity made a mockery of Hadowism; combined with an inherently imprecise form of selection, tripartism seemed to subject many 11 + children to a kind of educational Russian roulette – with most of the chambers loaded.

The abolition of the 11 + examination was included in the Labour Party's election programme of 1964 and the celebrated Circular 10/65 (which requested all L.E.A.s to produce schemes of comprehensive secondary education) followed its return to power.

The simple rejection of tripartism was not in itself likely to produce a credible form of secondary education. For decades England's educational system had been based (as Wilson had pointed out) upon the explicit assumptions that three-quarters of the country's children were mentally incapable of benefitting from higher education and that these children could be sorted out at the age of 11 + . A whole philosophy of theory and practice had been evolved to give support to these ideas. Between three and four thousand schools had been specifically designed to dispense a consciously limited form of education. The teachers in them had been trained to accept a corresponding1y circumscribed view of their pupils' needs, aspirations, and abilities. A dominating question of the post-1965 years would be whether the secondary modern schools could find within themselves the resources and the flexibility demanded by comprehensivization; or whether, lacking them, they would fail and in their failure jeopardize the whole structure of state secondary education.

THE COMPREHENSIVE ISSUE

It is sometimes a little difficult to realize that the idea of segregating children into schools specifically designed to accommodate only a restricted part of the normal range of academic ability is a relatively modern one. The clear-cut 11 + line drawn between grammar school children and those destined for the secondary moderns had no exact analogy either in the pre-1926 secondary school or in the schools of the independent sector. The tripartite classification formulated in the Taunton Report of 1868 assumed that social and financial considerations, rather than intellectual ones, would determine what kind of school, if any, a child of secondary age would attend.

That it was the aim of the Consultative Committee and its supporters in the interwar period to establish the grammar school as a preserve of the intellectually élite appears fairly evident, but in doing so they were destroying rather than maintaining the established tradition, which was based upon recruitment over a wide ability range (though of course a socially restricted one). It was hardly remarkable, consequently, that during the 1920s and 1930s a certain amount of disquiet was expressed about the implications of Hadowism. Some (though by no means all)* socialists were quick to discern dangers in the separation of bright children (and especially working-class ones) from their less able contemporaries; many educationalists felt equally strongly that interaction between children of a

---

* 'Until comparatively recently,' one C. E. O. observed in the early 1970s, 'the Labour Party in local authorities had little enthusiasm for comprehensive schools'. (See George Taylor in *County Hall*, ed. Kogan and van der Eyken, 1973, p. 171.)

wide spectrum of abilities was a vital element in the provision of true education. In the same year as the first Hadow Report, a joint Labour Party/T.U.C. document *(From Nursery School to University)* condemned any discrimination between schools based upon the leaving age of pupils as tending 'to accentuate undesirable class distinctions'. By 1929 the National Association of Labour Teachers (which was to prove one of the most tenacious supporters of comprehensive education) had come out in favour of the multilateral principle, considering that it would

. . . avoid premature determination of the adolescent training suitable for the child, and . . . prevent segregation in groups resulting in class differentiation.[43]

It is not perhaps surprising that there was a certain amount of left-wing opposition to Hadowism. Misgivings, however, were also voiced by less radical groups: the Association of Assistant Masters, for example, which gave its support to multilateralism* as early as 1925. Both the Association of Assistant Mistresses and the Association of Headmistresses took a strong line against 11 + differentiation. The latter flatly told Eustace Percy in 1929 that

the segregation of young people during adolescence in educational institutions of an acknowledged academic, or practical, or aesthetic type is artificial and restrictive, and is not in accordance with national interest.[44]

Indeed, the attitude of the board itself appears at times to have verged on the equivocal: Eustace Percy, replying to the Association of Headmistresses, maintained that

I have never contemplated the 'segregation of the different types of boy and girl mind' in different schools.[45]

And four years later the issue still appears to have been open. When the Consultative Committee was given instructions in 1933 to produce its report on the secondary school, the *Times Educational Supplement* printed a major front-page article on the merits of multi-bias schooling in which the writer surmised that:

The announcement may . . . possibly revive to some extent the controversy (which is always quietly raging) between those who advocate the 'single-track' secondary school and those who are in favour of the 'multi-bias' school . . .

and concluded:

The advantages of the 'multi-bias' school would seem to be indubitable. It affords opportunity for every variety of talent, and, this being developed, the resultant corporate body is in many ways superior to that in a more restricted secondary school,

---

*Multilateral (or 'multi-bias') schools were designed to admit all the 11 + children from a specific catchment area. But they might separate their pupils into 'sides' (for example, grammar, technical, and modern) for the purpose of instruction.

which of necessity cannot provide full outlet for the abilities of many of its members. On the other hand, there are very serious problems to be faced before such schools can become general. A 'multi-bias' school demands large numbers, and so far as capital expenditure is concerned a considerable outlay. It is hardly possible to run such a school with prospects of full success with an enrolment of less than 450. Laboratories of a superior quality are required and many practical rooms. It is not certain that the annual expenditure would have to be greater than that in an ordinary secondary school, but the probability is that it would be.

An even greater difficulty is the securing of suitable staff. . . .
(Times Educational Supplement, 21 October 1933, p. 349)

The line-up for Spens

The Consultative Committee's report on secondary education was published in 1938. After criticizing with some asperity the quality of the post-Hadow modern schools, it recommended a policy of tripartite selection even more discriminatory than the dual division advocated by Hadow. At the same time, it asserted, with apparent sincerity, that

the *multilateral idea*, although it may not be expressed by means of multilateral schools, must be inherent in any truly national system of secondary education.[46]

The committee had certainly gone to some trouble to examine the arguments in favour of multilateral schools. They had sought the advice of the Scottish Education Department on the organization of its 'omnibus' schools[47] and had sent an investigator to look at them. They had also collated the opinions of unions and other interested groups on the issue.[48] The resulting alignment revealed considerable and broad-based support for the multilateral school. Approval of multilateralism (or at least bilateralism) was expressed by the Association of Municipal Corporations, the Federation of Education Committees for Wales and Monmouthshire,* the Welsh Secondary Schools Association, the Headmasters' Conference ('In most cases it would be better to organize a variety of courses within one school'), the Association of Headmasters (which confined itself to approving a technical/grammar bilateralism), and, of course, the Association of Headmistresses ('. . . where a girl really does seem to have few talents, many a Head Mistress will testify that she is often, through character and grace, one whom the school would not willingly be without.'). Further support was given by the Association of Assistant Mistresses, the Association of Assistant Masters in Secondary Schools, the National Association of Labour Teachers, the T.U.C., and the Standing Joint Committee of Industrial Women's

---

*In 1936, for example, the education committee in Anglesey, on the initiative of its pro-comprehensive Director of Education, E. O. Humphreys, had recommended that 'the development of postprimary education in Anglesey should be based on the principle of multilateral secondary schools' at Amlwch, Beaumaris, Holyhead, and Llangefni.

Organizations. The National Union of Teachers also gave a measure of encouragement.

Teachers, then, showed themselves prepared in the late 1930s to give an impressive degree of approval to the principle of a unified form of schooling for 11 + children. Nevertheless the committed and opposing stance of the English L.E.A. associations was to prove more weighty. Given the decentralized structure of educational administration and government, it was their attitude which would almost certainly be decisive. Failing, therefore, a change of heart on the part of the L.E.A.s or the exercise of coercive pressure by the board (along, for example, the lines of Circular 1350), it was unlikely that the multilateral school would generally assume anything more than the subordinate and tentative role assigned to it in Spens:

We do not wish to deprecate experiments in multilateral schools, especially in areas where . . . difficulties do not arise,* as in areas of new population. We hope, too, that the various difficulties may be surmounted in sparsely populated rural areas where a Grammar School and a Modern School may be formed into a multilateral school.
(The Spens Report, Secondary Education, 1938, p. 292)

Moreover, as long as the twin justifications of parity of school status and accurate 11 + differentiation were to retain credibility, there would be relatively little incentive for either the board or the L.E.A.s to embark upon a policy which was conceded even by some of its supporters to be possibly more costly and less academically efficient than tripartism. Godfrey Thomson, whose 'own very strong predilection'[49] for comprehensive schools was based principally upon the argument that they were conducive to social solidarity, was prepared freely to admit that

The separate secondary school is very efficient in attaining its narrow aim. . . . In a school which catered not only for the demands of the university and the professions, but also for those of commerce, of art, of craft, and of the factory, it is very doubtful whether the same standard of efficiency could be reached which is attained today in separate secondary schools, commercial central schools, art schools, technical schools. . . . The ordinary process of organization would seem to lead to such separate institutions . . .

In America . . . there is sometimes heard the saying, 'A boy is entitled to his fair chance *even if* he is of superior intelligence.' The suggestion is that in a high school for all the general intellectual level is so lowered that the cleverer are handicapped, and are not receiving the kind of mental pabulum which is their due, that, in fact, they are being starved. While this, of course, need not be the case in a large and well-classified school with different kinds of courses for each category of pupil, it is

---

*i.e., where a multilateral school would not prejudice the success of preexisting grammar, technical, or modern schools.

certainly a danger if the schools must be small, and therefore cannot be well classified.
(Godfrey Thomson, A Modern Philosophy of Education, 1929, pp. 273-274)

Thomson was even prepared to concede that there was no absolute certainty of social integration under a system of comprehensive education:

But even when you have a common school with compulsory attendance, there will, of course, be social distinctions between a school in one district and that in another. This can hardly be laid at the door of the educational administration, but is rather another way of stating the larger fact that there are social distinctions in the world outside the school which lead to the segregation of classes in certain quarters of a city.
(Godfrey Thomson, A Modern Philosophy of Education, 1929, p. 276)

Thus even as early as 1929 two of the most controversial aspects of the comprehensive school – academic efficiency and social integration – were defined. It is perhaps a reflection upon the quality of English educational research that they are still being argued over almost half a century later: as late as 1964 (the year before comprehensive reorganization was initiated by the government) there were no D.E.S.-funded projects aimed at evaluating the new system (although £900,000 was being spent on research into other areas of education).

The drift from the comprehensive principle

The main recommendations of the Spens Report was backed up by those of the Norwood Report and the White Paper on Educational Reconstruction (1943); by 1944 the inference was that any initiative regarding comprehensivization on a national scale would have to come from the central government.

The 1944 Act, with its emphasis upon the powers of the new minister to modify or alter development plans submitted by individual L.E.A.s apparently made such a course of action more of a possibility than previously. In 1942, and again in 1943, moreover, the Labour Party annual conferences had approved resolutions demanding that the board should encourage

as a general policy, the development of a new type of multilateral school which would provide a variety of courses suited to children of all normal types.[50]

The return in 1945 of a strong Labour administration (with 'Red Ellen' Wilkinson as Minister of Education) might, therefore, have seemed auspicious for multilateralism's prospects. But there was a strong commitment within the party to the ideals of tripartism; the Hadow Report had, after all, been a socialist-inspired document. James Chuter Ede, who, as parliamentary secretary to the Board of Education, had been intimately involved with the drafting and ratification of the 1944 Act, apparently took a reserved and Spens-orientated view of secondary education:

Don't encourage this comprehensive school idea. Where it's sound educationally, O.K., where it's prompted by philosophical and political ideas, it's so much poppycock

he told Leah Manning.[51] A similar attitude was held both by Ellen Wilkinson and her successor, George Tomlinson. In 1949 the latter was to tell one pro-comprehensive L.E.A. (Middlesex) quite bluntly that he

. . . doubted . . . the wisdom of destroying the well-established system of grammar schools and of embarking upon a complete reorganization of secondary schools in the county on the basis of a system which, in this country, had no practical experience behind it.[52]

Support for selection in secondary education, indeed, was to remain an enduring feature of one section of socialist thought. Perhaps the best-publicized example of this was Harold Wilson's assertion that the grammar schools would be abolished only over his dead body. Another was the *Political Quarterly*'s editorial contribution of October-December 1951 which argued the case for the acceptance of the idea of 'an intellectual élite, an aristocracy of brains, based entirely upon ability and without regard to wealth, social standing, or other forms of privilege' and which condemned the L.C.C.'s adoption of comprehensive plans 'in the absence of any precise knowledge of the results' as 'scandalously irresponsible'. The point has more recently been reiterated in Iris Murdoch's 1975 Black Paper article entitled 'Socialism and Selection'.

During the immediate postwar period, tripartism seemed to offer a valid and indeed logical and praiseworthy structure for education. It was, moreover, becoming evident to many supporters of the grammar school that the terms 'multilateral' and 'comprehensive' were not at all the same thing, and that whereas the multilateral idea assumed an acceptable state of peaceful coexistence between grammar and less academic sides within a single institution, the comprehensive one implied amalgamation and the consequent end of differentiation. Circular 144 (1947) recognized the comprehensive school as one 'without an organization in three sides' – a definition that from then on was accepted as the main distinguishing feature of comprehensive education. It is the alleged advantages and disadvantages of this singularly exclusive form of education which have continued to form a semipermanent centre of controversy within which two principal issues have tended to remain dominant throughout: the first is concerned with the academic efficiency of the comprehensive school and the other with the question of its long-term influence upon the structure of society as a whole.

The issue of academic attainment

It has been noted that Godfrey Thomson, as early as 1929, had attempted to give a balanced assessment of the educational worth of the comprehensive school. In his estimation its greatest strength was that it promoted social unity; its weakness that it tended to underteach the gifted child. Shena Simon, writing in 1948, came down, like Thomson, on the side of comprehensive schools; but at the same time she voiced doubts which were to be reiterated time and again in the following years; although she could discover no falling-off of standards in the Scottish multilaterally organized 'omnibus' schools, in American comprehensives she observed that

The able, lazy child has little incentive to work his hardest, for, in addition to the lack of stimulus, which he would get from working with his equals – and superiors – there are, except in New York State, no external examinations and none, or very few, university entrance scholarships to be won. Experts who are in positions to judge both systems say that the American high school graduate is about two years behind the English sixth form boy or girl in actual knowledge, and that this lower standard is partly the result of putting all types of children together.
(*Lady Simon of Wythenshawe, Three Schools or One?*, 1948, p. 70)

Could it therefore be assumed that the mixed-ability grouping which was increasingly recognized as implicit in comprehensive schooling worked to the disadvantage of the more academic child? Sir Eric (later Lord) James and Harry Rée, two of the more prominent supporters of the grammar school, certainly believed so. James' thesis went well beyond the issue of school organization: 'the English grammar school,' he wrote in 1957, 'is quite simply, in our particular circumstances, one of the greatest hopes for our future national prosperity.'[53] In his book *Education and Leadership* (1951) he had forcefully advanced an unashamedly élitist doctrine:

. . . leadership in very widely different fields of activity is associated with high intelligence, and in particular with the small fraction of the population that includes the really outstanding individuals.[54]

There was real danger, James maintained, in 'frustrating the very intelligent by delaying his intellectual progress in the field of his choice';[55] he adduced psychiatric evidence that

Greater danger lies in failing to satisfy the child's natural needs than in encouraging him to use his capacities to the full.[56]

And he concluded that

For the brilliant child . . . there can be little doubt that it would be disastrous.[57]

H. A. Rée felt that there were strong positive arguments for the retention of grammar schools:*

*H. A. Rée was, however, in the course of time to become converted to the cause of comprehensive schools.

This . . . selection has meant that the clever child has been able to work alongside children equally clever, and has therefore gained from pitting his mind against a mind of like calibre; it has also meant that he has been able to pursue his studies in an atmosphere conducive to hard learning and serious application, and where a tradition of voluntary service and willing acceptance of responsibility has been growing up over the years.
(H. A. Rée, The Essential Grammar School, 1956, p. 83)

Attitudes such as these received some cogent support from the other side of the Atlantic. As early as 1948, Professor I. L. Kandel was complaining that, in the U.S.A.:

Quality has yielded to quantity and educational values have been lost sight of in a system which has been called the cafeteria plan of curricular organization.[58]

By 1965 the sociologist R. G. Corwin felt justified in putting his reservations under the dismissive heading of 'The eclipse of the comprehensive school':

Comprehensive schools have led to two major types of strain in the school system, each of which subverts intellectual functions. First, the comprehensiveness of the program results in a multiplicity of goals, ranging from teaching knowledge to teaching character training. Many of these goals are either logically inconsistent (e.g. teaching critical thinking along with uncritical patriotism), or they cannot be completely achieved simultaneously because of the limited time and energy of teachers and students.

But even if there were a single goal, the fact that the typical teacher, by design, faces a class of thirty students from different social class backgrounds, with differing motivations and interests, and with an IQ range of four to six years, considerably lessens his competence. Armed only with well-indoctrinated warnings to 'beware of individual differences', which he will find only too obvious, the teacher is not only unprepared but has insufficient time adequately to work with the one hundred and fifty individuals whom he will face daily in the high school. The situation condemns the teacher to inadequacy in most respects; it condemns the school to a nonspecialized, jack of all trades position.
(R. G. Corwin, A Sociology of Education, 1965, p. 141)

The situation in England was not, however, wholly analogous to that in the U.S.A. where, for example, a decentralized system of funding allowed greater discrepanices in the provision of schooling than was usual in Britain. As J. D. Koerner, an American critic of comprehensivization, pointed out, American comprehensives can be most impressive 'in any suburb that may spend £500 a year on each child, and they can be appalling fifteen miles away in a downtown slum.'[59] So it was to Sweden that British educationalists tended to turn for information about undifferentiated schooling. In that country a series of research projects concerned with comparative attainment levels in segregated and comprehensive schools had culminated in the mid-1950s with the decision of Stockholm City Council to initiate comprehensive education throughout the southern part of the city.[60] The progress of the children concerned was thereafter monitored against that of those who attended the differentiated schools in the north of Stockholm. Results published in 1962 by Nils-Eric Svensson appeared to be reassuring though hardly spectacular:[61] although the differentiated secondary environment seemed somewhat superior in the first years, it subsequently became less so and, in the long run, gave levels of attainment which were no better than those obtained in the comprehensive school. The findings were, however, inconclusive enough to be challenged in Sweden, where one of the best-known supporters of comprehensive schooling, Professor Torsten Husén, concluded in 1971 that:

The issue whether a school system (local or national) should 'go comprehensive' or not, cannot . . . be settled on the basis of purely pedagogical considerations only. Nor can it be settled by drawing mainly upon psychological evidence. Educators are wrong to feel that, because the issue is basically an educational one, it should be decided upon by educators themselves and that bodies such as national parliaments and governments are meddling when they decide the structure of a school system. Education does not operate in a socio-economic vacuum; it is today more than ever a vital part of the socio-economic fabric. Education is too important to society to be shaped chiefly on the basis of pedagogical considerations.
(T. Husén, The Comprehensive versus Selective School Issue, in International Review of Education XVII/1971/1, p. 9.)

The social solidarity issue

Torsten Husén's last point – that educational policy making should not be principally determined by teaching considerations – opens up the second basic issue concerning comprehensive education. Indeed, the question of social engineering, rather than that of the narrowly educational function of the comprehensive school, has apparently played a dominant part in the thinking of many of its supporters. In Anthony Crosland's words:

Our belief in comprehensive reorganization was a product of fundamental value-judgements about equity and equal opportunity and social division as well as about education. Research can help you to achieve your objectives. . . . But research can't tell you whether you should go comprehensive or not – that's a basic value-judgement.
(E. Boyle and A. Crosland, The Politics of Education, 1971, p. 190)

It has already been mentioned that this line of approach was by no means novel. Shena Simon had noted American opinion in 1948 that

. . . our high schools are not institutions for instruction – not primarily at least. . . . In most communities the high school is the chief symbol of democracy . . .[62]

while even twenty years before that, Godfrey Thomson had argued that the chief merit of comprehensive education was that 'it leads to social solidarity'.[63]

The argument is undoubtedly an emotive and (to many) an attractive one, in spite of – or perhaps because of – its incompatibility with the grammar school's assumption that priority should rest with high academic attainment. Any educational programme likely to contribute to the easing of social tension would have much to recommend it in a country as self-conscious about its class rivalries as England. The question, of course, is whether there exists any conclusive proof that comprehensive education can genuinely be regarded as an engine for social equality.

This assumption is contradicted by many opponents of comprehensive education. In the succinct words of Lord James:

Actually the whole argument based on the evils of segregation is a fallacious one. If the children for selective schools are drawn from every social class such schools are among the strongest solvents of class division. . . . Further, nothing could accentuate class divisions more effectively than comprehensive schools drawing on limited localities, where the whole tone and prestige of the school is completely coloured by the social status of the particular neighbourhood, as American experience shows. *(Eric James, Education and Leadership, 1951, p. 45)*

American comprehensives have not infrequently been criticized for their allegedly low levels of academic attainment; James' last sentence carries the implication that there have been equal deficiencies in the fulfilment of their social role. Indeed, in a passage which must have brought joy to contemporary supporters of the grammar school, one popular sociologist, Vance Packard, contrasted American social attitudes in the late 1950s unfavourably with those of (amongst other countries) tripartite England:

Although we still tend to think of equality as being peculiarly American, and of class barriers as being peculiarly foreign, the evidence indicates that several European nations (such as Holland, England, and Denmark) have gone further than America in developing an open-class system, where the poor but talented young can rise on their merits.

Referring specifically to the American scene, Packard remarked that:

Youngsters, by the time they reach the fifth or sixth grade, have absorbed the social-class origins of their playmates, and know whom they shouldn't associate with, except on a polite basis . . .

In many schools, the youngsters from the higher-prestige families form tight cliques. An eighth-grade teacher in a Connecticut school voiced to me her discouragement because she had in her home room 'a snippy little clique of girls' from the upper level of classes 'who outlaw everyone who doesn't seem to belong to their group and do what they do'. One girl in the clique fell by the wayside because her parents neglected to send her to dancing school. 'She was dropped from everything,' the teacher relates. *(V. Packard, The Status Seekers, 1961 ed., pp. 16-17 and 202-203)*

The preceding extracts express what might be termed the 'confrontation' argument against claims that comprehensive schooling is conducive to social integration. Events at Kent State University (Ohio) in May 1970 seemed further to weaken such suppositions, at least as far as America was concerned. There, a series of almost unbelievably acrimonious encounters between students and National Guardsmen culminated in the shooting of thirteen or fourteen of the former. Many of those involved on both sides were of about the same age,[64] but accounts of the affair emphasize the extreme social tensions and the unbridgeable cultural gaps which somehow had come to exist within the comprehensively educated society of the United States. Indeed, deschoolers such as Everett Reimer and Ivan Illich claimed vociferously and sometimes persuasively that schools – whatever their type – could only exacerbate existing social and economic problems.

A more subtle denial of the social advantages of comprehensive schooling (though one less acceptable to hard-core educationalists of all shades of opinion) is the 'reflection' hypothesis, which casts doubt upon the assumption that schooling can modify society as a whole. The logical conclusion of this premise is that educational planners should base their systems upon existing social attitudes and not delude themselves with any *folie de grandeur* about social engineering. 'Social equality in the community,' concisely remarked Shena Simon,[65] 'is the prerequisite of social equality in the school, and not the reverse.' By the mid-1940s, some American commentators were claiming to discern very real dangers in any attempt to modify society through its schools:

As long as we have our present social structure education must be adapted to it or we will produce a generation or more of maladjusted children and unhappy adults. The school in America, whether we like it or not, must function to make democracy work in a status system that is only partially equalitarian. Only as our social order changes can the school indoctrinate its pupils with economic and political philosophies of human relationship which are now in sharp conflict with the prevailing social system. The thesis of some educators that American schools should be the instruments of propaganda for a particular kind of economic or political thought is wrong and must be discouraged. Although the guiding philosophy of such propagandists may be democratic, the methods advanced are unreal and dangerous. Propaganda education that conflicts with the prevailing mores produces conflict in the lives of those taught and does not provide growing children with a realistic orientation to the social world in which they must compete for a living and for status.
(*W. L. Warner, R. J. Havighurst and M. B. Loeb, Who shall be Educated?, 1946, p. 140*)

Yet more barbed in its criticism is the argument, aimed less at comprehensive schooling itself than at the alleged hypocrisy of some of its supporters, whose radicalism may be no more than skin deep. In the passage below R. G. Corwin taxes such crypto-conservative attitudes and the widespread but ingenuous belief in the omnipotence of school upon which they depend for credibility:

> . . . sociologists and the public in general continue to expect the public* schools to generate a classless society, do away with racial prejudice, improve table manners, make happy marriages, reverse the national habit of smoking, prepare trained workers for the professions, and produce patriotic and religious citizens who are at the same time critical and independent thinkers! It should be noted that this reliance on education as a means of improving the world may be so popular because it seems to be a safe way to institute change: when stressing the potential of education eventually to change individuals, reformers need not concern themselves with the dreadful prospect of altering entrenched social structures.
> (R. G. Corwin, A Sociology of Education, 1965, p. 57)

The British experience

During the late 1960s and early 1970s, research data based upon British (rather than American or Swedish) comprehensive schools began to be published. In 1969 Dr. Julienne Ford's survey of three London schools (a streamed comprehensive, 'Cherry Dale'; 'South Moleberry' Secondary Modern School; 'Gammer Wiggins' Grammar School) appeared, while between 1968 and 1972 the National Foundation for Educational Research brought out an elaborate three-phase study of comprehensive education in England and Wales. This analysed groups of 385, 59, and eventually 12 comprehensives in increasing detail.

Dr. Ford's work was concerned with the social aspects of comprehensive education. The results she obtained were not encouraging, though the narrowness of the study and the fact that the comprehensive school studied was a streamed one argued against any conclusive interpretation:

> The evidence from the three schools, then, far from revealing a greater equality of opportunity for the comprehensive school pupil, shows a persistence of class bias in educational attainment under the comprehensive system. Indeed there is some indication that 'wastage of ability' among bright working-class pupils may be occurring on an even larger scale in Cherry Dale comprehensive school than in Gammer Wiggins grammar school.
>
> For where comprehensive school children are taught in ability groups or streams as nearly all of them are, the 'self-fulfilling prophecy' characteristic of the tripartite system is still very much in evidence.
> (Julienne Ford, Social Class and the Comprehensive School, 1969, p. 40)

Regarding the hoped-for breakdown of class consciousness and division, Dr. Ford's research only confirmed the arguments which such people as Lord James had been advancing for some time:

---

*i.e. state-controlled.

The evidence from this sample then suggests that if any type of schooling diminishes the likelihood of class bias in informal social relations within the classroom this is not the comprehensive but the grammar school.

And as for the anticipated erosion of social exclusiveness in the comprehensive school . . .

. . . there is no evidence whatever from this study of three schools that this is the case. In Cherry Dale as in most comprehensive schools, children are taught in doubly homogeneous social groups. They, like tripartite children, mix during lesson time mainly with those from similar social background and those who are bound for similar eventual social status. The option for social mixing which is supposedly created in the comprehensive school by the house system is simply not taken up:[66] children are more likely to choose their 'real friends' from their own academic streams than any others in the same school, and houses and house tutor groups have no impact on friendship formation. Within these homogeneous academic streams children apparently prefer to mix with those from similar social background. *(Julienne Ford, Social Class and the Comprehensive School, 1969, pp. 103-105)*

Julienne Ford had remarked upon the initial difficulty she had experienced in finding a genuinely comprehensive school. This point was reiterated in the second part of the N.F.E.R. survey: out of the 45 schools which completed the first-year attainment tests

. . . only nine schools had what might be regarded as fully 'comprehensive' or balanced ability intakes in 1967/68. Of these, only seven schools can be considered fully comprehensive, since two are junior high schools of the type from which not *all* pupils transfer to senior high schools. *(P. Evison, in Comprehensive Education in Action, N.F.E.R., 1970, p. 107)*

The final part of the N.F.E.R. survey – 'A Critical Appraisal of Comprehensive Education' – was in some ways the most informative. It dealt with twelve comprehensive schools which between them contained a wide variation of internal organization and structure. This factor, combined with the relatively small number of schools in the survey, effectively inhibited the kind of conclusive and credible generalization for which there was so great a need. For example, as far as the crucial issue of social integration was concerned, the only conclusions which could be safely drawn were as follows:

Few of the schools provide straightforward situations for social mixing to occur. Three are in urban areas which are predominantly working class, one with the additional burden of creaming by grammar schools. Ability grouping (streaming or banding) further restricts mixing and the already numerous ill-behaved children, of either sex, tend to form delinquent sub-cultures. The Leicestershire plan system produces some segregation by ability and related factors in different schools in the fourth year, and a hard division by previous attendance at separate feeder schools occurs in the senior high school, though this division may soften in time.

The one urban school which is nearly comprehensive in intake is banded and displays a clear polarity between the abler, higher social class, well-behaved pupils and the less able, lower social class, ill-behaved (though there are, of course, exceptions to these generalizations).

Two small Welsh rural schools and a larger English rural school are streamed and show a similar polarity, but fewer pupils are classed as ill-behaved by their teachers. An English rural school which has introduced unstreaming has shown almost complete disappearance of the delinquent sub-culture, but this one example cannot be taken as conclusive.

In two schools only, serving well-defined English communities, does a satisfactory level of social mixing appear to have been achieved. In this, pupils of each sex display one continuous extensive friendship network. Within the network are sub-groups, each of which has usually some common feature, whether of ability, social class, sport participation, aspiration, behaviour or home proximity. It is the many cross-links between these sub-groups which break down the divisions implied by them. Both a streamed and an unstreamed school display this pattern.
(J. M. Ross, W. J. Bunton, P. Evison and T. S. Robertson, A Critical Appraisal of Comprehensive Education, N.F.E.R., 1972, p. 111)

The concluding paragraph of the passage above did not appear to give much consolation to the advocates of comprehensive education for the sake of social solidarity. On the issue of overall academic attainment, however, the N.F.E.R. survey did give a measure of reassurance. Of the eleven schools which provided the relevant statistics only one had more than its theoretical due of high-ability students while no fewer than five had a more than average proportion of low-ability ones. Nevertheless,

At the fifth-year level the comprehensive schools in this study have more pupils remaining at school and gaining qualifications than expected from national statistics. Indeed, in only two of the 11 schools were the proportions lower than the national average. These findings are important, for they mean that the pupils of average ability and below, in addition to the more able, are being tempted to stay on at school voluntarily beyond the school leaving age and this in some school populations that are deprived of the more able pupils.

Compared with national standards, sixth-form records for all pupils staying on at school may be described as average or above but examination passes at the higher level, are average or below. However, when the characteristics of the pupils are borne in mind, sixth-form examination standards appear satisfactory.
(J. M. Ross, W. J. Bunton, P. Evison and T. S. Robertson, A Critical Appraisal of Comprehensive Education, N.F.E.R., 1972, p. 67)

This conclusion was broadly consistent with that arrived at in Sweden a decade earlier. But it left unanswered the important question of the effect of comprehensive schooling upon the academic achievement of the intelligent child. The N.F.E.R. survey took an elaborately noncommittal line on this and it has remained for many an unresolved issue and one still open to evidence of a highly conflicting nature. As late as July 1974 the *Times Educational Supplement* could feature, under a headline that ran 'Manchester shaken by survey of comprehensives', an article which began by announcing that 'The proportion of Manchester schoolchildren going in for G.C.E. "O" levels has been falling steeply since comprehensive reorganization in 1967.' This was followed three months later by one which read 'Exam passes up in all-in Sheffield'[67] and continued: 'Exam entries and passes in Sheffield's maintained schools have gone up following comprehensive reorganization.' Then, in March 1977, a report based upon attainment within Leicestershire schools soberly claimed that 'it is plain that well-established comprehensives can hold their own in terms of exam performance, at least up to about average national standards . . .' Even the apparent decline in O-level examination achievement within the maintained sector between 1971 and 1975[68] was open to various and conflicting interpretations. The Tory government's decision to initiate a scheme enabling bright children to move to independent schools seemed to be an admission that comprehensive education did not develop the intellects of brainy pupils.

The latitudinarian approach of Circular 10/65 (which, apart from giving some measure of toleration to no fewer than six varieties of school organization, carefully omitted any instructions about banding, streaming, setting, or mixed-ability grouping) was, no doubt, in part responsible for the difficulties experienced in obtaining conclusive evidence regarding the social and academic consequences of comprehensive reorganization. The ensuing policy of wide-spectrum pragmatism (which might perhaps be less sympathetically described as one of muddling through) has made it difficult to predict whether any particular variant of comprehensive schooling will ultimately become dominant. In March, 1975, the *Times Educational Supplement* reported that of the 104 L.E.A.s in England and Wales, only 20 were 'truly comprehensive'. Forty hoped to be comprehensive by September 1975, but 46 came into the 'sometime', 'possibly never', or 'never' categories. Governmental dissatisfaction at the rate of progress was shown in the following year by the passing of an act designed to require L.E.A.s to submit to the Secretary of State proposals for comprehensive reorganization and to implement such plans within five years of their being submitted. The deadline for such submission was subsequently fixed for the end of May, 1977. Only one L.E.A. of the eight which had so far refused (Bexley, Buckinghamshire, Essex, Kingston-upon-Thames, Redbridge, Sutton, Tameside, and Trafford) remained recalcitrant. This, perhaps not surprisingly, was Tameside; the other seven with some reluctance drew up plans for the phasing-out of selection over periods of up to fifteen years (Bexley)[70] — an empty gesture in the context of British politics.

One thing, however, does seem fairly certain: comprehensive education has come to stay. For, as Harold Wilson explained in 1963, no acceptable alternative form of secondary education exists at the moment. This is not to say that differentiation will vanish. It might be surmised, for example, that economic stringency will encourage an increasingly tolerant attitude towards the erosion of the R.O.S.L.A. concept; this might possibly take the form of semiofficial toleration of truancy or, perhaps, a willingness on the part of authority to permit reluctant students to absent themselves in order to pursue 'vocational project work' in shops and factories. Simultaneously, falling roles and competition for pupils between individual comprehensives seem likely to accelerate the evolution of high status, 'prestige' schools.

There is also a possibility that differentiation within the comprehensive school will increasingly appear in a socially and politically acceptable guise. In 1974 the Royal Commission on Working Conditions in Swedish Schools, for example, concluded that the prevailing mixed-ability class system in that country needed modification and suggested that a new structure, based upon flexible 'work units', should be substituted for it:

Today school work is dominated by a single teacher system. This creates many problems, e.g. from the point of view of the teacher, who has to try to individualize his teaching within the class. This has led to the development of a parallel organization for remedial teaching which now involves roughly 40 per cent of the pupils. This organization has also led to the practice of a pre-eminently written methodology based on work books and stencils. A methodology of this kind creates considerable difficulties among large groups of pupils and its monotony can have a devastating effect on the motivation of many pupils.

Active work in various pupil groups requires the organization of school into smaller and partially autonomous work units. One such work unit can include a variable number of pupils. For instance, it can include the same number of pupils as two present-day classes. It is proposed that the school management be allowed to determine the number of work units in the individual school.

The pupils within a work unit will belong to teaching groups of varying size and composition. These groups are not to be streamed, although there is nothing to prevent e.g. a number of children with reading disabilities being collected in a group and given special training. The group is only to be retained for as long as it is needed for this purpose. For other purposes the pupils in it will belong to other groups.
(*Proposals of the Royal Commission on Working Conditions in Swedish Schools, Stockholm, 1974, p. 4*)

The work unit concept was strongly opposed by the teachers' unions and subsequently modified in the 1975 Education Bill. But Swedish concern about comprehensive curriculum and standards was reechoed in Britain, where in 1976 the D.E.S. *Yellow Book* memorandum noted criticisms that schools 'have become too easy going and demand too little work, and inadequate standards of performance in formal subjects, from their pupils'. The D.E.S. document also referred to the results of low pupil motivation and wide curriculular variation:

One consequence of teacher inexperience (in some cases, incapacity) may have been over-compensation for their worries over disciplinary problems. Many teachers have felt these to have been accentuated by comprehensive re-organization and the raising of the school-leaving age. In an almost desperate attempt to modify styles of teaching and learning so as to capture the imagination and enlist the co-operation of their more difficult pupils, some of them have possibly been too ready to drop their sights in setting standards of performance and have failed to develop new styles of assessment.

And it concluded that the time had probably come for the establishment of a common 'core curriculum' for all pupils.[71] A little later, the Prime Minister, Mr. Callaghan, went so far as to concede in a speech at Ruskin College that he was 'inclined to think that there should be' a basic curriculum with universal standards.[72] The ensuing 'great debate' on education was followed in July, 1977, by the Green Paper *Education in Schools*, which announced that the Secretaries of State were intending to initiate a 'review of curricular arrangements' and to establish 'a broad agreement with their partners in the education service on a framework for the curriculum, and on whether part of the curriculum should be protected because there are aims common to all schools and pupils at certain stages.'[73] The spirit of 1904, banished for half a century, was abroad once more.

Notes

1   Parl. Papers 1897, Vol. LXX, *Return of the Pupils in Secondary and Other Schools, etc.*, p. 557 seq.

2   Sadler Correspondence: M.E.S. to Sir Hugh Orange, 19 April 1904.

3   Report of Board of Education for 1905-1906, p. 63. At that time there were 178 L.E.A. secondary schools.

4   Report of Board of Education for 1924-1925, pp. 97 and 108. There were in addition 100 Welsh Intermediate Schools.

5   See below, p. 89.

6   Spens Report, 1938, p. 270.

7   Ibid., p. 65, note.

8   Report of Board of Education, 1900-1901, pp. 53-54.

9   Three boys' and four girls' schools.

10   For details of changes in the secondary school Regulations see O. Banks, *Parity and Prestige in English Secondary Education*, London, 1955, Chapter 6, and J. Graves, *Policy and Progress in Secondary Education*, 1943, Chapter IX.

11   Board of Education Report for 1905-1906, p. 53.

12   J. Graves, op. cit., pp. 146-147.

13   S.S.E.C. Report on Secondary School Examinations other than G.C.E. (Beloe), p. 5.

14   For an account of these grants, see A. D. Edwards, *The Changing Sixth Form in the Twentieth Century*, 1970, pp. 12-13.

15   Report of Board of Education for 1938, p. 16.

16   J. G. Legge, *The Rising Tide*, 1929, pp. 47-48. The actual figures were for boys in

secondary schools whose fathers were traders' assistants, postmen, policemen, seamen, soldiers, domestic and other servants, and unskilled workmen: in 1909 there were 4,893 (6.7%) boys from such families out of 73,270; by 1926 the total had risen to 22,844 (12%) out of 189,657.

17 Report of the Board of Education for 1938, p. 17.

18 R. H. Tawney, *Secondary Education for All*, 1922, p. 7.

19 J. Graves, op. cit., 1943, p. 127.

20 Norwood Report, 1943, p. 2.

21 Hansard, Fifth Series, Vol. 396, pp. 469-470 (20 January 1944).

22 Leah Manning in her autobiography *(A Life for Education,* 1970, pp. 203-204) alleges that W. G. Cove's attack on Ellen Wilkinson was at least partly motivated by personal jealousy.

23 E. Boyle and A. Crosland, *The Politics of Education,* 1971, p. 94.

24 The literature dealing with secondary modern schools is considered in M. Mathieson and M. T. Whiteside, 'The Secondary Modern School in Fiction', *British Journal of Educational Studies,* Vol. XIX, No. 3 (October 1971). The rapid turnover of staff in secondary modern schools was investigated by the Newsom Committee, which found that 31% of the male teachers on the staff of the secondary modern schools concerned in 1958 had left by 1961. The figure of women teachers was 50%. The proportion of leavers in slum schools was 48% and 67% respectively (see *Half Our Future,* p. 23). The committee concluded that wastage figures indicated 'an unhealthy state of affairs in modern schools generally'. (p. 245)

25 Secondary Capitation Allowances (N.U.T. policy statement), 1973, p. 4.

26 For a full account of the 'points' system during this period see W. Taylor, *The Secondary Modern School,* 1963, pp. 228-231.

27 J. Vaizey, *The Costs of Education,* 1958, p. 102.

28 H. C. Dent, *Secondary Modern Schools, An Interim Report,* 1958, p. 82.

29 R. M. T. Kneebone, *I Work in a Secondary Modern School,* 1957, pp. 66 and 100.

30 Beloe Report, *Secondary School Examinations other than G.C.E.,* 1960, pp. 7-8.

31 Ibid., p. 55.

32 Ibid., p. 60, Table 3.

33 Ibid., pp. 13-15 and Appendix 7.

34 For an account of the assumption of comprehensive reorganization policy by the Labour Party which stresses the influence exercised by certain pressure groups, see I.G.K. Fenwick, *The Comprehensive School 1944-1970,* 1976. A shorter work on the same general subject is M. Parkinson, *The Labour Party and the Organization of Secondary Education 1918-65,* 1970.

35 Report of the 1963 Labour Party Conference, p. 136.

36 Parl. Papers 1920, Vol. XV, *Report of the Departmental Committee on Scholarships and Free Places,* p. 25.

37 P. E. Vernon (ed.), *Secondary School Selection,* 1957, p. 24.

38 Ibid., note on p. 24.

39 A. Yates and D. A. Pidgeon, *Admission to Grammar Schools,* 1957, p. 179.

40 J. E. Floud (ed.), *Social Class and Education Opportunity,* 1956, pp. 142-143.

41 P. E. Vernon, op. cit., p. 8.

42 A. Yates and D. A. Pidgeon, op. cit., p. 181.

43 T. G. Miller, *Values in the Comprehensive School,* 1961, p. 3.

44   *Times Educational Supplement*, 30 March 1929, p. 145.

45   Ibid.

46   Spens Report, 1938, pp. xxxv-xxxvi.

47   These schools catered for 'all types of postprimary courses in parallel'. See P.R.O. Ed. 10/153, papers U.94 and U.95.

48   P.R.O. Ed. 10/153, Paper U.53.

49   Godfrey H. Thomson, *A Modern Philosophy of Education*, 1929, p. 209.

50   Report of the 41st Annual Conference of the Labour Party, 1942, p. 141.

51   Leah Manning, op. cit., p. 188.

52   *Times Educational Supplement*, 29 July 1949, p. 521. The divisions within the Labour Party over the issue of the relative merits of grammar and comprehensive schools during the period 1945-1951 are analysed in Rodney Barker, *Education and Politics 1900-1951*, 1952, Chapter V.

53   Cited in R. Davies, *The Grammar School*, 1967, p. 189.

54   E. James, *Education and Leadership*, 1951, p. 42.

55   Ibid., p. 55.

56   Ibid.

57   Ibid., p. 48.

58   *Times Educational Supplement*, 10 January 1948, p. 17.

59   J. D. Koerner, *Reform in Education*, 1968, p. 255.

60   Torsten Husén in *Educational Research and Policy-Making*, N.F.E.R., 1968, p. 14.

61   Sixten Marklund in *International Review of Education*, XVII/1971, p. 43.

62   Lady Simon of Wythenshawe, *Three Schools or One?* 1948, p. 60.

63   Godfrey Thomson, op. cit., p. 209.

64   The 'average' National Guardsman was described by J. A. Michener *(Kent State, What Happened and Why*, 1971, p. 226) as being in his early twenties.

65   Lady Simon of Wythenshawe, op. cit., p. 44.

66   For a more recent assessment of the effectiveness of the house system see R. B. Dierenfield, 'The House System in Comprehensive Schools', *British Journal of Educational Studies*, Vol. XXIV (February-October 1976).

67   *Times Educational Supplement*, 25 October 1974, p. 1.

68   Ibid., 25 March 1977, p. 20 and 15 April 1977, p. 80.

70   *Times Educational Supplement*, 20 May 1977, p. 5.

71   Ibid., 15 October 1976, pp. 2-3.

72   Ibid., 22 October 1976, p. 72.

73   Ibid., 22 July 1977, p. 5.

CHAPTER 7

THE PUBLIC SCHOOL SECTOR : A
CONSIDERATION OF PUBLIC SCHOOL,
PREPARATORY AND PREPREP EDUCATION

'Baited, trampled, desolate, distracted'?—governesses in the nineteenth century

In one of the picture galleries of the Victoria and Albert Museum, placed incongruously between two rather lurid Etty nudes, there hangs a painting entitled *The Governess*.[1] True to its genre, it masterfully depicts a story: in the background two happy girls skip unconcernedly together in a sunlit garden; inside a french window and in the right foreground is another – inattentive and fractious over a book; opposite her sits the principal subject of the picture – a young lady at once appealing and refined – clad in a black dress. She seems lost in sorrowful reverie; a tear shows on her cheek and she holds a black-edged letter from home which apparently carries news of a family bereavement. Behind her on a music rack is the score of 'Home Sweet Home'. The whole feeling of the picture is one of fair maidenhood uprooted and spent unappreciated amid strangers.

Governesses are fairly common in the nineteenth-century fiction; real accounts of their lives are less in evidence. In the three extracts given here, two women with experience of the work discuss its theory and its practice, while in the last Lord Curzon distastefully recalls his experiences under the tutelage of his governess at Kedleston.

First, then, Charlotte Brontë, whose career as a governess does not appear to have been a particularly happy one. A. C. Benson recalled that she had

. . . acted as governess to my cousins at Stonegappe for a few months in 1839. . . . She was, according to her own account, very unkindly treated, but it is clear that she had no gifts for the management of children and was also in a very morbid condition the whole time. My cousin Benson Sidgwick, now Vicar of Ashby Parva, certainly on one occasion threw a Bible at Miss Brontë: and all that another cousin can recollect of her is that if she was invited to walk to Church with them, she thought she was being ordered about like a slave; if she was not invited, she imagined she was excluded from the family circle.
(*A. C. Benson, The Life of Edward White Benson, 1899, Vol. I, p.12*)

Charlotte Brontë's own assessment of the demands and rewards of a governess's task has an exasperated and bitter tone. She may, understandably, have found the dependent and shabby-genteel status of the job humiliating, or perhaps, as A. C. Benson asserted, she may have lacked to a greater or lesser degree what she herself described as

. . . the great qualification – I had almost said the *one* qualification – necessary to the task: the faculty, not merely of *acquiring* but of imparting knowledge – the powers of influencing young minds – that natural fondness for, that innate sympathy with, children. . . . He or she who possesses this faculty, this sympathy – though perhaps not otherwise highly accomplished – need never fear failure in the career of instruction. Children will be docile with them, will improve

under them; parents will consequently repose in them confidence. Their task will be comparatively light, their path comparatively smooth. If the faculty be absent, the life of a teacher will be a struggle from beginning to end. No matter how amiable the disposition, how strong the sense of duty, how active the desire to please; no matter how brilliant and varied the accomplishments; if the governess has not the power to win her young charge, the secret to instil gently and surely her own knowledge into the growing mind intrusted to her, she will have a wearing, wasting existence of it. . . . Her deficiency will harass her not so much in school-time as in play-hours; the moments that would be rest and recreation to the governess who understood and could adapt herself to children, will be almost torture to her who has not that power. Many a time, when her charge turns unruly on her hands, when the responsibility which she would wish to discharge faithfully and perfectly, becomes unmanageable to her, she will wish herself a housemaid or kitchen girl, rather than a baited, trampled, desolate, distracted governess.
(Shakespeare Head Brontë, 1932, Life and Letters, Volume II, pp. 212-213 passim. Letter from Charlotte Brontë to W. S. Williams, 12 May 1848)

Charlotte Brontë writes of governesses in general terms. Ellen Weeton, by contrast, gives in her journal and letters a specific account of the vicissitudes of her career as a governess with two fairly wealthy middle-class families in the north of England. Ellen can hardly be described as one of Fortune's favourites: born on Christmas Day, 1776, she had started teaching at the age of twelve in a private school run by her mother. The latter's illness and death left her in sole charge of this shaky enterprise, which she finally relinquished in 1808, when her weekly income was down to 7/-. In December of the subsequent year she obtained, at thirty guineas per annum, the post of governess in the household of Edward Pedder of Dove's Nest near Ambleside.

Elements of Gothick tragedy were latent in the circumstances of the Pedder family: a cowardly, drunken, and violent husband, an ex-dairymaid child-wife (recently elevated to gentility by a Gretna Green marriage), and an afflicted stepdaughter who was to be Ellen Weeton's main charge and who was to die in tragic circumstances within a few months of Ellen's arrival. A riveting account of the latter's two-year stay with this strange family is to be found in her journal. Then, in the summer of 1812, Ellen accepted a situation with a far more stable and mundane family – the Armitages of High Royd near Huddersfield. Joseph Armitage was a hard man in the wool trade whose estates abounded in coal seams and Luddites; his wife, not yet thirty, with six children, another on the way ('Heaven help them' wrote Ellen of the parents) and a further eight as yet unconceived, ran her house like clockwork, though becoming recurrently ill-tempered as each pregnancy progressed.

In the two years that followed her appointment, Ellen wrote a series of sensitive and penetrating reports upon her position as governess, its frustrations and rewards. First, the daily programme:

My time is totally taken up with the children; from 7 o'clock in the morning, till half past 7, or 8 at night. I cannot lie any longer than 6 o'clock in a morning; and, if I have anything to do for myself, in sewing, writing, etc., I must rise sooner. At 7, I go into the nursery, to hear the children their prayers, and remain with them till after they have breakfasted, when I go out with them whilst they play; and am often so cold, that I join in their sports, to warm myself. About half past 8, I breakfast with Mr. & Mrs. Armitage, and then return again to the children till 9, when we go into the school-room till 12. We then bustle on our bonnets, etc., for play, or a short walk. At One, we bustle them off again, to dress for dinner, to which we sit down at a quarter past; the children always dine with their parents. By the time dinner is well over, it is 2 o'clock, when we go into school, and remain till 5. Whilst I am at tea in the parlour, the children eat their suppers in the nursery. I then go to them, and remain with them till 7, either walking out of doors, or playing within, as the weather may permit. I then hear their prayers, and see them washed; at half past 7, they are generally in bed.
(*Miss Weeton's Journal of a Governess, edited by Edward Hall, Vol. II, 1939, p. 58. Letter to Mrs. Price, undated, 1812*)

Next, the children themselves and the problems of their upbringing:

I feel more at home here now than I have done any time since I came first into Yorkshire; and could be very comfortable if it were not for the perverse and violent tempers of the children. And they really are terrible; whether I can ever subdue them, is doubtful. For a few months before the holidays, I flattered myself that I had reduced my pupils to greater order than they had ever been before; but – the holidays have undone all, and again have I all to do. Such screaming and shouting and incessant loud talking I dare say you never heard in any family before; and such everlasting quarrelling. For a month since my return, the two boys *never* attempted to say a lesson without throwing themselves into violent fits of passion; screaming dreadfully, if I persisted in making them say it. I have at last resorted to the rod, notwithstanding it is so repugnant to the present mild system of education; and if you had heard their screams, you would have thought I was really killing them, when frequently I had only struck their clothes; but for the last week, I have made them feel it, and I have found the benefit of it, though my reward from the two Mrs. Armitages, is sour looks and cool treatment. A mother must indeed feel for her children, and so do I feel for them; my spirit droops under such a task; but my duty to God is to fulfil the duties of my present situation, which I cannot do by indulging the children in their own perverse ways, as their mother has done. The oldest girl, for some weeks, would not study a single lesson. She sat with the book or slate before her, doing nothing. What would you have done in such a case? I requested, persuaded, insisted; but she would only smile carelessly in my face, and toss her head. I then incessantly confined her at play hours, till she had finished not only her present lessons, but all which were in arrears. Cool looks from Mrs. A., were the consequence; Sarah Anne's health would suffer, she thought. So I thought; but something must be done, and as Mrs. A. did not propose any better way, I persevered, notwithstanding her unjust treatment, though a frequent fit of weeping

was the consequence; and I think I have conquered. Miss A. is again become not only tractable, but affectionate.
(Miss Weeton's Journal of a Governess, edited by Edward Hall, Vol. II., 1939, pp. 99-100. Letter to Mrs. Price, dated 4 September 1813.)

So much for Ellen Weeton's actual work. Here are her reflections upon the peculiar and parsimonious semiequality which seems to have characterized the governess's position in a nineteenth-century household:

There has been a good deal of company since I came; but, though I dine or drink tea with them, I am obliged to leave the room so immediately after I have swallowed it, that I may truly be said to see little of them.

. . .

Mr. and Mrs. A. are pleasant and easy in their temper and manners, and make my situation as comfortable as such a one can be; for it is rather an awkward one for a female of any reflection or feeling. A *governess* is almost shut out of society; not choosing to associate with servants, and not being treated as an equal by the heads of the house or their visitors, she must possess some fortitude and strength of mind to render herself tranquil or happy; but indeed, the master or mistress of a house, if they have any goodness of heart, would take pains to prevent her feeling her inferiority. For my own part, I have no cause of just complaint; but I know some that are treated in a most mortifying manner.
(Miss Weeton's Journal of a Governess, edited by Edward Hall, Vol. II, 1939, pp. 58 and 62)

Ellen's admiration for Mrs. Armitage's competence slowly grew, and together they endured and overcame one of the more-or-less inevitable nursery crises which punctuated family life:

We have a sad house just now; five of the children have got the hooping cough; the two who are worst sleep in my room, so that I have but little rest night or day. Mrs. A. always takes the youngest at night, and has less rest for the time than any of us; indeed, as a wife and a mother, she is really an exemplary character.
(Miss Weeton's Journal of a Governess, edited by Edward Hall, Vol. II, 1939, p. 119. Letter to Miss C. Braithwaite, dated 4 February 1814)

But Mrs. Armitage became pregnant again, and, as usual, pusillanimous on account of it. More important, Ellen herself decided to leave High Royd in order to get married. It is a pity that the touching farewell scene which follows was not the prelude to happiness for Ellen; but her husband – as her later writings poignantly reveal – was to prove a singularly nasty piece of work.

I could weep now when I think of our parting the night before I left. I had seen them all put to bed, when, hearing some noise, I thought they were quarrelling, and went to see. I found them all weeping at the idea that that was the last night I should be with them; and the next morning they rose at five, and walked with me part of the way (I had 4 miles to walk to the coach), and when they left me, went weeping home; the servants were very angry that I was not sent in the Car.
(Miss Weeton's Journal of a Governess, edited by Edward Hall, Vol. II, 1939, pp. 123-124)

Not all governesses were so well loved by their charges as Ellen Weeton. Winston Churchill, in his own terse words, 'took to the woods' on the arrival of his, while George Nathaniel Curzon appears to have profoundly abhorred the governess at Kedleston, Miss Paraman:

In her savage moments she was a brutal and vindictive tyrant; and I have often thought since that she must have been insane. She persecuted and beat us in the most cruel way and established over us a system of terrorism so complete that not one of us ever mustered up the courage to walk upstairs and tell our father or mother. She spanked us with the sole of her slipper on the bare back, beat us with her brushes, tied us for long hours to chairs in uncomfortable positions with our hands holding a pole or a blackboard behind our backs, shut us up in darkness, practised on us every kind of petty persecution, wounded our pride by dressing us (me in particular) in red shining calico petticoats (I was obliged to make my own) with an immense conical cap on our heads round which, as well as on our breasts and backs, were sewn strips of paper bearing in enormous characters, written by ourselves, the words Liar, Sneak, Coward, Lubber and the like. In this guise she compelled us to go out in the pleasure ground and show ourselves to the gardeners. She forced us to walk through the park at even distances, never communicating with each other, to the village and show ourselves to the villagers. It never occurred to us that these good folk sympathised intensely with us and regarded her as a fiend. Our pride was much too deeply hurt.

She made me write a letter to the butler asking him to make a birch for me with which I was to be punished for lying and requesting him to read it out in the Servant's Hall. When he came round one day with a letter and saw me standing in my red petticoat with my face to the wall on a chair outside the schoolroom and said, 'Why, you look like a Cardinal!' I could have died of shame.

She made us trundle our hoops as young children, all alone, up and down a place in the grounds near the hermitage where were tall black fir trees and a general air of gloom and of which we were intensely afraid. She forced us to confess to lies which we had never told, to sins which we had never committed, and then punished us savagely, as being self-condemned. For weeks we were not allowed to speak to each other or to a human soul.
(Manuscript notes of the Marquis Curzon of Kedleston, quoted in K. Rose, Superior Person, 1969, p. 20)

A postscript on dame schools

The vast majority of parents could not, of course, afford a governess for their children. Many had to be satisfied with a dame school. The latter do not appear to have been highly regarded by educational commentators, some of whom, however, had a certain vested interest in the expansion of the state-backed system.[2] Many dame schools were doubtless absolutely deficient; others lacked materials and learning, though not, perhaps, kindness. Nevertheless, it should be remembered that one of the most discerning educationalists of the nineteenth century, Richard Dawes, officially approved of a dame school in King's Somborne acting as the preparatory department for his own celebrated establishment. Thomas Cooper remembered with affection the working-class dame school which he attended around 1810 and it is hard to believe that decent though unpretentious schools like the one which he describes below were a rarity:

As soon as I was strong enough, I was sent to a dame's school, near at hand, kept by aged Gertrude Aram: 'Old Gatty', as she was usually called. Her school-room – that is to say, the larger lower-room of her two storied cottage – was always full; and she was an expert and laborious teacher of the art of reading and spelling. Her knitting, too – for she taught girls as well as boys – was the wonder of the town. I soon became her favourite scholar, and could read the tenth chapter of Nehemiah, with all its hard names, 'like the parson in the church', – as she used to say, – and could spell wondrously.
(The Life of Thomas Cooper, written by himself, 1872, p. 7)

Prep schools in the nineteenth century

The public schools of the nineteenth century and their preparatory satellites formed, as they do today, a system of schooling parallel to, and essentially separate from, the one used by the mass of the population. By the last decades of the century, a child of wealthy parents would often be taught by a governess up to the age of seven or eight, sent to a prep school* until he was twelve or thirteen, and thence to a public school, end-on to this there would frequently be a university course. Coherent and purposeful,[3] the whole sequence stood in significant contrast to the ill-defined paths of the state-connected system.

The retrospective gaze of ex-pupils has not always rested kindly upon prep schools.[4] Lord Randolph Churchill was apparently happy at his, and this may have contributed to his lack of discrimination in selecting the Reverend H.W. Sneyd-Kynnersley's dread establishment for his elder son Winston. H. C. Barnard likewise found most aspects of his day prep school congenial enough (but then he was to become a professor of education); he wrote later that

The school consisted entirely of day-boys, and was carried on in a large and convenient house, with a small playing-field attached. The headmaster was an enthusiast for good literature and was able to make us share his enthusiasm. It was through him that I was introduced to *The Tempest, Twelfth Night, Henry V*, and *A Midsummer Night's Dream* – though it was some years later that I paid my first visit to the theatre and saw Frank Benson and his company in *Antony and Cleopatra*. This was rather a concession because it was something of a tradition in the puritanical section of the Victorian middle class to look with severe disapproval on the theatre. But the best part of the week at Henderson's was on Friday afternoon when the Head

---

*The syllabus really did prepare the pupil for his public school. *The Preparatory Schools Review* (Vol. I, No. 1) of July 1895 analysed the average time allocated per week to individual subjects in 43 prep schools: Latin – 10 hrs 6 mins; Greek – 6 hrs 12 mins; German – 5 hrs; Maths – 5 hrs 45 mins; French – 3 hrs 20 mins; History – 1 hr 27 mins; Geography – 1 hr 27 mins; English – 1 hr 40 mins; Div. – 2 hrs 10 mins; Catechism – 48 mins.

used to read to us the novels of Stevenson and Dumas. The only punishment in vogue in the school was to be debarred from 'reading'; and that in itself was sufficient to ensure that breaches of the school rules were rarely committed.

In spite of this emphasis on English we were well grounded in arithmetic, algebra and geometry (which we learnt from Euclid's *Elements*). History and geography continued to be taught by the memorisation of sheer facts. Latin bulked largely in the timetable; and as I had already started this subject at the dame's school I continued to make some progress with it. In a year or two I also began Greek, and was soon learning a new series of declensions and paradigms from W. Gunion Rutherford's grammar, or translating sentences from Ritchie's *First Steps in Greek*. With all this I started yet another language – French. This was taught by a lady who visited the school periodically (until she eventually married the headmaster). . . . The headmaster was assisted by a series of young men who usually stayed for a year or less and then departed. They were for the most part candidates for Holy Orders, who were filling in the time until they were old enough to be made deacon; or else they were mere youths who had recently left school and were about to proceed to the University. Some of them were quite effective and some completely incompetent. One of the best – and I remember him with gratitude – in due course became a prison chaplain. I hope that his experience as an usher in a preparatory school for small boys was of some assistance to him in such a capacity.
(*H. C. Barnard, Were those the Days?, 1970, pp. 58-59*)

But the autobiographies of George Cornwallis-West and Winston Churchill, both of whom attended boarding prep schools, have a different tenor – one, indeed, of blood, toil, tears, and sweat. The rigours of public school appeared unexceptionable by comparison. As George Cornwallis-West put it:

I had not been at Eton more than a day or two before I began to appreciate the comparative freedom which can be enjoyed there. After my private school, I felt as a prisoner must feel who has been released from a term of imprisonment . . .

The justification for this euphoric mood can be seen in his recollections:

I was sent . . . to a preparatory school at Farnborough – I refrain from mentioning which, but there are three schools there; suffice it to say that it contained so many sprigs of aristocracy that it went by the name of 'the House of Lordlings'. I have often discussed the past with men of my own age who were at that school, and we have all agreed that we would not go back there for a million pounds. Hardly one of the masters was a gentleman. We were taught well, I admit, but if it had not been for the fact that our parents sent us hampers of food which we were supposed to share with the other boys seated at the same table, we should scarcely have been fed at all. As it was, if one happened to be unpopular with the boy whose hamper was being shared, one got nothing at breakfast or tea but bread and butter. The only meal actually provided by the school was mid-day meal, with its everlasting stringy beef or mutton, both invariably over-roasted.

Bullying at that school had developed into a fine art. I was a very delicate child, in fact an overgrown slab of misery, unable to take part to any great extent in games; I was in consequence made to suffer. One of the chief amusements of the bullies in our bedrooms was to tie scarves to each wrist and ankle, stretch the unfortunate

The public school sector   135

victim on the bed and pretending that he was 'on the rack', only there wasn't much pretence about it. Another form of amusement was to make small boys eat flies.

The headmaster himself was, I honestly believe, a sadist; I am certain it afforded him intense pleasure to administer the severest thrashings, having first deprived the boy of any form of protection. He once, while I was there, thrashed a boy until he fainted.

Unfortunately for the bullies, I completely upset their apple cart by attempting to commit suicide, not entirely on my own initiative, as it was suggested by one of my aggressors, who said, 'Let's make young West drink ink.' Before I could be prevented I swallowed most of the contents of one of the desk inkpots. Then they really were frightened. A master came in, realised that something was amiss, saw my mouth covered with ink and was told what had happened. I was promptly given an emetic.

(George Cornwallis-West, Edwardian Hey-Days, 1930, pp. 17-19)

St. George's School at Ascot, however, was destined for a more widespread and lasting notoriety than the 'House of Lordlings'. For it numbered among its more intractable pupils the articulate and implacable Winston Churchill: *

. . . I was told that 'school days were the happiest time in one's life'. Several grown-up people added that in their day, when they were young, schools were very rough: there was bullying, they didn't get enough to eat, they had 'to break the ice in their pitchers' each morning (a thing I have never seen done in my life). But now it was all changed. School life nowadays was one long treat. All the boys enjoyed it. Some of my cousins who were a little older had been quite sorry – I was told – to come home for the holidays. Cross-examined, the cousins did not confirm this; they only grinned. Anyhow I was perfectly helpless. Irresistible tides drew me swiftly forward. I was no more consulted about leaving home than I had been about coming into the world.

It was very interesting buying all the things one had to have for going to school. No less than fourteen pairs of socks were on the list. Mrs. Everest† thought this was very extravagant. She said that with care ten pairs would do quite well. Still it was a good thing to have some to spare, as one could then make sure of avoiding the very great dangers inseparable from 'sitting in wet feet'.

The fateful day arrived. My mother took me to the station in a hansom cab. She gave me three half-crowns, which I dropped on to the floor of the cab, and we had to scramble about in the straw to find them again. We only just caught the train. If we had missed it, it would have been the end of the world. However, we didn't, and the world went on.

The school my parents had selected for my education was one of the most fashionable and expensive in the country. It modelled itself upon Eton and aimed at being preparatory for that Public School above all others. It was supposed to be the very last thing in schools. Only ten boys in a class; electric light (then a wonder); a swimming pond; spacious football and cricket grounds; two or three school treats, or 'expeditions' as they were called, every term; the masters all M.A.'s in gowns and

---

* 'He has no ambition,' complained the headmaster on his 1884 summer term report.

† Winston Churchill's nurse.

mortar-boards; a chapel of its own; no hampers allowed; everything provided by the authorities. It was a dark November afternoon when we arrived at this establishment. We had tea with the Headmaster, with whom my mother conversed in the most easy manner. I was preoccupied with the fear of spilling my cup and so making 'a bad start'. I was also miserable at the idea of being left alone among all these strangers in this great, fierce, formidable place. After all I was only seven, and I had been so happy in my nursery with all my toys. I had such wonderful toys: a real steam engine, a magic lantern, and a collection of soldiers already nearly a thousand strong. Now it was to be all lessons. Seven or eight hours of lessons every day except half-holidays, and football or cricket in addition.

When the last sounds of my mother's departing wheels had died away, the Headmaster invited me to hand over any money I had in my possession. I produced my three half-crowns which were duly entered in a book, and I was told that from time to time there would be a 'shop' at the school with all sorts of things which one would like to have, and that I could choose what I liked up to the limit of the seven and sixpence. Then we quitted the Headmaster's parlour and the comfortable private side of the house, and entered the more bleak apartments reserved for the instruction and accommodation of the pupils. I was taken into a Form Room and told to sit at a desk. All the other boys were out of doors, and I was alone with the Form Master. He produced a thin greeny-brown, covered book filled with words in different types of print.

'You have never done any Latin before, have you?' he said.

'No, sir.'

'This is a Latin grammar.' He opened it at a well-thumbed page. 'You must learn this', he said, pointing to a number of words in a frame of lines. 'I will come back in half an hour and see what you know.'

Behold me then on a gloomy evening, with an aching heart, seated in front of the First Declension.

Mensa	a table
Mensa	O table
Mensam	a table
Mensae	of a table
Mensae	to or for a table
Mensa	by, with or from a table

What on earth did it mean? Where was the sense in it? It seemed absolute rigmarole to me. However, there was one thing I could always do: I could learn by heart. And I thereupon proceeded, as far as my private sorrows would allow, to memorise the acrostic-looking task which had been set me.

In due course the Master returned.

'Have you learnt it?' he asked.

'I think I can *say* it, sir,' I replied; and I gabbled it off.

He seemed so satisfied with this that I was emboldened to ask a question.

'What does it mean, sir?'

'It means what it says. Mensa, a table. Mensa is a noun of the First Declension. There are five declensions. You have learnt the singular of the First Declension.'

'But,' I repeated, 'what does it mean?'

'Mensa means a table,' he answered.

'Then why does mensa also mean O table,' I enquired, 'and what does O table mean?'

'Mensa, O table, is the vocative case,' he replied.

'But why O table?' I persisted in genuine curiosity.

'O table, – you would use that in addressing a table, in invoking a table.' And then seeing he was not carrying me with him, 'You would use it in speaking to a table.'

'But I never do,' I blurted out in honest amazement.

'If you are impertinent, you will be punished, and punished, let me tell you, very severely,' was his conclusive rejoinder.

Such was my first introduction to the classics from which, I have been told, many of our cleverest men have derived so much solace and profit.

The Form Master's observations about punishment were by no means without their warrant at St. James's School.* Flogging with the birch in accordance with the Eton fashion was a great feature in its curriculum. But I am sure no Eton boy, and certainly no Harrow boy of my day, ever received such a cruel flogging as this Head-master was accustomed to inflict upon the little boys who were in his care and power. They exceeded in severity anything that would be tolerated in any of the Reformatories under the Home Office . . .
(Winston L. S. Churchill, My Early Life, 1930, pp. 22-26 passim)

The public schools up to 1914

'I felt that my heart would break as I scrunched the muddy gravel, beneath the boughs of budding trees. . . . But I said to my heart: "I have to be made a man here." ' So wrote John Addington Symonds of his feelings as he prepared to enter his new school in 1854, sharing, no doubt, the sentiments of thousands of public schoolboys before and since.

In Symonds' case the apprehension was justified. Disenchantment lay ahead of him, culminating eventually in a conviction that the headmaster was having an affair with one of his friends. Such deviation was hardly, of course, a subject for wide discussion in Victorian society; an oblique reference to it as late as 1917 in Alec Waugh's book *The Loom of Youth* caused an extreme reaction in the public school world.[5] Physical violence, by contrast, was an accepted, even ritualized feature of public school life. Corporal punishment was widely regarded as a valid method of keeping original sin at bay; Gordon Hake feelingly recalled one particular ordained master at Christ's Hospital around 1820 who

. . . beat the boys with a fury worthy of a bastard son of the Eumenides.
To see that man of the fist, rod, and cane spending his force on a little boy, now leaving the autograph of his four fingers, in red and white, on the infant's cheek,

---

*The real name of Churchill's school was St. George's.

sending him reeling halfway up the room, while the robes he wore were flung
fluttering into the air, was a sight worthy of the demons . . .
(Gordon Hake, Memoirs of Eighty Years, 1892, pp. 30-31)

At schoolboy level violence was, perhaps more naturally, widely regarded as
a convenient, even entertaining way of settling personal differences. Here is
G. F. Lamb's account of a notorious encounter at Eton in 1825 between
Ashley-Cooper minimus and C. A. Wood:

The battle had started at four o'clock. They were still fighting an hour later. At one
stage in the contest Cooper received a blow on the temple which felled him to the
ground, where he lay for fully half a minute. Some of the boys were afraid that this
was going to stop the fun; some (though apparently they kept silent) may even have
felt that it ought to be stopped. But there was plenty of brandy still left in the
bottles, and presently the battered loser was able to continue. At least he had the
satisfaction of knowing, if he was conscious of anything at all, that his opponent was
pretty exhausted also; which was not surprising seeing that they had by this time
fought over fifty rounds.

About the sixtieth round, when they had been battling for just under two hours, the
smaller boy collapsed and fell heavily on his head. The fight was over, and brandy no
longer had any power to revitalise an insensible fourteen-year-old boy.

The victim's two older brothers carried him back to the boarding-house of the Rev.
Mr. Knapp, himself a keen follower of prize-fighting, but seemingly engaged on his
own pursuits elsewhere during the whole of this afternoon and evening. No other
master or senior was in charge of the House during his absence in these very casual
days; there was only a woman servant with no authority.

She at least had a little more sense than the boys. When the unconscious loser was
carried in and put to bed she asked his brothers whether she had better send for the
doctor.

'There's no need to,' said Ashley-Cooper major. 'He's fast asleep. He'll be all right
when he wakes up.'

But he was not fast asleep. He was in a dying coma; and when, some hours later,
somebody thought that medical assistance had better be sought after all, it was too
late. The boy died just after the doctor's arrival.

. . .

Wood was charged with manslaughter, but eventually acquitted on the ground that
the contest was conducted in accordance with the rules of regular prize-fights.
(G. F. Lamb, The Happiest Days, 1959, pp. 38-40)

Queer headmasters and fatal battles were, as far as the evidence indicates,
exceptional in the context of nineteenth-century public school education. A
more representative account of mundane school life (this time at
Winchester) was written by Robert Lowe, whose acidulous gaze rested no less
coldly upon the supposed deficiencies of the élite public schools than upon
those of the genuinely public elementary variety:

We were expected to be down at six in summer and a quarter to seven in winter; we
went into school at half-past seven and stayed there till ten, then we had
breakfast – bread as much as we could eat, a pat of butter each, and one pail of milk

among 130 boys, for this we made a *queue,* every fag* with his jug. Occasionally when the competition was more than ordinarily severe, the pail was upset, and the school went milkless to breakfast. Tea and sugar we might find for ourselves if we had the money, they were sold to us at the buttery hatch on account of whom it might concern. We went into school from eleven to twelve, from twelve to one was our play hour; the field was half a mile off, so that to make the most of it we usually ran there and back and came in streaming with perspiration. At one we dined! At two we went into school, where we remained till six, then supper – bread and cheese and beer, then work in the hall till half-past eight, then to bed. Twice a week we had what was called a 'remedy' – I suppose because it was worse than the disease, applying that name to the ordinary school days, – we were marched two and two to the hill a mile off, and in consideration of this airing were shut up in the hall for four hours. Sunday was a particularly miserable day; two hours in chapel, nearly three in the cathedral, one hour to walk, and the rest shut up in our court and hall.

It will be seen from this statement that we fasted from seven o'clock in the evening till half-past ten in the morning; that four hours and a half were interposed between rising and breakfast; that we had no food for breakfast but bread; that we dined three hours after breakfast and immediately after an hour of violent exercise. The result may be easily imagined – we were ravenous at breakfast and there was nothing but bread to eat unless we had pocket money to buy food; out of breath and reeking with perspiration we loathed our dinner, and it was only when in school that we felt hunger which there was no means of appeasing for hours, and then with the (to gentlemen's children) uncongenial fare of bread and cheese. Our pocket money, as long at it lasted, went in buying the food with which we ought to have been supplied, and when that was gone we bore our loss as best we could, only too happy if we could coax a colleger to impart to us something from his comparatively liberal dietary.

We were, it will be observed, never alone by day or by night, so that the power that one boy possessed to annoy another was almost boundless. We were, besides, debarred of our natural liberty, and the high spirits of youth, missing their natural vent, found employment in mutual torment.

. . .

In the fourth year of my residence at Winchester, I became a prefect. As this institution still exists, and has drawn upon itself no little public notice, I will say a few words about it, and should be very glad if anything I can say shall draw renewed attention to the subject. It will be gathered from what I have already said that the school was conducted with a view to make the expenses to the Master as small as possible. We had only two men-servants to wait on 130 boys; of course it followed that in a similar spirit there were not enough masters to do the work, and one reason why we were so unmercifully long in school was the want of more masters, and the consequent impossibility of a subdivision of classes.

The result was that a good deal of the discipline of the school was entrusted to the prefects; they had to keep order, and as a reward for thus doing the duty of under-masters, were invested with personal inviolability, besides the power of fagging the other boys as before mentioned. Thus I found myself at the mature age of sixteen invested with infinitely more power, with infinitely less control, than I have ever had since. A stick was put into my hand, and I had to walk up and down the hall and

---

*The term 'fag' was applied to junior pupils in public schools who were obliged to act in certain respects as servants to the senior boys.

keep silence by applying the said stick to the back of any boy whose voice or conduct disturbed the silence of 130 boys. I had besides the power of tunding, a punishment far more severe than that of flogging, which was in fact little better than a farce. I do not think that at first, at any rate, I abused my new power. I had no great zeal for the discipline of the school, which I not unreasonably considered was no affair of mine.

. . .

. . . I cannot help thinking that however economical or convenient it may be to put a stick into the hand of a boy of sixteen and allow him to use it upon his schoolfellows, it is neither fair on the tunder nor the tunded. If servants are wanted they ought to be supplied from some other source than the junior scholars, and if more masters are wanted they ought to be supplied from some other source than the senior boys.
(A. Patchett Martin, Life and Letters of the Right Honourable Robert Lowe, Viscount Sherbrooke, 1893, Vol. I, pp. 8-12 passim)

Morally suspect, physically violent, pervasively mediocre in attainment, and on occasion run with financial ineptitude if not corruption* – the obloquy hurled at public schools by disillusioned ex-pupils might be taken in some degree to justify one writer's estimate that the school years of as many as 25 percent of their pupils were 'shockingly wasted'.[6] Adverse criticism, in fact, seems only to be exceeded in volume by the panegyrics of loyal old boys. So great, indeed, is the quantity of material (pro., con., and fiction) relating to nineteenth-century public schools that an observer might well conclude that hardly any other form of education then existed in England. But in justice to the supporters of the system it should be said that abuses which may have been painfully obtrusive to an individual were quite possibly unperceived by the mass of his contemporaries. It is perhaps significant that Augustus Hare, who was at Harrow under the same headmaster as John Addington Symonds (and certainly little enamoured of the place) could write that 'I have often heard since much of the immoralities of a public-school life, but I can truly say that when I was there, I saw nothing of them.'[7] George Melly, who went to Rugby soon after the death of Thomas Arnold,[8] later described his life there in measured terms of warm approval. In his view

. . . where a large number of boys are gathered together, there must inevitably be much oppression and tyranny; it is, therefore, better freely to sanction and strictly to legalize the power which you cannot withold from the bigger boys, by entrusting it to those who combine influence with knowledge, and age with high character. By making them responsible for its impartial exercise, and rendering it their interest, as well as their duty, to protect all who are in need of their protection, you at once enlist them on the right side.

It has been urged that it is bad for the morals of monitors† to be, as boys, entrusted with such absolute power. I reply that they naturally possess it already, and nothing

---

*At Eton the provost and fellows had adopted the dubious habit of sharing out between themselves the renewal fines payable upon the leases of college land. As the Clarendon Report (p. 104) put it: 'A large proportion, therefore, of the actual income of the College is thus diverted from the purposes to which that income is by the Statutes directed to be applied.'

†i.e., prefects

can prevent their exercising it, and that the monitorial system only places it under due regulation. In every community – be it a family or a township, a school or a nation – the strong will, the powerful intellect, the matured judgement, exert a predominating influence over the weak, the thoughtless, and the inexperienced; this superior force is not only innate, but acknowledged, and under due regulation it is beneficial to all . . .

. . .

When taxes shall be considered robbery, or the law of the land an arbitrary exercise of power, then will fagging be considered degrading to fags; for it is the taxation and the law of the little world in which they live.
(George Melly, School Experiences of a Fag, 1854, pp. 305-307)

Melly's views are particularly interesting in that they are based upon his experiences at Rugby in the immediate post-Arnold era (he became in fact a friend of the family). His microcosmic concept of public-school society was doubtless to some extent fostered by the social exclusivity and isolation for which Arnold himself had striven. Equally noteworthy, though, is Melly's attitude towards the prefectorial system, contrasting as it does so markedly with that of Robert Lowe, to whom it was an unjustifiable consequence of the meanness and irresponsibility of the school authorities, and with that of Gordon Hake, to whom it seemed an (almost) unmitigated evil: at Christ's Hospital, the steward

. . . presided at meal-time, seated at a desk on the large daïs at the upper end of the hall, like a modern Pontius Pilate. There he was, to receive criminals led to judgement by the monitors, and to flog them without mercy. . . . No complaint was made to him of the boys, by beadles or monitors, but what was believed by him; he required no proof.

It was a sort of Russian system; every official, every monitor, was a spy, and the steward was the willing knout, a creature emotional as a reptile, servile as a dog, and as a cat cruel.

Nevertheless, there was one extenuating circumstance – he had a pretty daughter . . .
(Gordon Hake, Memoirs of Eighty Years, 1892, p. 33)

It is arguable that the transmutation of the indifferent and cut-price ushers of Lowe's time and the obsequious informers of Hake's into Melly's judicious and upright preservers of law and order can be read as evidence of the benign influence of Thomas Arnold. For although it appears doubtful whether the latter contributed a great deal to either the curriculum or the internal organization of his school,[9] he does seem to have tried to recast the insentient authoritarianism which prevailed at the turn of the century into terms of nineteenth-century Christian morality. The change was acceptable, above all, to the wealthy God-fearing mercantile and professional upper classes, and its impact was probably less apparent upon established aristocratically biased public schools like Eton and Winchester than upon the new proprietary schools and those endowed schools whose headmasters saw, in Arnold's way, the road to solvency and prestige. Such a course usually meant that recruitment of pupils had to be based upon the criterion of parental wealth rather than upon residence in the school's locality. Inevitable sequels were a greatly increased emphasis upon boarding facilities and the conscious fostering of a self-contained social existence. Alienation from the local population was to become so complete that after 1902 some L.E.A.s were compelled to build maintained grammar schools in proximity to endowed public schools in order to refulfil the aims for which the latter had themselves originally been founded. One writer has described the situation of the public schools in these terms:

They had broken their links with the local community even to the extent of building their own chapels and not using the village church. Organized games now restricted the boys to school grounds during their leisure time, whereas formerly they often used to roam the countryside at will. There was now no reason why the boys should leave the total institution either for worship or leisure. The authoritarian structure of a total institution had been established by an accretion of power to the headmaster, and the centralization of control in his hands. The reformed prefect system operated directly under his control so that he could direct in minute detail the activities of the boys. . . . The total institutional structure became a powerful device for insulating and socializing an élite, and for protecting the values of aristocracy, moral fervor, and Gentlemanliness. Like their massive neo-Gothic architecture the public schools seemed both immovable and impregnable. The success of the Victorian reformers was to cause immense strain later because the Victorian public school was too unchanging and stable. It could save the élite in the nineteeth century but how long could it work?

(Ian Weinberg, The English Public Schools, 1967, p. 52)

During the early years of the nineteenth century, seven boarding schools – Westminster, Eton, Winchester, Charterhouse, Harrow, Rugby, and Shrewsbury – had a widely recognized right to public school status; Merchant Taylors' and St. Paul's were day schools; Christ's Hospital, a boarding school resembling the others in its classical curriculum, differed in that it catered for less wealthy boys.

The seven principal boarding schools* had some 2500 pupils by the mid-1860s.[10] Their headmasters were apparently concerned to preserve the traditional social pattern of individual schools even if it meant turning away incompatible applicants when places were vacant.[11] So the increased demand for boarding school education was in the first instance often answered by the newly founded proprietary schools – Cheltenham (1841), Marlborough (1843), Rossall (1844), Clifton (1862), and Haileybury (1862)[12] — upon which the Taunton Commission was to comment so favourably.

---

*Whose primacy was recognized by the government, which appointed the Clarendon Commission to investigate them (together with Merchant Taylors' and St. Paul's). Other secondary schools were dealt with by the Taunton Commission.

A second wave of select establishments was made up of a number of old endowed schools which, from the 1850s onwards, began to compete for upper-class clients. Possibly the best known of these was Uppingham. This school, founded in the late sixteenth century as a 'faire, free grammar school', had only 25 pupils[13] when Edward Thring was appointed headmaster in 1853. He was determined to develop the boarding-school idea. Sincerely convinced of its advantages, he wrote, with the unconscious presumption of his class, that 'The English school in all instances started in early days as a local school, and has been pushed out of this by the judgement of the English people. . . . England has not chosen to have its education carried on at home, but deliberately prefers, when it can be had, a boarding school.'[14]

With the moral and financial help of a few dedicated colleagues (in 1884 he could claim that between them they had spent in the region of £91,000 on the school),[15] Thring was able to increase greatly both the size and the prestige of Uppingham School. By mid-1863 there were 200 boys; by 1869 over 300. In his determination to fight off governmental interference threatened by the Endowed Schools Bill he initiated the Headmasters' Conference and, had he lived until 1889, would doubtless have noted with satisfaction that the editors of its first year book – all from Clarendon schools – overtly recognized Uppingham (together with six other English endowed schools)[16] as being of the same *genus* as their own.

The public school curriculum

The public school curriculum was, throughout the period, heavily biased towards the classics – that is, Latin and Greek. It is difficult for anyone educated in a modern state school to conceive how extreme the situation was: with the exception of arithmetic, writing, and the copying of a few geographical texts,

> . . . the school was purely classical; nothing whatever was taught but Greek and Latin. History, geography, English, and its grammar, were unheard of . . .

wrote Gordon Hake of Christ's Hospital around 1820.

> . . . But what is more remarkable than all the other omissions in the school is, that the boys were never, individually, taught a word of religion.
> *(Gordon Hake, Memoirs of Eighty Years, 1892, pp. 32-33)*

By 1864 the Clarendon Report was able thus to summarize the situation in the nine schools with which it dealt:

> The school course at every school now includes arithmetic and mathematics, as well as classics. At every school except Eton it includes also one modern language, either French or German. At Rugby (and practically, as it seems, at the Charterhouse) it

includes both French and German; at Rugby, however, modern languages are not studied by those whose parents prefer that they should study natural science. *(The Clarendon Report, on nine principal public schools, 1864, p. 13)*

The Clarendon Report, though it recommended that classics should continue to dominate the public school curriculum, suggested that mathematics, a modern language, some natural science, and either drawing or music should be included in all syllabuses, as should some measure of general knowledge in history and geography. It also observed that the effectiveness of the actual teaching was open to question. This view was endorsed by A. C. Benson, who remembered that:

. . . I began Latin at seven and Greek at nine, and, when I left Cambridge, I did not know either of them well. I could not sit in an arm-chair and read either a Greek or a Latin book, and I had no desire to do it. I knew a very little French, a very little mathematics, a very little science; I knew no history, no German, no Italian: I knew nothing of art or music; my ideas of geography were childish. . . . It is nothing short of infamous that any one should, after an elaborate education, have been so grossly uneducated.
(A.C. Benson, The Upton Letters, 2nd ed., 1906, p. 158)

During the latter part of the nineteenth century, the concept of a 'modern' (as opposed to a 'classical') side began to take form. An experimental 'modern' side, in which the boys learned history, modern languages, mathematics and science as well as Latin, was started at Harrow in 1869.[17] But here the success of the course depended upon the support given by the headmaster (Butler), and it apparently languished upon his retirement. Similarly the strong scientific and technical orientation for which Oundle School became notable at the end of the century was due essentially to the convictions of the headmaster there, F. W. Sanderson. More representative was the situation described by H. B. Gray:

Out of the thirty-two 'periods' (or hours) in the week devoted to study in class-rooms (i.e. exclusive of preparation time, which was mainly appropriated to classics), about twenty to twenty-four were given up to Latin and Greek, the remaining twelve or eight being distributed between Mathematics, Scripture, French, and German (the last-named a later importation). From this educational dole, Mathematics seized about half, Scripture a quarter: for the miserable residuum there was a scramble. In two ancient and illustrious schools with which I was intimately connected in the 'sixties' and 'seventies' there was practically no teaching in the mother tongue, and literally none in Natural Science, though, later on, some sporadic study in English Literature for the upper forms was certainly hailed as a reform.
(H. B. Gray, The Public Schools and the Empire, 1913, p. 111)

According to Gray's book, the curriculum changed little in the years before 1913, though he did point out that 'modern' sides were developed in the younger schools.[18]

The public school image
1   There is only one God, and the captain of football is His prophet.
2   My school is the best in the world.
3   Without big muscles, strong will, and proper collars, there is no salvation.
4   I must wash much, and in accordance with tradition.
5   I must speak the truth even to a master, if he believes everything I tell him.
6   I must play games with all my heart, with all my soul, and with all my strength.
7   To work outside class-hours is indecent.
8   Enthusiasm, except for games, is in bad taste.
9   I must look up to the older fellows, and pour contempt on new-comers.
10   I must show no emotion, and not kiss my mother in public.

The 'Ten Commandments of the English public school boy', quoted above[19] emphasize two dominant aspects of public school life during the latter part of the nineteenth century: social conformity and the cult of games. The one, of course, implied the other, and Arnold Lunn, in observing that 'Conform or be kicked' is the command written over the portals of every school[20] might have added that the option was in reality almost nonexistent. The only choice was whether the hacking and battering should assume a more-or-less legitimate form on the games field or the equally painful kind associated with the bullying of misfits off it.

By the turn of the century, the teaching of games in the public schools seemed in some cases to have assumed, in the words of H. B. Gray, the author of the following passage, the form of a 'mind-numbing, unwholesome cult' whose spurious importance was warping the judgement of England's future leaders:[21]

... the general recognition of games by high and low in our public schools as 'the one thing needful' goes on apace, and is connected with the false estimate of their importance prevailing among the people at large. What was half a century ago regarded in our 'seminaries of religious and useful learning' as a healthy outlet for the physical energies of youth has degenerated into a mind-numbing, unwholesome cult. Men in our leading classes, destined to play prominent parts in national life, have become obsessed, through their early training, with the craze for athletic competitions, and have imbibed the false creed that a Higher Power 'delighteth in men's legs'.
(H. B. Gray, The Public Schools and the Empire, 1913, p. 193)

The theme is reiterated by Alec Waugh (who, in his own words, 'loved cricket and football and was reasonably good at them') in his autobiographical novel The Loom of Youth:

Gordon went to Fernhurst with the determination to excel, and at once was brought face to face with the fact that success lay in a blind worship at the shrine of the god of Athleticism. Honesty, virtue, moral determination – these mattered not at all. . . . He who wishes to get to the front has to strive after success on the field, and success on the field alone. This is the way that the future leaders of England are being trained to take their proper place in the national struggle for a right and far-sighted civilisation. On this alone the system stands condemned. For the history of a nation is the history of its great men, and the one object of the Public School is to produce not great men, but a satisfactory type.
(Alec Waugh, The Loom of Youth, 1917, 1955 ed., pp. 126-127)

It is hard to challenge the success of the public schools in their traditional function – in Waugh's words the production of a 'satisfactory type' who could automatically assume the role of an acceptable and viable member of the 'establishment'. The worth of the public schools' curriculum might be questioned, as was their scholastic efficiency. But it goes without saying that there was more to the public school than snobbish social exclusiveness and an insistence upon a Billy Bunteresque conformity of mores and language. Their prime function was the contribution which they made to the perpetuation of the English upper class: a celebrated purple passage of the Clarendon Report expressed it this way:

It is not easy to estimate the degree in which the English people are indebted to these schools for the qualities on which they pique themselves most – for their capacity to govern others and control themselves, their aptitude for combining freedom with order, their public spirit, their vigour and manliness of character, their strong but not slavish respect for public opinion, their love of healthy sports and exercise.* These schools have been the chief nurseries of our statesmen; in them, and in schools modelled after them, men of all the various classes that make up English society, destined for every profession and career, have been brought up on a footing of social equality, and have contracted the most enduring friendships, and some of the ruling habits, of their lives; and they have had perhaps the largest share in moulding the character of an English gentleman.
(The Clarendon Report, on nine principal public schools, 1864, p. 56)

More succinctly, a public school man was 'in'. And aspiring upper middle-class parents were every bit as aware of this fact as were those who had already arrived. In Alec Waugh's words:

. . . the Freemasonry of a Public School is amazing. No man who has been through a good school can be an outsider. He may hang round the Empire bar, he may cheat at business; but you can be certain of one thing, he will never let you down. Very few Public School men ever do a mean thing to their friends. And for a system that produces such a spirit there is something to be said after all.
(Alec Waugh, The Loom of Youth, 1917, 1955 ed., p. 80)

---

*One witness before the Clarendon Commission 'when asked what was the boy's opinion of intellectual distinction, replied that if it was accompanied by success in games, it did not stand much in a boy's way'.[22]

A yet more positive view was taken by Arnold Lunn in his controversial book *The Harrovians*:

The somewhat trite accusation that schools do not foster originality is scarcely just. . . . The eccentric may suffer, but if he has any genuine originality it will be submerged – perhaps – but not destroyed. The worst that a school can do is to transform an inefficient artist into a humdrum useful member of society. They teach the lesson that the brilliant individualist if often a nuisance in the game of life. They train men to become efficient cogs in the social machinery. So long as they fail to extinguish talent while developing mediocre ability, we may forgive them if they relieve the overcrowded literary market by transforming a bad poet into an indifferent civil servant.
(Arnold Lunn, The Harrovians, 1913, pp. 44-45)

Arguments over alleged defects in nineteenth-century public school education should not be permitted to conceal the fact that the function of these institutions was above all a *social* one. In this sense their curriculum was irrelevant. As an integral part of English upper-class life, they provided a *milieu* in which the 'right' people could, at an early stage, get to know one another. An idealized account of the role of the public school in the cycle of upper-class life appeared in the *Church Quarterly Review* of early 1905:

. . . to refuse to send a boy to a public school because he might be better taught elsewhere is far too dangerous an experiment to play. He is sent accordingly; and a few years later is discharged, much as his father was before him, honest, unaffected, agreeable, capable of dealing with men, not afraid of responsibility; and with all this, phenomenally ignorant of all the subjects he is supposed to have been taught. So the story is begun anew again. He thinks his school is the finest in the world, he thinks the teaching he has received there contemptible, he cannot imagine sending his own sons anywhere else.

But in the last analysis it was their customers that made the public schools what they were, not the reverse. As Cecil Spring Rice perceptively commented, one might as well talk of the P&O boats breeding viceroys as of Eton breeding governor-generals: it was the only line for them to go by.[23]

The public schools in a changing society

The rate of increase in the number of boys' public schools* slackened off appreciably after 1900. Within the independent sector as a whole the most publicized twentieth-century foundations perhaps tended to be 'progressive' schools such as Dartington Hall and Summerhill, most of which, initially at any rate, were ostentatiously to reject the traditional public school ethos.

---

*The 'official' or governmental definition of a public school is one which is in membership of the Headmasters' Conference, Governing Bodies' Association or Governing Bodies of Girls' Schools' Association. The Public Schools Commission stated that in 1967 there were 140 girls' public schools and three coeducational ones in addition to the 130 boys' schools mentioned above.[24]

From the beginning of the century until 1967 only twelve new boys' public schools were established; one of the best known of these (and one which from the start set out to establish a contemporary image for itself) was Stowe School, founded in 1923 under the headmastership of J. F. Roxburgh. The actor David Niven joined the school soon after it had opened. This is how he described it:

Stowe School was established not, as were the others, by Kings, Archbishops or Lord Mayors but by a consortium of educators and hard-headed businessmen who saw the possibilities for a new public school and hoped to make a good thing out of it . . .

In these early post-war years, a whole stratum of suddenly well-to-do industrialists found the established public schools, to which they longed to send their sons, already bulging at the seams, so the consortium had no problem whatever in finding clients. Discovering a young aggressive headmaster with new ideas was far more difficult. They made a most fortunate choice – a young housemaster from Lancing College – J. F. Roxburgh . . .

. . .

One of Roxburgh's better new ideas was to break with the traditional prison garb of the older establishments; no top hats, stiff collars or straw boaters for us . . . the boys wore grey flannel suits on weekdays and blue suits on Sunday.

Rules were sensible and good manners were encouraged: for instance hands had to be removed from pockets when passing masters or visiting parents. There were no 'bounds' and boys were allowed to have bicycles. As, however, one had to pedal three miles to get out of the school grounds, this was a little more strenuous than it sounded.

. . .

Roxburgh dominated the scene and I worshipped the man. The first to notice some special interest being shown by a boy, Roxburgh nurtured it, fostered it and made the boy feel a little bit special because of it. How he did this, I shall never know, but he made every single boy at that school feel that they, and what they did, were of real importance to the Headmaster. Boys were always addressed by their first names and encouraged to build radio sets, to fence and play golf and tennis besides the usual school games, to paint, play the piano or the bagpipes and to keep pets, though this last got a little out of control as the boys grew older and instead of rabbits and ferrets being status symbols, monkeys, bears, hyenas and skunks filled the cages. Finally the school zoo was shut down for reasons of noise and smell.

. . .

I studied fairly hard, though permanently stymied by mathematics, and my immediate goal was the School Certificate . . .
(D. Niven, The Moon's a Balloon, 1971, pp. 21-24 passim)

Stowe School, then, directed its teaching towards the School Certificate rather than the traditional classically biased timetable. This adoption of the grammar school curriculum was in the course of time to become almost universal among the public schools. David Niven's attention, however, was by no means centred exclusively upon his academic work; during his holidays he had struck up a relationship with an attractive girl of cockney origins and easy virtue called Nessie. She visited him at Stowe and in the following extract Niven describes her encounter with his headmaster:

Nessie came down to Stowe to see me in the summer and brought a picnic basket and a tartan rug. Together we took full advantage of the beauties of the school grounds. . . . She took a great interest in my progress at the school and became so intrigued by my hero worship of Roxburgh, that she insisted on meeting him. Basely, I tried to avoid this confrontation but Nessie was not easily put off. . . .

'That's 'im, innit?' she cried one Saturday afternoon, looking across towards the cricket pavilion. Roxburgh was approaching our tartan rug, resplendent in a pale grey suit topped by the inevitable spotted bow tie.

Nessie stood up, bathed in sunlight. She was wearing a short white silk summer dress that clung lovingly to her beautiful body; her honey coloured hair was cut in the fashion of the time – the shingle; she had a small upturned nose; she looked wonderfully young and fresh.

Roxburgh came over smiling his famous smile, 'May I join you?'

I introduced him.

' 'e's just like you told me,' said Nessie in a stage whisper.

' 'e's beautiful,' and then to Roxburgh, 'Don't look a bit like a schoolmaster dew yew, dear?'

J. F. settling himself on the rug missed a tiny beat but thereafter never gave any indication that he was not talking to a beautiful duchess.

He stayed about ten minutes, extolling the glories of Stowe House and its history, and Nessie bathed in the full glow of his charm. Never once did he ask any loaded questions and when he got up to leave he said, 'David is very lucky to have such a charming visitor.'

(D. Niven, The Moon's a Balloon, 1971, pp. 31-32)

The public schools and the state

People like David Niven might enterprisingly build up informal contacts with outsiders, but public schools generally have usually acknowledged the social divisiveness implicit in their ethos. As early as 1861 Gladstone had referred to the existing public schools as being 'what in a large sense is certainly public property'.[25] Suggestions that the state ought to involve itself in the control of the public schools have generally been countered by an expressed willingness on the part of the schools themselves to receive a number of pupils selected from L.E.A. schools (and paid for wholly or in part) by the state authorities. An offer along these lines was made in 1919 by the headmasters of Charterhouse, Eton and Marlborough; a similar suggestion[26] – under which tuition would be provided free while the state paid boarding fees – was put forward by Cyril Norwood in 1928.[27] And it was ideas of this kind that provided the basis of the Fleming Committee's Scheme B of 1944.

The Fleming Committee had been appointed in 1942 'to consider means whereby the association between the Public Schools . . . and the general educational system of the country could be developed and extended'. Its

Scheme A was intended to replace the direct grant system; Scheme B, open only to boarding schools, proposed a minimum of 25 percent of places should be offered to pupils from grant-aided primary schools.[28] Bursaries calculated according to parental income should be payable by the board to some of the children selected, while local L.E.A.s could similarly finance other pupils (and recoup their expenditure from the central authority). Final acceptance would rest with the schools themselves, though 'they would be expected to satisfy the Board of Education as to their reasons, in the event of their rejecting recommended candidates'.[*] At the same time it was proposed that not more than one-third of the governors of a participating school would be nominated by the board and the L.E.A.

The Fleming proposals were subsequently rejected, but Section 8 of the 1944 Act specifically instructed L.E.A.s to consider the provision of boarding accommodation for children who needed it. Circulars 90 and 120 confirmed this policy,[29] and in 1961 the minister revealed that 9700 boys attending independent schools were having their fees paid in full;[†] the Public Schools Commission further reported that in 1966 there were just over 20,000 pupils assisted by L.E.A.s and government departments (such as the diplomatic service and the forces) at independent schools in England and Wales. By 1976-1977 the number of L.E.A.-assisted pupils at independent schools had apparently increased to 40,000; one county – Lancashire – was giving aid to no fewer than 6275.[30]

An association of the kind envisaged by Fleming would probably have made the schools of the independent sector more élitist than ever by enabling them to 'cream' the grammar schools at the 11 + and 13 + stages (points at which, of course, the grammar schools themselves effectively creamed the modern schools). A more thorough solution to the problem would be compulsorily to absorb the independent schools into the state system. Socialist threats to do this have tended so far to have a hollow echo; indeed, the unwillingness of Labour administrations to take resolute action against the independent schools (as opposed to their greatest rivals in the state-controlled sector, the grammar schools) has been criticized by Emmanuel Shinwell:

We are afraid to tackle the public schools to which wealthy people send their sons, but at the same time we are ready to throw overboard the grammar schools which are for many working class boys the stepping-stones to universities and a useful career.

I would rather abandon Eton, Winchester, Harrow and all the rest of them than sacrifice the advantage of the grammar school.[31]

---

[*] But the head teacher of the school concerned would be on the interviewing board.
[†] There were about ten applications for each award in one county (Middlesex).

But it was perhaps not without significance that the Secretary of State upon whom the policy of comprehensivisation devolved in 1967, Patrick Gordon Walker, had sent his twin sons to Wellington, one of the more élitist of the public schools: 'It is hard not to choose what you think is the best within what is permitted you by the law,' he remarked when taxed upon the point,[32] though he did claim that he was 'not at all sure we would do the same thing again.' Lord Snow, another Labour supporter, accounted for his approval of public schools more bluntly; he had sent his own son to Eton, he explained, because 'it seems to me that if you are living in a fairly prosperous home it is a mistake to educate your child differently from most of the people he knows socially.'[33] An uncompromisingly hostile attitude, however, was taken by Roy Hattersley, Labour spokesman on education, in 1973; after rejecting Fleming-style solutions on the grounds that

A better social mix in no way makes the private schools more acceptable. It merely gives them a spurious political respectability,

he stated that he saw

no objection to presenting a Bill which prohibits both the charging of fees for full-time education and the subsidy of full-time education by public companies or private individuals,

and concluded with the apparently unequivocal statement that

If I am to give you* an accurate picture of both the policy of the Labour Party and the prospects for independent schools during the lifetime of the next Labour Government I must, above all else, leave you with no doubts about our intention initially to reduce and eventually to abolish private education in this country.
(Roy Hattersley in The Times, 8 September 1973, p. 2 and Times Educational Supplement, 14 September 1973, p. 10)

Hattersley's speech caused a good deal of alarm and there was talk of transferring some of the independent schools to countries outside the United Kingdom: the policy he advocated 'could be very helpful to those larger country mansions in the Irish Republic for which it is difficult to find a social function' commented *The Times*.[34] In the event, however, Roy Hattersley was not offered a post in education when the Labour Party returned to power in 1974; Reg Prentice, who had previously displayed a notably accommodating attitude towards the independent schools, became the new Secretary of State for Education and Science.

Official Labour Party policy towards the independent schools has generally been fairly cautious; in 1947 Ellen Wilkinson stated that

. . . if people prefer to pay high fees for education less good or no better than that

---

*His speech was made to the I.A.P.S. (preparatory schools' association).

which the state provides free of charge to its taxpayers, there is certainly no reason, in a free country, why they should not spend their money that way. Variety in education is a needed spice.
(E. Wilkinson, The New Secondary Education, 1947, foreword)

And almost twenty years later Reg Prentice, as Minister of State for Education and Science, could reiterate that

We do respect parents' freedom of choice. It is not our intention to remove the private sector in education. It is not our intention to make private payment of school fees illegal.[35]

Statements in this vein by Reginald Prentice and Anthony Crosland to some extent forestalled the report produced in 1968 by the Public Schools Commission. The latter had been set up in 1965 with Sir John Newsom as chairman 'to advise on the best way of integrating the public schools with the State system of education'. Its first report (on the independent boarding schools) embodied an emphatic extension of the Fleming Report's recommendations. No coercion was envisaged; only schools 'suitable and willing' would be expected to participate in its schemes. But whereas Fleming had talked of a 25 percent intake from state schools, the commission recommended a minimum of 50 percent. More importantly, admission was to be based upon principles which were at once intellectually comprehensive and socially selective in a way that was perhaps not caluated to appeal greatly to the public-school tradition:

Most schools, and especially boys' schools, should admit pupils of a wider range of ability. With very few exceptions, they should cater for pupils including those of an ability level corresponding with that required for courses leading to the Certificate of Secondary Education. They should be encouraged where possible also to admit children below this level of ability . . .

. . .

The only justification for public expenditure on boarding education should be need for boarding, for either social or academic reasons. Social grounds would include circumstances in which a child is seriously deprived of reasonable possibilities of educational development because of the absence of a home in this country or because of adverse home or family conditions . . .
(Public Schools Commission, First Report, 1968, Recommendations 2 and 21)

The commission recommended that by 1980 some 45,000 state places should be sought in the independent schools. Many of the children selected would inevitably be of low academic ability and of poor and inadequate home background.

The report was received with a marked lack of enthusiasm. No significant action was taken and Roy Hattersley's subsequent threats to the independent sector were disregarded by the Labour administration of 1974 onwards; in 1976 the government (after some hesitation) actually ratified

Article 13 of the Covenant of the General Assembly of the United Nations, Section 3 of which guarantees that

The States Parties to the present Covenant undertake to have respect for the liberty of parents and, when applicable, legal guardians, to choose for their children schools, other than those established by the public authorities, which conform to such minimum educational standards as may be laid down or approved by the State and to ensure the religious and moral education of their children in conformity with their own convictions.

The implication of this action – assuming it has any significance at all – would appear to be that the continued existence of the independent schools has been openly accepted, in principle at least, by the British government.

The direct grant schools

But if the first report of the Public Schools Commission was largely disregarded, the second was not. The latter dealt with the 178 direct grant schools – a group which, while accepting financial aid from the central authority and offering a minimum of 25 percent free places to children from state schools, nevertheless remained outside the state-owned system. Fees, when not remitted *in toto*, were adjusted according to parental income and were usually well below those of comparable fully independent schools.[36] Direct grant schools tended in consequence to be highly selective academically and their existence had been widely accepted as compatible with a national policy of tripartism (though the Fleming Report had recommended they adopt a 100 percent scholarship system). The implementation of a comprehensive policy by the Labour government in 1965, however, changed this. The direct grant schools, being selective, became anomalous; and in their second report (1970) the Public Schools Commission recommended that

Day schools receiving grants from central or local authorities should participate in the movement towards comprehensive reorganisation.[37]

The members of the commission disagreed on the future position of the direct grant schools, but eight (almost half) considered that they should adopt some form of locally maintained status.[38] Action was delayed until after the return to power of the Labour Party in 1974. Given until the end of 1975 to decide whether to become comprehensive or to forgo state aid altogether, about fifty (almost all of them Catholic schools) chose the former course. Practically all the remainder, in what amounted to a massive vote of confidence in the independent sector of education, decided to cut all ties with the state system.[39] Within a year these direct grant schools were being followed into the independent sector by a trickle of state-maintained voluntary grammar schools: Emanuel School in early 1976 was the first of three London schools to ask their LEA to obtain a 'cease to maintain' order from the Secretary of State under Section 13 of the 1944 Act. Within a year or so, three of the four Surrey voluntary-controlled grammar schools had also successfully negotiated independent status. The 1976 Education Act seemed to strengthen the government's hand by giving the secretary power to compel voluntary grammar schools to go comprehensive. Nevertheless, by late 1977 a further four or five London schools, together with two in Hampshire and seven in Birmingham, were reported to be asking for independent status.[40]

The future of the public schools

It remains to be seen whether or not the confidence of the direct grant schools will prove to be misplaced. But there are some indications that the public schools generally may face the future with cautious optimism. Even the removal of their charitable status (one of Roy Hattersley's more immediate threats) seemed less likely to materialize after the failure of the Goodman Committee to recommend such a step. The traditional status of the public schools shows few signs of erosion. Academically they continue to dominate the Oxbridge open-award table, gaining in 1974-1975 a total of 746 scholarships and exhibitions. This compares favourably with the grammar and comprehensive school totals of 303 and 90 respectively.[41] At the same time they appear to offer encouraging prospects to the less academic pupil: a survey of over 1000 public schoolboys known to have failed their 11 + indicated that 'about 70 percent got 5 or more passes at "O" level . . . the average number per boy being between 5.5 and 6 . . .' About a quarter of them eventually went to university.[42]

Perhaps such results were only to be expected. The staff ratios of public schools are good: 1 to 11.6 compared to 1 to 16.8 in maintained grammar schools[43] – yet at the same time the fees charged tend, at least according to one source, to be much the same (or even less) than the average unit cost per pupil in a state secondary boarding school.

There is little evidence that the public schools are losing their social function as educational institutions for the top people. The following table indicates some weakening of their hold over senior civil service posts since 1939, but no relaxation in other vital areas:

Percentage of élite groups educated at public schools

	1939	1970-71
Civil Service (under secretaries and above)	84.5	61.7
Ambassadors (heads of embassies and legations)	73.5	82.5
Judiciary (high court judges and above)	80.0	80.2
Royal Navy (rear-admirals and above)	18.6	37.5
Army (major-generals and above)	63.6	86.1
R.A.F. (air vice-marshals and above)	66.7	62.5
Church of England (assistant bishops and above)	70.8	67.4
Clearing Banks (directors)	68.2	79.9

(Figures extracted from D. Boyd, Elites and their Education, N.F.E.R., 1973, pp. 80-84)

Between 1946 and 1971, the number of boys in the public schools increased from 39,000 to 54,000. The schools as a whole have shown a degree of flexibility and opportunism by increasing the number of day boys and in some cases admitting a small number of girls. According to one observer, this pattern may develop to the extent that 'A typical public school of the future might well be one-third boy boarders, one-third day boys, and one-third day girls.'[45]

If the possibility of drastic government action is excluded, the future of the public schools appears reasonably assured; in the opinion of Royston Lambert (whose work as director of the government-financed Research Unit into Boarding Education was used extensively by the Public Schools Commission):

As long as the association of certain kinds of boarding with various kinds of elite continues there is no likelihood of any dramatic decline in demand for such schools. In them costs have risen even more than elsewhere but, such are the benefits they are considered to bestow, parents are still prepared to pay and eager to enter their sons. There seems little likelihood that the function of such schools will alter rapidly. The failure of the Labour Government of 1964-70, which entered into office pledged to alter the public school system so as to eliminate its social divisiveness, to take action beyond setting up a commission whose report it subsequently ignored is indicative. It is improbable that any effective political action will occur to alter the allocative role of this sort of boarding: it will therefore continue to command a market whatever the price it charges. Changes will occur from within the schools and there may be over the years some decline in high status boarding schools as independent day schools prosper and assume a more secure position in the process of upward social allocation.
(R. Lambert, The Chance of a Lifetime?, 1975, pp. 350-351)

Notes

1   By Richard Redgrave, dated 1844.

2   A plea for the reassessment of the value of the dame school as an institution has been advanced by A.F.B. Roberts in 'A New View of the Infant School Movement', *British Journal of Educational Studies*, Vol. XX (February-October 1972), who

suggests (p. 164) that 'Give us back our dame schools!' might be an appropriate demand for the post-Plowden era. Other articles dealing with the subject are by J. H. Higginson and D. P. Leinster-Mackay in *British Journal of Educational Studies*, Vol. XXII (February-October 1974) and Vol. XXIV (February-October 1976) respectively.

3   For an examination of some of the links between nineteenth-century prep schools, public schools and universities, see T. W. Bamford, 'Public School Masters: A Nineteenth-Century Profession', in T. G. Cook (ed.), *Education and the Professions*, 1973.

4   The developmental history of the prep school is considered in some detail by Donald Leinster-Mackay in 'The evolution of t'other schools: an examination of the nineteenth-century development of the private preparatory school', in *History of Education*, Vol. 5, No. 3 (October 1976).

5   In the preface to the 1955 edition of his book, Alec Waugh recalled that 'In many schools the book was banned and several boys were caned for reading it. Canon Edward Lyttleton, the ex-headmaster of Eton, wrote a ten-page article in *The Contemporary* – then an influential monthly – explaining how biased and partial a picture the school gave. *The Spectator* ran for ten weeks and *The Nation* for six a correspondence filling three or four pages an issue in which schoolmaster after schoolmaster said that whatever might be true of "Fernhurst", at his school it was all very different.

6   D. Crichton-Miller, 'The Public Schools and the Welfare State', *British Journal of Educational Studies*, Vol. III, No. 1 (November 1954), p. 7.

7   Augustus J. C. Hare, *The Story of My Life*, 1896, Vol. I, p. 245.

8   George Melly, *Recollections*, 1893, p. 86.

9   T. W. Bamford, *Thomas Arnold*, 1960, Chapter XVII *passim*.

10   T. W. Bamford, *The Rise of the Public Schools*, 1967, p. 38.

11   Ibid., p. 6.

12   E. C. Mack, *Public Schools and British Opinion 1780-1860*, 1938, p. 346.

13   See G. R. Parkin, *Life of Edward Thring*, 1898, Volume I, pp. 59 and 79. For a sympathetic modern appraisal of Edward Thring see Alicia C. Percival, *Very Superior Men*, 1973, pp. 177-198.

14   G. R. Parkin, op. cit., Vol. I, p. 67.

15   Ibid., Volume II, p. 150.

16   T. W. Bamford, op. cit., 1967, pp. 188-189. Besides the seven boarding schools and two day schools of Clarendon, the 1889 list included Bedford, Dulwich, Repton, Sherborne, Tonbridge, and Uppingham (endowed schools), and the recent foundations of Bradfield, Brighton, Cheltenham, Clifton, Dover, Haileybury, Lancing, Malvern, Marlborough, Radley, Rossall, and Wellington. The Scottish schools Fettes, Glenalmond, and Loretto were other establishments named.

17   Vivian Ogilvie, *The English Public School*, 1957, p. 177.

18   Cheltenham appears to have had a nonclassical side from its earliest days. See T. W. Bamford (1967), pp. 25-26.

19   H. B. Gray, *The Public Schools and the Empire*, 1913, pp. 172-173 (footnote).

20   Arnold Lunn, *The Harrovians*, 1913, p. 43.

21   There are some indications that the cult of athleticism was on the wane after the turn of the century. See J. A. Mangan in *The Victorian Public School*, ed. by B. Simon and I. Bradley, 1975, pp. 127-128.

22   H. B. Gray, op. cit., p. 192 (footnote).

23   Kenneth Rose, *Superior Person, A Portrait of Curzon and his Circle in late Victorian England*, 1969, p. 58.

24   Public Schools Commission, First Report, p. 31 and diagram 6, p. 54.

25   Ibid., p. 76.

26   T. W. Bamford, op.cit., 1967, p. 288.

27   Ibid., p. 292.

28   Fleming Report, 1944, p. 66.

29   G. Robinson, *Private Schools and Public Policy*, 1971, pp. 94-95.

30   Public Schools Commission, First Report, Table 27, p. 99, and *Times Educational Supplement*, 18 February 1977.

31   *The Times*, 30 June 1958, p. 6. Attitudes towards the public schools within the Labour Party generally are discussed in G. Robinson, op.cit. and Rodney Barker, *Education and Politics 1900-1951*, 1972, Chapter VI.

32   Quoted in *Times Educational Supplement.*, 8 September 1967, p. 394.

33   Quoted in D. Boyd, *Elites and their Education*, N.F.E.R., 1973, p. 141.

34   *The Times*, 8 September 1973, p. 13.

35   Quoted in G. Robinson, op.cit., p. 121.

36   The Public Schools Commission (First Report, p. 44) stated that the average fee for day pupils in public schools was £192 p.a. In the Second Report (p. 73) the average fee for day pupils in H.M.C. direct grant schools was given as £144 p.a.

37   Recommendation 1.

38   Recommendation 7.

39   *Times Educational Supplement.*, 9 January 1976, p. 4. The relative willingness of Roman Catholic schools to accept comprehensive reorganization is considered in Marjorie Cruickshank, 'The Denominational Schools Issue in the Twentieth Century', *History of Education*, Vol. 1, No. 2 (June 1972).

40   *Times Educational Supplement.*, 21 January 1977, p. 22 and 10 June 1977, p. 3.

41   *Times Educational Supplement.*, 31 October 1975, p. 12.

42   *Times Educational Supplement.*, 17 May 1963, p. 1061.

43   Public Schools Commission, First Report, Table 13, p. 43.

44   Figures quoted in *Times Educational Supplement* (17 September 1976, p. 3) gave the average cost of a pupil in a state secondary school as £1303. The highest regional variation was in Bromley (£2368) and the lowest was in Tameside (£741).

45   Philip Venning, in *Times Educational Supplement.*, 23 June 1972, p. 16.

CHAPTER 8

THE TRAINING OF TEACHERS IN THE NINETEENTH AND TWENTIETH CENTURIES

'A LATENT INJUSTICE UNPERCEIVED' – THE TRAINING OF ELEMENTARY SCHOOL TEACHERS IN THE NINETEENTH-CENTURY

The formal training of would-be teachers for English working-class schools generally remained rather sketchy and haphazard until the 1840s. Earlier in the century both of the principal religious societies had indeed initiated schemes under which their metropolitan centres – at Borough Road or Baldwin's Gardens and Westminster – accommodated intending teachers. But the courses were uniformly restricted in scope and consisted essentially of a short period of participation in each of the monitorial classes underpinned on occasion by extra instruction of a practical or theoretical nature. When Lancaster could spare the time (which was not very often) he apparently gave 'lectures on the passions'; Bell's approach, however, remained firmly down-to-earth:

My suggestion is

That certain classes be set apart for the instruction of masters. . . . It is proposed that each master in succession shall remain in charge of one of these classes for a given time (say one week or a fortnight) at the end of which the summary of his report of its comparative progress and present state be read, and that a brief examination take place, in the presence of all the masters which, (if the primary law of perfect instruction has been observed) will require only a very few minutes; and that, according to the conduct of the master and the progress of the class, he be ranked in the list of candidates for pay and for an appointment to a school, due attention however being paid to any other pretensions.
(Minutes of the National Society School Committee, July 20, 1821)

Students were kept under a censorious eye; when some from Baldwin's Gardens frivolously attended a dance and then a water party, their teacher received (and doubtless passed on) a reprimand from the Bishop of London, no less.[1] From a slightly later period, F. Crampton recalled the perfunctory training which a student received at the Anglican Central Schools:

He was generally what was called trained at Westminster, where you might see him with a little slate round his neck, going up and down in the class with the little boys with whom he was practising the various dodges of Dr. Bell's system, and at twelve o'clock placed in a row, waiting to be bowed to by the Head Master as a sign of dismissal. For about six months he underwent this ordeal, and then went to practise in a school all that he had observed in training. For the most part he had diligently to instil into his pupils the duty of behaving themselves 'lowly and reverently to all their betters'.
(The School and the Teacher, August, 1861, pp. 202-203)

Nonconformists likewise had a classroom-centred course. According to Henry Dunn (secretary of the British and Foreign School Society), they were admitted to Borough Road between the ages of 19 and 24 and stayed there for a minimum of three months, spending the first fortnight on probation.

The annual total of students of both sexes, stated Dunn in 1834, had always been less than one hundred:

They are required to rise every morning at five o'clock, and spend an hour before seven in private study. They have access to a good library. At seven they are assembled together in a Bible class and questioned as to their knowledge of the Scriptures; from nine to twelve they are employed as monitors in the school, learning to communicate that which they already know or are supposed to know; from two to five they are employed in a similar way; and from five to seven they are engaged under a master who instructs them in arithmetic and the elements of geometry, geography and the globes, or in any other branches in which they may be deficient. The remainder of the evening is generally occupied in preparing exercises for the subsequent day. Our object is to keep them incessantly employed from five in the morning until nine or ten at night.
(Parl. Papers, 1834, Vol. IX, Minutes of Evidence before the Select Committee on Education, etc., p. 17)

Thus established at an early date were the twin characteristics of querulous paternalism and academic superficiality which were to prove such persistent features of so much training college instruction.

Formal teacher training, however, was not confined to London; the diocesan local training schools and the Barrington School at Bishop Auckland supplemented the output of Anglican teachers. But nonconformists, after the failure of Lancaster's grandiose training scheme at Maiden Bradley in 1809, appear to have concentrated upon the Borough Road institution, though connections did exist with the model school at Kildare Place in Dublin and attempts were made to establish monitorial training schools in places as far apart as Weimar and Madrid.

Although the brevity of the courses provided by the religious societies was freely admitted to be a drawback, there was a certain reluctance to acknowledge that their whole basis – the monitorial system itself – was becoming, as time passed, increasingly outmoded. The Wesleyans were already during the 1830s sending would-be teachers to David Stow's Normal Seminary in Glasgow, while the Home and Colonial Infant School Society's training college, founded in 1836, was understandably orientated towards more congenial methods of teaching than those generally practised under the monitorial system.

But it was James Kay (Kay Shuttleworth after 1842) who emerged during the 1840s as the dominant figure in English teacher training. The celebrated institution which he was instrumental in founding at Battersea served as a prototype for subsequent nineteenth-century training colleges; and in his capacity as secretary to the Committee of Council he was able in large measure to overcome the basic failure of the monitorial system to provide financial and intellectual incentive for the monitors themselves. The great achievement of Kay Shuttleworth was that he created a continuous, state-financed process by which an aspiring girl or boy of thirteen or more in an inspected school could become a pupil teacher for five years and then, as a Queen's Scholar, attend college for one, two, or even three years. Such a student would be subsidized throughout from government resources, annually tested in government examinations and, when certificated, rewarded with a salary augmentation from government funds and a rent-free house. The 1846 *Minutes* even held out the prospect (though rather a delusory one as it turned out) of a noncontributory retirement pension. Teachers who had not followed the approved course of training were eligible for these benefits provided that they were able to pass the examinations leading to certification.

In the circumstances it is hardly surprising that Kay Shuttleworth's régime from 1839 to 1849 was often regarded with admiration and later with nostalgia by qualified elementary teachers. As one of them was to write in 1861, 'He was the man who saw the schoolmaster in the mud, and tried to help him out – like a poor Crossing Sweeper, he got more kicks than half-pence . . .'[2]

The pupil teachers

The pupil teacher system provided the foundation and much of the superstructure of the nineteenth-century teaching profession. From the outset, the Committee of Council was careful to provide a direct means of certificate qualification for pupil teachers and others who, for one reason or another, had not undergone a course in a training college. This attitude was only realistic as throughout the period the number of pupil teachers successfully completing their courses far exceeded the number of places available in the colleges. As the Board of Education Report for 1912-1913 was to point out:

For some years previous to 1889, the number of persons admitted as Pupil-Teachers ran from 8,000 to 9,000 per annum, and the number who completed their apprenticeships each year was over 6,000; while the Colleges could not admit more than about 1,600 persons per annum.

As late as 1898, in fact, over half (50.9 per cent) of women teachers in inspected schools and over a quarter (28.1 per cent) of the men had had no college training. The day training colleges of the final decade of the century alleviated this position but they did not change it radically. In 1903, for example, before what has been described, perhaps with more realism than tact, as 'the gradual elimination of the nondegree student',[3] their output was limited to around 830 students.

The Kay Shuttleworth conception of a pupil teacher appears to have derived from Holland and from the secretary's own poor law experiences in East Anglia and Norwood. The following extracts are taken from the *Minutes* of 1846 which gave material form to these ideas:

Pupil Teachers – Qualifications of Candidates

The following qualifications will be required from candidates for apprenticeship:

They must be at least thirteen years of age, and must not be subject to any bodily infirmity likely to impair their usefulness as pupil teachers.

In schools connected with the Church of England, the clergyman and managers, and, in other schools, the managers must certify that the moral character of the candidates and of their families justify an expectation that the instruction and training of the school will be seconded by their own efforts and by the example of their parents. If this cannot be certified of the family, the apprentice will be required to board in some approved household.

Candidates will also be required –

1   To read with fluency, ease, and expression.

2   To write in a neat hand, with correct spelling and punctuation, a simple prose narrative slowly read to them.

3   To write from dictation sums in the first four rules of arithmetic, simple and compound; to work them correctly, and to know the tables of weights and measures.

4   To point out the parts of speech in a simple sentence.

5   To have an elementary knowledge of geography.

6   *In schools connected with the Church of England* they will be required to repeat the Catechism, and to show that they understand its meaning, and are acquainted with the outline of Scripture history. The parochial clergyman will assist in this part of the examination.

In other schools the state of the religious knowledge will be certified by the managers.

7   To teach a junior class to the satisfaction of the Inspector.

8   Girls should also be able to sew neatly and to knit.

. . .

At the close of each year, pupil teachers or stipendiary monitors will be required to present certificates of good conduct from the managers of the school, and of punctuality, diligence, obedience, and attention to their duties from the master or mistress.

In *Church of England Schools,* the parochial clergyman, and *in other schools,* the managers, will also certify that the pupils teachers or stipendiary monitors have been attentive to their religious duties.

Salaries of Pupil Teachers and Stipendiary Monitors *

If these certificates be presented, and if the Inspector certify, at the close of each year, that he is satisfied with the oral examination and the examination papers of the pupil teachers or stipendiary monitors, and if those papers be satisfactory to their

---

* Stipendiary monitors were to serve in schools where the staff were not qualified to give the instruction specified for pupil teachers in the 1846 *Minutes.*

Lordships, the following stipends will be paid, irrespectively of any sum that may be received from the school or from any other source:

	For a Pupil Teacher		For a Stipendiary Monitor	
	£.	s.	£.	s.
At the end of the 1st year	10	0	5	0
At the end of the 2nd year	12	10	7	10
At the end of the 3rd year	15	0	10	0
At the end of the 4th year	17	10	12	10
At the end of the 5th year	20	0	0	0

(Committee of Council Minutes, 1846, Vol. I., pp. 2-9 passim)

A later *Minute,* that of 10 December 1851, equated three years' service as a principal or assistant teacher with a one-year course at a training college, thus more closely defining the twin procedures by which a pupil teacher could qualify to take the certificate examination and, if successful, obtain the resultant augmentation grant.

The Revised Code bore with particular harshness upon the pupil teachers, for the Education Department's responsibility towards them was firmly shifted on to the managers of the individual schools. The payment of pupil teachers (and of the staff who instructed them) became a matter for direct negotiation between the parties concerned. Symptomatic, perhaps, of the department's policy of disengagement is Article 90 of the Revised Code, rather callously listed under 'Disposal of Pupil Teachers at the end of their apprenticeship':

At the close of the apprenticeship pupil-teachers are perfectly free in the choice of empolyment . . . the pupil-teacher, if willing to continue in the work of education, may become an assistant in an elementary school (Article 91), or may become a Queen's scholar in a normal shcool (Articles 103-118), or may be provisionally certificated for immediate service in charge of small rural schools (Articles 132, 133).

Article 132, mentioned above, is worthy of note. By instituting a lower, provisional form of certification it made it possible to increase the number of qualified teachers without extra expense. But Article 132 was also intended to serve the useful purpose of channelling qualified staff into small, impoverished country schools with one hundred or fewer pupils, thus making them eligible for annual inspection and grant.

In larger schools, however, qualified teachers sometimes tended to exploit their superior status and greater maturity in order to secure for themselves a disproportionate amount of the total money available. And the pupil teacher suffered accordingly. As HMI Watts regretfully observed:

In collective examinations of pupil-teachers I often meet with candidates of a very unpromising stamp. On one occasion out of eight candidates only one was admitted.

Upon inquiry I found that most of the unsuccessful candidates were only in the second class in the schools in which they were intended to be articled; the reason why some of the most advanced boys could not be induced to become pupil-teachers was the small payment of 1l. a quarter offered to such as would accept it, with far less regard to their efficiency than to the means of securing the maximum grant at the least possible expense, without any intention on the part of the master to prepare the pupil-teacher, or on the part of the pupil-teacher to be prepared for admission in due time into a training college.

These cases are confined, I believe, to schools where unwisely, in my opinion, in consideration of a fixed stipend plus all the pence, and a portion, if not the whole of the Government Grant, the responsibility of providing pupil-teachers is either sought by or thrust upon the master, who is not always capable of resisting the temptation to swell out his own salary by employing the cheapest and most probably therefore the most inferior article; thus injuring in a degree which it is difficult to measure the actual welfare of his own school as well as the future welfare of a system which it is strictly his duty to promote.

(Mr. Watts' General Report for 1868)

HMI Swinburne gives several instances of the results of this short-sighted (but tempting) policy as demonstrated in the examination answers of pupil teachers. Here is one of the more curious examples:

Wolfe was a very able man, he was sent out by the honourable East India Co. to take Calcutta, this he did, then he died. He is reported as he led his men to the charge to have quoted those memorable lines from 'Graves Energy'. 'Up, Guards, and at 'em,' and to have said, 'Gentlemen, I would rather be the editor of these lines than take Calcutta'.

(A. J. Swinburne, Memories of a School Inspector, 1912, p. 184)

The Education Department was by no means unaware of the situation but nevertheless remained adamant in insisting upon its own lack of responsibility – thus imparting a slightly crocodilian air to its lamentations:

We frequently receive complaints from managers of the difficulty of finding male pupil-teachers, when a reference to their yearly returns of income and expenditure shows that, while the masters may be drawing very liberal salaries from the schools, a stipend of 5l. a year, to begin with, is all that is offered to candidates for engagement as pupil-teachers. The Revised Code purposely leaves all matters of this kind to be settled in each case on the spot, according to the general rate of wages in the district; but the object of doing so is defeated if the local authorities do not interfere to prevent even the suspicion that any interested influence has affected too exclusively the scale of remuneration enjoyed by the various classes of teachers in their schools.

(Committee of Council Report, 1869-1870, p. xxiv)

The figures mentioned above – an initial £4 or £5 per annum – represent of course a reduction of 50 percent or more from the stipends originally payable under the 1846 *Minutes*. Fortunately, the actual situation was not quite as disastrous as these figures imply: by 1867, for example, the average stipends of pupil teachers were £13.9s. for boys and £12.15s. for girls. But things were nevertheless quite bad enough. The suggested pupil teacher/scholar ratio had originally been 1:25; by 1859 this had been modified to 1:40. In 1861 the real ratio stood at 1:36. By 1866 it had declined to 1:54. This meant an absolute reduction in the number of pupil teachers from 13,871 (1861) to 8,866 (1866).

These daunting figures appear to have produced a prompt and positive reaction from the Education Department. 'Mr. Corry's Minute' of 20 February 1867 made a fairly radical modification to the capitation grant system by introducing an additional sum of 1/4d for each pass in reading, writing, or arithmetic (to a maximum of £8) in efficient schools which were able to maintain a full complement of certificated assistant teachers or pupil teachers. Further grants, moreover, were to be payable to any schools whose male ex-pupil teachers achieved a place in the first or second class of their college entrance or first year examination. Pupil teacher statistics thereupon took a more encouraging turn: by 1868 numbers had risen to 11,031 and in 1870 they reached 14,612, though girls formed an increasing proportion of the new enrolments.

The following account of life as a pupil teacher is taken from F. H. Spencer's autobiography. The author came from a skilled working-class background in the railway town of Swindon. For him, the only means of extending formal education beyond higher elementary standards was through the pupil teacher-training college system. Later he was to gain a degree and spend almost all his working life in posts connected with state-aided education. Spencer's wide experience lends validity to the measured criticisms which he presents in this extract; his comments on the academic standards (or rather on the lack of them) required of pupil teachers and training college students certainly merit serious consideration:

The early autumn of 1886 witnessed my apprenticeship. I still remember walking with my father, who had to take a half-day off work for the purpose, on a Saturday morning up the hill to the office of the dignified old solicitor, who acted as clerk to the School Board. We saw, not the great man, who may, for all I know, have been shooting partridges with some of the squirearchy of the neighbourhood for whom he acted, but the respectable little man of the managing-clerk type, who ran the School Board business for him. There were regular indentures, and I had to put my finger on a red seal and give something or other, I knew not what, as my act and deed. So did my father. Then I was a pupil teacher. . . . No one asked me whether or not I wished to teach. If they had asked, I should probably have said 'No', the natural answer for a boy of fourteen.

. . .

A pupil teacher was precisely what the name implies. The pupil teacher was the pupil of the head master in things academic, and he was a teacher. No doubt the theory was that he was trained to teach. In fact, he taught as best he could, his practice being based on what he remembered of how he had been taught, and on the tricks of the trade picked up from those among whom he worked. In these respects at fourteen he was like the normal public-school master of twenty-three. In the circumstances of those times the system was not without its advantages. You sank or swam. Either you could 'hold' a class of thirty, fifty, or sixty boys or you could not. If you could, and you passed an annual examination of a rudimentary 'Secondary' level, you survived, and, in due course, at the age of eighteen or nineteen, proceeded to a training-college to take a two years' course, principally concerned with the content of a decent secondary education, or, in some directions, rather more than that, with a tincture of actual training for the work of teaching.

So far as the academic side was concerned, my pupilage was largely a fraud. The Code laid down that a pupil teacher was to have at least one hour's instruction a day from the head master, who apparently could delegate this duty, or part of it, to certificated assistants. In our school these 'lessons' purported to take place every day from Monday to Friday inclusive from seven to eight in the morning. (The Headmaster) himself was down for Wednesday mornings. One or other of the assistants attended on the other four days. In fact, (the Headmaster), who took English, chiefly grammar and the reading of a play of Shakespeare, could be relied upon never to arrive before 7.30. On the other mornings things varied according to the conscientiousness of the various masters, of whom the more intelligent were, as a rule, the less conscientious.

On Wednesdays, therefore, I would often struggle to arrive by 7.30; but I was not infrequently late. On the other mornings I turned up chiefly according to my interest in the subject taken and the degree of respect which each particular assistant master inspired. Sometimes sleep or laziness would ensnare me and I would not attend at all.

. . .

. . . As an education, therefore, the instruction of the pupil teacher was a futile sham. And the Government programme of annual P.T. Examinations was far too easy, unambitious and dull for any lively-minded lad. Many, of course, in other schools were better taught than I was.

Pupil teachers, however, were regarded not as pupils or students, but primarily as teachers; and I was plunged into the pedagogic business at once and at the top of the school.

(F. H. Spencer, An Inspector's Testament, 1938, pp. 74-79 passim)

F. H. Spencer was by no means alone in his doubts about the quality of education commonly given to pupil teachers: 'our pupil-teachers are a sort of child-drudge' complained Sir John Gorst in the House of Commons, '. . . this is not the way to bring up teachers'. (Cheers).[4] A minority view in the Cross Report had expressed sweeping criticisms of the pupil teacher system a few years earlier:

. . . the complaint is general that pupil-teachers teach badly, and are badly taught. The wretched state of their preparation when they enter the training colleges will be dwelt on when that part of our educational system is dealt with, and the remarkable thing is that the witnesses, while complaining generally of the backwardness and ignorance of pupil-teachers, lay special stress on their inability to teach, and on their ignorance of school management.

(The Cross Report, on the working of the Elementary Education Acts, 1888, p. 270)

And though the majority acquiesced to the continuance of the system, it did so in terms which were something less than enthusiastic:

On the whole we concur in the opinion . . . that, having regard to moral qualifications, there is no other available or, as we prefer to say, equally trustworthy source from which an adequate supply of teachers is likely to be forthcoming; and with modifications, tending to the improvement of their education, the apprenticeship of pupil-teachers, we think, ought to be upheld.
(The Cross Report, on the working of the Elementary Education Acts, 1888, p. 88)

So there took place in the last decades of the nineteenth century and in the early years of the twentieth a progressive reduction in the teaching commitment of pupil teachers coupled with a raising of their minimum age of entry. In 1878 the normal length of the course was shortened from five to four years, the minimum age increased from thirteen to fourteen, and the teaching load confined to between fifteen and thirty hours per week. Four years later the maximum time to be spent in teaching was reduced to 25 hours and a new grade – that of probationer – was instituted for intending pupil teachers aged from thirteen to fourteen, who were to teach no more than half-time. Next, in 1896, the usual minimum age for the pupil teachers was again raised – to fifteen. Then finally a series of new regulations which became effective between 1903 and 1907 put up the age of entry to between sixteen and seventeen, strictly limited teaching to half-time and stipulated that at least three hundred hours a year should normally be spent in study at an approved centre.

Pupil teachers' centres and the 'block system'

Pupil teachers' centres, at which the time available due to the moderated demands of teaching was intended to be spent, were to prove a relatively ephemeral species of educational institution. Like the pupil teacher concept itself, they had long been an integral part of the Dutch system. In England, one of the earliest centres had existed since 1859 at Wantage, and during the 1870s similar projects had been organized in Liverpool, Birmingham, and London. But the legality of these ventures was open to question on two counts: the instruction provided went beyond that specified in the code, while at the same time pupil teachers could officially be taught only by the certificated staff of the school to which they themselves belonged.

The 1880 Code removed these objections, at least to the satisfaction of the Education Department and the school boards (though not to that of the legal profession, as the Cockerton Judgement was later to show), and many centres were subsequently established. When, in 1894, they were placed on the visiting list of H.M. Inspectorate, their respectability seemed assured. By 1902, 17,000 pupil teachers and probationers (out of 32,000) were receiving some measure of instruction at pupil teachers' centres.

The vicissitudes of the pupil teachers' centres in London are related below by

G. A. Christian, who was deeply involved in their work from 1882 until their eventual demise in 1911:

. . . in January 1885, a dozen day-centres were established in London. As my work at the evening-centre had attracted favourable attention, I was one of the fortunate dozen principals selected after a severe competition, and the Southwark Pupil-Teachers' Centre was assigned to my charge. All the centres were, I think, relegated to temporary buildings, such as disused voluntary schools, private houses, and one floor of a school-building, etc. Our quarters were the old national school at the back of St. Paul's Church, Bermondsey, very near to Guy's Hospital, and on Saturday morning, when the whole of the students were present, we were allowed to overflow into the near Laxon Street School.

. . .

The premises and the material equipment were poor, and the Rev. Stewart Headlam on one of his visits described the place with a literal truth of which he was unconscious, as a 'rat-hole'. However, we teachers endeavoured to make up by enthusiasm and good teaching for the defects of the place, and especially among the younger students our efforts were eagerly reciprocated. We were handicapped by the quarterly examinations of the pupil-teachers, and what with these, with the science and art examinations in May, our own necessary internal examinations, and – most important of all – the Queen's Scholarship Examination, which was the final test so far as the Centre was concerned, we were always hard pressed.

. . .

At Easter, 1894, our specially-designed permanent building on the grounds of the Alma School, Bermondsey, was ready for occupation, and the transfer was eagerly made. The fine hall, the chemical laboratory, the art-room, the commodious class-rooms, and the luxury of teachers' rooms, provided a contrast to our former habitation, and we celebrated the opening (by the Rev. Joseph W. Diggle, Chairman of the School Board) in high spirits. It would be incorrect to say that our work under the new conditions was of better quality, but the increased comfort and pleasure to teachers and students cannot be fully understood except by those who have made a similar change. We made good use of our new resources, and as principal, I particularly appreciated the commodious hall – for the school-hall effectively utilised is an important factor in promoting and sustaining corporate life and that unity of feeling which differentiates a school from a mere collection of classes.

. . .

No serious attempt, however, in any quarter was made to widen the scope of the centres, but subsequent Education Codes definitely decided for the secondary schools as the main places for the instruction of pupil-teachers. As long as the London School Board lasted, the London centres went on as usual, but as soon as the County Council assumed authority the new batches of probationers (or beginners) were allocated to the secondary schools. I well recollect going to the Embankment to point out the serious consequences to the centres of this step and to plead for delay at least until the new Committee had had time to acquaint itself with the problem. Our plea was overruled and the probationers were drafted to the secondary schools.
(G. A. Christian, English Education from Within, 1922, pp. 23-38 passim)

The centres were instrumental in altering the balance of the training given to pupil teachers. As F. H. Spencer had pointed out, the traditional emphasis had always been upon the teaching element rather than the academic. By 1907 this situation no longer obtained. But by then the independent pupil teachers' centres, failing to establish their own position, were being absorbed into, or superseded by, secondary grammar schools.

Even before 1902 some intending teachers were in attendance at secondary schools rather than at the segregated pupil teachers' centres. At Scarborough, for example, they were enrolled as ordinary scholars at the secondary school up to the age of about sixteen. Then as pupil teachers for the following two years they divided their time equally between their secondary studies and elementary teaching.

The Cockerton Judgement, the 1902 Act, and the attitude of the board itself combined to ensure that such experiments would ultimately become the rule. By 1906 this process was well under way: out of just under 11,000 pupil teachers, 6260 remained in independent centres, 4280 were attending secondary schools, and only about 360 exclusively received instruction on the old pattern at the elementary schools in which they taught. The dissonant requirements of half-time teaching and full-time secondary attendance were resolved by the so-called 'block system' ('sandwich course' in modern terms) which allowed pupil teachers to spend one or more terms continuously at each of their schools. But, as some of their older colleagues were already discovering in the university day-training colleges, true social integration was not always easy. An ex-H.M.I. recalled in 1911 how

. . . a few years ago when pupil teachers were to be educated at secondary schools what a gross distinction was made between them and other pupils, how they were separated from the others, had separate playtimes, and so forth.
(H. Holman in The Schoolmaster, 28 October 1911, p. 722)

In 1907 a novel and alternative method of financing would-be teachers was introduced. Bursary grants, as they were called, aimed at providing them with a sufficiency of government money until the age of seventeen or eighteen when they could qualify to enter a training college. In conjunction with L.E.A. teaching scholarships to secondary schools, the new grants provided a free and subsidised (but not, as before, remunerative) course of preparation. This innovation, officially described as 'a better way' of teacher training, was a fair indication that the days of the old pupil teacher system were numbered.

Training colleges
The first state grant towards teacher training – £10,000 for the erection of normal schools – was made available in 1835; still unused in 1839, it was offered, divided equally, to the two religious societies. But the controversy over the Committee of Council's own scheme for a state-run normal school

at Kneller Hall supervened, and even when this had died down matters were further deferred by the committee's insistence upon the right of inspection as a necessary condition of aid. So it was not until November, 1843, that training colleges were systematically offered building grants at the rate of £50 per student place. The *Minutes* of 1846 greatly extended government help by the provision of payments to inspected training colleges in respect of 'every student trained therein concerning whose character and conduct the Principal shall give a favourable report' and whose examination results and general aptitude for teaching received H.M.I.'s approval. Thus, for each successful first, second, or third year student the sum of £20, £25, or £30 was awarded directly to the college.

Battersea Training School, founded in 1840 by a defiant Kay and his friend Carleton Tufnell as a *faute de mieux* consequence of the defeat of the Committee of Council's normal school plans of the previous year, became in some measure a prototype for later foundations. But its beginnings, if not exactly humble, were hardly conceived on the grand, even elephantine scale of some twentieth-century colleges of education. The following is a description of Battersea when, after a rapid conversion, it was ready to receive its first students in early 1840:

In the month of January all the preparations were completed. The spacious old manor-house of Sir Walter St. John emerged from the hands of the workmen duly altered and fitted for its new career, one part being set apart as a residence for Dr. Kay, and the rest being given up to the school. . . . (The latter) was divided into two class-rooms, one on the ground-floor . . . and the other above it; the top of the house was converted into dormitories, the beds being placed round the rooms; the kitchen of the old house became a dining-room and an occasional lecture room; the stables were turned into a kitchen, and the room above the stables into a laboratory.
(T. Adkins, the History of St. John's College, Battersea, 1906, pp. 47-48).

Though structural alterations were minimal, the ambiance of the place must have been totally changed. For Battersea under the new order was anything but redolent of leisured manorial life. A student there was to be left in no doubt as to the lowly and austere nature of his vocation. In Kay Shuttleworth's own words:

In the formation of the character of the school-master, the discipline of the training school should be so devised as to prepare him for the modest respectability of his lot. He is to be a Christian teacher, following him who said, 'he that will be my disciple, let him take up his cross'. Without the spirit of self-denial, he is nothing. His reward must be in his work. There should be great simplicity in the life of such a man.

Obscure and secluded schools need masters of a contented spirit, to whom the training of the children committed to their charge, has charms sufficient to concentrate their thoughts and exertions on the humble sphere in which they live, notwithstanding the privations of a life but little superior to the level of the surrounding peasantry. When the scene of the teacher's exertions is in a neighbourhood which brings him into association with the middle and upper classes of society, his emoluments will be greater, and he will be surrounded by temptations which, in the absence of a suitable preparation of mind, might rob him of that humility and gentleness, which are among the most necessary qualifications of the teacher of a common school.

In the training school, habits should be formed consistent with the modesty of his future life. On this account we attach peculiar importance to the discipline which we have established at Battersea. Only one servant, besides a cook, has been kept for the domestic duties of the household . . . you will perceive that the whole household work, with the exception of the scouring of the floors and cooking, is performed by the students, and that they likewise not only milk and clean the cows, feed and tend the pigs, but have charge of the stores, wait upon each other, and cultivate the garden. We cannot too emphatically state our opinion that no portion of this work could be omitted, without a proportionate injury to that contentment of spirit, without which the character of the student is liable to be overgrown with the errors we have described. He has to be prepared for a humble and subordinate position, and though master of his school, to his scholars he is to be a parent, and to his supervisors an intelligent servant and minister.

. . .

We have also adhered to the frugal diet which we at first selected for the school. Some little variety has been introduced, but we attach great importance to the students being accustomed to a diet so plain and economical, and to arrangements in their dormitories so simple and devoid of luxury, that in after life they will not in a humble school be visited with a sense of privation, when their scanty fare and mean furniture are compared with the more abundant food and comforts of the training school. We have therefore met every rising complaint respecting either the quantity or quality of the food, or the humble accommodation in the dormitories, with explanations of the importance of forming, in the school, habits of frugality, and of the paramount duty of nurturing a patient spirit, to meet the future privations of the life of a teacher of the poor.
(Committee of Council Minutes, 1842-1843, pp. 261-263)

Condescending attitudes such as those adopted by the founders of Battersea did not go wholly uncriticized; the Rev. Derwent Coleridge, principal of St. Mark's College at Chelsea, remarked in 1862 that:

Humbling and laborious discipline; a rigid simplicity in dress, diet, and external accommodation; sound elementary instruction; above all, the substitution of religious principle for wordly motive: all this looked well upon paper, and recommended itself strongly to the religious mind of the country. . . . In itself it was a noble scheme . . . (but) there lay in the scheme itself . . . a latent injustice unperceived, and unintended by its authors and abettors, but sure to be keenly felt by those to whom it was addressed. It seemed to say, 'We are about to bestow upon you a privilege of a high and spiritual nature, but we do not intend that you shall reap the wordly advantages with which it is ordinarily accompanied . . . in outward circumstances you must remain as you are . . .'
(Rev. Derwent Coleridge, The Teachers of the People, 1862, pp. 29-30)

Training colleges in the later nineteenth century

A pervasive meanness of spirit appears in many cases to have characterized the *ethos* of later nineteenth-century training colleges. F. H. Spencer, with typical honesty and balance, recalled that at Borough Road he had 'according to my then standards (and perhaps relatively any standards), a good time'. His assessment of the instruction there was more qualified but, in part at least, warm:

The professional training . . . was inadequate, and the school practice worthless, where not positively harmful. But our real concern was the academic instruction. Though necessarily this connoted preparation for examinations and little more, I have no doubt at all that the teaching we got was generally good, often stimulating, and sometimes inspiring.[5]

Others were less fortunate in their choice of college: for example, the moustachioed Battersea student who was commanded by the principal to 'Shave off that bit of hair. It makes you look like a twopenny-halfpenny caricature' – an unfeeling remark, to say the least, while, on occasion teaching was conducted with an inadequacy which appears to have verged on the cynical. As one woman ex-student ruefully recalled:

Once in the week a certain number repaired to the Laundry, where they scrubbed huckaback towels for an hour. This was called 'Practical Instruction in Domestic Economy'.
(Report of the Board of Education, 1912-1913, p. 64)

Another was reluctant to dignify with its official title the kind of instruction which he had received:

I use the term 'lectures', for thus was the teaching described; but I must take exception to it altogether, for with two exceptions, the Vice-Principal's Mathematics and the Third Master's Perspective Drawing, the instruction was entirely the text-book with notes dictated to, and copied by, each student.

The Principal's Holy Scripture, Liturgy, and English were simply the text and notes often gathered together then and there, and with, I am sure, little or no preparation.

The Vice-Principal's subjects – Euclid, Arithmetic, and Algebra – did not lend themselves to much lecturing, but he was especially clever, could, and did, come down to our level, took much interest in us individually, and earned our gratitude. His Second Year History was, however, confined to the text-book and the reading to us of long chapters from Hallam's Constitutional History.

The Third Master's Geography was purely the getting-up of several pages of the text-book and being questioned upon them. We drew what maps we thought most useful. The only Geography lecture he ever gave us was on 'the tides' at the annual inspection of H.M. Inspector. So good was it that I took copious notes, and was afterwards reprimanded for my inattention. Like little boys we were expected 'to look at teacher'. First Year History was taken similarly, and the Theory of Music was a series of wholly dictated notes which I still have by me.

The Method Master's School management 'took the cake', for it consisted solely of notes lifted bodily from two or three text-books and dictated. This was an absolute waste of time, for some of us had read much of this during our apprenticeship, and

had the books by us. This Master was also Head of the Practising School, and it was fortunate that most of us had had serious practice in teaching previously, for we learnt none here.
(Report of the Board of Education, 1912-1913, pp. 58-59)

But the student's academic life in college was not wholly passive. His role might be abruptly transformed into an embarrassingly prominent one:

An important feature of the College routine (wrote Thomas Adkins) is the weekly criticism lessons. Everybody is assembled in the theatre, both the bodies of students and the whole of the staff, under the presidency of the Principal, all being critics to a man. Before them is a class of little boys from the practising school, and in front of the class, the cynosure of all eyes, stands the victim. A copy of the notes of the lesson prepared is handed to the Principal; and then, a hundred pencils being ready to jot down his deficiencies, and an equal number of tongues awaiting the opportunity of declaring them, the teacher of the occasion addresses himself to his task. The majority stand the ordeal excellently, and many very fine lessons are given. Occasionally, however, somebody suffers from nerves, and, though anything but happy himself, is the cause of much quiet enjoyment to his audience. Here, for instance, is our friend giving a lesson on milk, and seeking now and then to fortify himself by taking a drink from his specimen, and further, in a burst of generosity, handing it on to his class of little boys, with 'Here, take a drink all round!' Then here is another who, absent-mindedly, keeps putting his specimens into his pockets and losing them. . . . Or, yet again, another who, in a moment of forgetfulness, assists a lazy little boy with an application of his foot from behind . . .
(Thomas Adkins, The History of St. John's College, Battersea, 1906, pp. 198-199)

James Runciman, drawing upon his own experiences at the old Borough Road institution, paints a portrait of college life during the 1870s which has a touch of the Grand Guignol about it:

At half-past nine a bell rang, and the young men, to the number of a hundred and twenty, trooped into a lecture-room, which looked like a squalid model of one end of the Coliseum. Tiers of rickety, narrow desks rose from the floor and sloped upwards to a height of about fourteen feet. The walls were greasy, leprous, bedizened with tattered maps. A vast blackboard stood in one corner, and an oaken table curved within the lowermost row of desks. It was hard to sit in the queer seats, for they were contrived, like everything in the building, with a view to combining discomfort and ugliness in the most appalling proportions.

. . .

The stairs were bare, and the hoarse winds that moaned around the building forced their way in, and swept shrieking over the cold stones. . . . Long lines of cells stretched like rows of horse-boxes from right to left. Each cell was open at the top, and the men were only separated from each other by a low partition, so that privacy was practically unknown. The frolicsome winds whisked merrily round each bare inhospitable compartment, and the murmur of conversation echoed along the ceiling. . . . No candles were allowed, and the men who were farthest away from the gas had to grope their way to bed amid lurching shadows and chance lights. Reeking slums surrounded the building. . . . Reeling figures moved along the foul pavement; the beer-house windows glimmered dimly, and the murmur of drunken babble rose softly to the ear. Frowsy women came to uncurtained windows and calmly proceeded to undress; sharp silhouettes were marked on the few blinds that appeared in the ghastly row. There came a sound of shrill scolding; then a growl like that of a beast, then the thud of a blow, then a long quavering shriek, and a trample of many feet; then a strained throbbing silence . . .

A bell rattled with impatient clamour; a dragging chorus of yawns resounded. Thumps on the floor showed that the reluctant youngsters were rising, and the splash of many basins tinkled oddly. The British notions of cleanliness were sternly set at naught at the Russell Street College; each youth washed himself as best he could in a minute basin, but the cold tub was unknown. The pious founders apparently considered that washing takes the stamina out of a man, and they arranged so as to let every student cleanse himself in the orthodox way about once a month.

. . .

There was not a picture or an ornament in any room; the asceticism of a workhouse was blended with the solidity and ugliness of a gaol, and the combination formed the abode of a hundred and twenty eager, hopeful lads . . .

The students lived the repressed, arid, bleak life of charity-children. No man could have a moment of privacy until he was in bed. The barren, foetid rooms, with their greasy forms and notched desks, were the only places where a letter could be written, and many a poor fellow, sick with heartache, had to sit down in a miserable class-room and compose his letters while lively comrades shouted and carried on horseplay all round him. If a man had tried to go up to his bedroom for an hour of quiet thought, he would, in all probability, have been dismissed for the offence . . .

At night there was a sorrowful interval between half-past eight and half-past nine. The hard-reading men ground on in spite of the clamour; the others squatted listlessly on tables or crowded around the dismal grates.

Smoking was regarded as a crime too serious for mention, but, of course, the men who had learned to smoke could not be prevented from taking their pipes after hours. No grounds were attached to the melancholy place, but at the back there was a narrow flagged yard, like the square in which Millbank prisoners take exercise, and there the smokers gathered when the weather was warm enough. On bitter winter nights the school of smokers hid themselves in any filthy corner where they happened to be secure from observation, and they chatted and puffed with doleful satisfaction . . .

At dinner the position of refined men was humiliating. Silence was enforced, and the rows of students sat like images on the mean forms, and the food was passed down in rough platefuls. The meat was of the best, and an unwholesome mouthful of any kind never appeared on the table; but the mode of serving was brutally coarse. Manners were forgotten, and the greediest men grabbed at the vegetables with silent vulture-like eagerness. An ugly white mug was put down beside each plate, and only water was allowed . . .

Good, sound, plentiful food was spoiled by the piggish service, and the ceremony of dining was something to be remembered in grey, unhappy dreams.*
(James Runciman, Schools and Scholars, 1887, pp. 136-139, 155-158)

---

*James Runciman and Matthew Arnold had their differences, but at least they agreed in condemning the uncouth way in which training college meals were served. In *A French Eton* Arnold reflects disapprovingly upon '. . . the stained cloth, napkinless knives and forks, jacks and mugs, hacked joints of meat, and stumps of loaves, which I have seen on dinner-tables of normal schools in England.'

Day training colleges

Day training colleges, of which the present university departments of education constitute mutated forms, originated in England and Wales subsequent to the reports of the Cross Commission. Their creation, enthusiastically described by R. W. Rich as 'one of the most important points in the history of teachers' training in England', initiated the process which was ultimately to lead to the theoretical withdrawal of central authority control over the certification of teachers. A concise account of the foundation and early problems of these new colleges was given in the Board of Education Report of 1912-1913:

Both majority and minority (reports of the Cross Commission) recommended that experiments should be made in the training of non-residential students attending institutions of higher learning. The majority were in favour of the training being given in University Colleges, and against the establishment of rate-supported Colleges. The minority considered that the training of teachers might well be aided by local rates, and were in favour of the establishment of Day Training Colleges under local authorities as well as in connection with Universities. Both parties, however, recommended that day students should be admitted to residential Colleges without any denominational test, and that the training of certain selected students should be extended for a third year.

. . .

The regulations issued by the Education Department in 1890 substantially embodied the recommendations of the majority report. For the first time Day Training Colleges attached to some University or College of University rank received recognition and day students were admitted to residential Colleges. But the total number of day students was not allowed to exceed 200 in all.

In addition to this very important departure from the system which had been in force since 1846, the regulations of 1890 also sanctioned a third year of training for certain selected students. Before long, the extra year came to be granted freely to students reading for a final Degree Examination.

The restriction of the number of day students to 200 disappeared from the Code of 1891, and the Day Colleges soon began to increase in number and size. The first Colleges which had taken advantage of the new regulations in 1890 were King's College, London (recognised for 25 men students), Mason's College, Birmingham (40 women students), Durham College (20 men and women students), Owen's College, Manchester (25 men students), University College, Nottingham (30 men and women students), and University College, Cardiff (31 men and women students). In the year 1891-92, with the removal of the restriction in number, each of these Colleges was recognised for about twice the number of students. In addition, Cambridge University (25 men), Yorkshire College, Leeds (15 men), University College, Liverpool (30 men), and Sheffield, Firth College (20 men and women), first obtained recognition in 1891. In the following year, 1892-93, recognition was accorded to Oxford University (25 men), Bristol University College (30 women), London University College (25 men), and Aberystwyth University College (30 men and women). In subsequent years, Day Training Colleges were recognised at Bangor, Reading, Southampton, Exeter, and in Southampton Street, London; new departments for men or women were opened at some of the Colleges already mentioned, and the number of recognised students generally increased. By the year 1903, the total number of students for which the Day Training Colleges were recognised amounted to over 2,000.

. . .

Changes in the Residential Colleges . . .

Whilst the stronger students in the Day Colleges fared better than they could have done in the old Residential Colleges, the weaker probably fared worse. In the first place, many of the Day College students neither obtained University degrees nor even made progress towards them. On the contrary, not more than about 130 passed degree examinations in 1903, a year in which about 830 completed their period of training, and about 230 more passed the Intermediate Examination of a Univeristy. Moreover, 81 of the degrees were obtained in five Colleges, and in several Colleges the work for University examinations amounted to very little.

. . .

Other difficulties were due to the conditions of life in the new Colleges. Their students, if they gained in some ways by not residing in College, undoubtedly lost in others.

Even if their homes were within easy reach of the College, they did not always enjoy the privacy and facilities for uninterrupted study which a Residential College ought to provide. The case of students living at a distance – especially women students – was worse. They had either to make a tiring journey to and from College daily or to live in lodgings. Rules for the supervision of lodgings were introduced from the first, but life in such lodgings as were available for students of narrow means, was often less pleasant and healthy than life in College. Further, the intending teachers did not enjoy, so commonly as had been expected, the advantages of contact with students of other types. The fact that they could not confine themselves to the University course but had to study also certain professional subjects, tended to keep them apart from the other students.

(Report of the Board of Education, 1912-1913, pp. 28-33 passim)

This last point – the lack of integration of education students with the generality of the undergraduate body – was reiterated by Elspeth Huxley, who studied (with increasing disillusion) at Reading University in the mid-1920s. Her comments provide a sad and perhaps cautionary epitaph to that first period of training college-university flirtation which had resulted from the Cross Commission's recommendations.

I soon discovered that, as in all walks of English life, this unpretentious university of some eight hundred lower middle class students was honeycombed with subtle snobberies. There was a pecking order among studies as well as among people; agriculture ranked high, not because farming was regarded as a snob pursuit – very few of the 'agri' students were likely to plough a furrow or hoe a field of roots, and we had no sons of landowners – but because most of the graduates would join the staff of some local authority or government department, the latter often in the Empire as it then was . . .

So to be an 'agri' was all right, and so was a 'horti'; pure scientists, historians and classicists occupied a middle range, and at the bottom, I regret to say, came the future teachers, who read for a two-years' diploma instead of for a three or four-years' degree. Why future teachers should have been so poorly thought of, I do not know – I suppose because they were so poorly paid. 'Edu's' tended to cluster together looking earnest, pallid (probably from malnutrition) and even more

drearily dressed than the rest of us; to dodge coffees in the buttery because twopence was beyond their means; and, if girls, to live in a remote hall called St. George's that no one else ever visited.
(Elspeth Huxley, Love Among the Daughters, 1968, p. 49)

CONFUSED ALARMS: TEACHER-TRAINING IN THE TWENTIETH CENTURY

Throughout the nineteenth century, the training colleges had functioned as *ad hoc* institutions for intending teachers. Their courses consisted of two elements – a vocational course of classroom skills and an adacemic education whose programme, as F. H. Spencer observed, initially at least 'resembled what we should now call a general secondary education of the non-specialized sixth form order'.[6]

In the late nineteenth and early twentieth centuries, however, this latter function became increasingly overshadowed by the expansion of advanced courses within the secondary grammar schools. At the same time, the failure of the university-linked day training college schemes seemed to illustrate the general inability of the training colleges to participate in academic work of a genuinely postsecondary standard. Lacking the standing necessary to establish an unquestioned academic identity of their own, the training colleges began to appear as isolated and anomalous institutions in what was developing into a unified and continuous system of secondary and higher education. Professionally their reputation was not particularly high: 'The professional training . . . was inadequate,' reflected F. H. Spencer, 'and the school practice worthless, where not positively harmful.'[7] By the 1880s doubts were being voiced about the viability of training colleges as independent institutions. James Runciman, that forceful critic, saw only one solution to the problem:

You have sent the schoolmaster abroad, but before sending him, you allow priests and potterers to ruin his intellect, to lower his manhood, to deny him almost all humanising culture, to deprive him of the polish that makes social intercourse graceful and charming . . .
Get rid of priestly interference; affiliate all (colleges) to the great universities; give the teachers a fair chance; and in twenty years the British artisans will have reason to be proud of themselves.
(J. Runciman, Schools and Scholars, 1887, pp. 169-170)

Runciman's advocacy of a connection between the training colleges and the universities was, of course, to be reflected in the day training college schemes of the 1890s. The theme was to become a constant one. Indeed, the anxiety of the training colleges to secure a university connection was only to be exceeded by the reluctance of the universities themselves to be inveigled into a relationship which seemed to threaten their status as élitist academic and nonvocational institutions. The comment of one vice-chancellor in 1944 that the training colleges were 'an unlovely lot to ask the universities to take an interest in'[8] was perhaps no more than a crude statement of widely held university opinion. From about 1911, moreover, the universities themselves began to provide vocational postgraduate courses for intending teachers.[9] Though many of their students were destined for secondary posts, the university training departments contained, by the early 1920s, more than one-quarter of the students training to be elementary teachers.[10] The 3 + 1 degree-based training course had thus come to represent an alternative with whose academic status the concurrent training college courses could hardly hope to compete.

In the circumstances, it was not surprising, therefore, that in 1923 a departmental committee was set up under Lord Burnham to investigate the training of teachers for public elementary schools. In its report (which appeared two years later) the committee noted the incompatibility of training colleges with the developing pattern of state-aided education; examining the changes from the 1890s onward, it claimed that:

The common element in all these movements is clear, the tendency to merge the arrangements for the education and training of teachers in the general organisation of the national system. They suggest the principle that the general education (if not the professional training) of those who are to be teachers in Elementary Schools should follow the same lines and be pursued in the same circumstances as the general education of their contemporaries.

The committee therefore suggested that students who had obtained a Higher School Certificate at secondary school should be exempted from further academic work in college:

We think that, broadly speaking, the Secondary Schools may fairly be expected, from now on, to take over a large and increasing share of the work for all students of less than degree standard, and that the Training Colleges should become, *pari passu*, institutions for vocational education primarily.
(*Report of the Departmental Committee on the Training of Teachers for Public Elementary Schools, 1925, pp. 24 and 84*)

The implication of these suggestions was that training colleges should become academically low-grade replicas of the existing postgraduate university departments of education. The board, however, unhesitatingly approved them, accepting in part the even more radical minority recommendation that courses should be reduced in length to one year. The proposed new scheme was outlined in Circular 1377 (1926): students whose level of attainment was limited to the School Certificate would undergo a two-year course at training college, while those who had reached Higher School Certificate level could qualify for admission to a course 'wholly consisting of one year's professional training'.

Had Circular 1377 and the Draft Regulations of 1926 been enforced, training colleges would by implication have been excluded from the sector of higher education. As it was, however, the colleges' opposition persuaded the board to refer a final decision on the matter to the new joint boards which were being set up in accordance with the departmental committee's 38th recommendation:

That the establishment of examining boards should be encouraged, representative of universities and the Governing Bodies of Training Colleges, to examine students of a College or of a group of Colleges for the purpose of the recognition of the students by the Board as Certificated Teachers.

The joint board compromise

The joint boards represented the committee's attempt to replace the Board of Education's control of certification by creating area coordination committees to determine syllabuses and administer certificate examinations. The presence of university representatives would, it was hoped, enhance the academic respectability of the certificate without entangling the universities in a direct relationship with the training colleges. As the committee itself bluntly pointed out, there could be no question of the universities amalgamating with the colleges; to give all student teachers a full four-year course would almost double the numbers and radically change the character of the universities. An experiment to provide a four-year course leading to a London University degree was in fact instituted at Westminster College in 1930, but this was an exceptional case and recognized as such.[11] By 1930, the year in which a Central Advisory Committee was appointed to standardize their work, eleven joint boards had been set up, thereby establishing a real though tenuous connection between the colleges and the universities. S. H. Wood, later head of the Board's Teacher Training Branch and an influential member of the McNair Committee of 1942-1944, was to analyse the situation in these terms:

. . . it cannot be said that the present relationship is, at any rate constitutionally, a relationship with a university, but only with a Joint Board to which the university appoints representatives. The Joint Board has no authority to deal with anything except examinations and the syllabus of study which examinations involve. In short, the Colleges, having properly been released from the Board's apron strings, have evolved no disciplined adult relationship with any other body.
(S. W. Wood, Memorandum of 12 March 1943, McNair Committee Papers No. 102, PRO Ed. 86/94)

The McNair Report

In March 1942 a committee was appointed under the chairmanship of Sir Arnold McNair (the vice-chancellor of Liverpool University) 'to investigate the present sources of supply and the methods of recruitment and training of teachers and youth leaders and to report what principles should guide the board in these matters in the future'. The basic reason for this step was that the anticipated postwar expansion of the state system of education would require the training of between 50,000 and 90,000 additional teachers, many of whom would be required in the relatively specialized fields of nursery, secondary, and further education.[12] The McNair Committee worked under the shadow of the Norwood Report, the White Paper on Educational Reconstruction and the Education Bill itself. On one vital point its conclusions were unanimous:

We realise the immense importance to the country of securing as teachers an adequate supply of men and women of character, and we are convinced that nothing but drastic reforms involving the expenditure of considerable additional sums of public money will secure what the schools need and what children and young people deserve.[13]

But there was an irreconcilable cleavage of opinion within the committee as to the nature of the 'drastic reforms' necessary. In his covering letter to R. A. Butler (the president of the Board of Education) McNair felt compelled to write that

. . . I greatly regret that in one respect (the report) contains a headache for you, namely, our difference of opinion on the subject of the relation of the Universities to the new area training organisations. It is a fundamental difference and it was not possible to bridge it.

Training colleges, the committee had agreed, were in general inadequate on a number of counts. But the members were split down the middle when it came to formulating a solution. Five, led by S. H. Wood, advocated an intimate college-university relationship: 'The "idea" of a separate, wholly autonomous self-contained Training College must disappear and be replaced by the idea of a component part of a service . . .' argued Wood, and he suggested that pressure should be brought upon the universities 'to accept a special responsibility' for the training of teachers.[14] This group subsequently proposed that each university should establish a school of education which 'should consist of an organic federation of approved training institutions working in cooperation with other approved educational institutions . . .'[15]

McNair himself and his supporters, on the other hand, viewed any idea of 'organic federation' between training colleges and universities with alarm. In a classic exposition of the university view, McNair himself pointed out that if training college students were to be associated with universities on anything less than a basis of full equality they would constitute 'a helot class of student'. But if, on the other hand, they were to be genuinely absorbed into the undergraduate body 'the total number of university students in

England and Wales would be virtually doubled'. This, uncompromisingly argued McNair, would be deleterious to the true interests of the universities:

I think that probably the main point on which I differ from Mr. Wood is as to the true function of the Universities. That is, in my opinion, to advance knowledge and to *educate the leaders* in every walk of life to which University education can make a contribution – teachers of all kinds, administrators, clergy, doctors, divines, lawyers, scientists, etc., but it is unlikely that they will ever educate all of these persons. A University is not capable of infinite expansion, and it is only very slowly that the Universities can be enlarged, or new Universities established without destroying their real national value. Moreover, Universities must continually be vigilant lest they become too much training establishments and too little educational institutions.
(A. McNair, Supply and Training of Teachers, 12 April 1943, McNair Committee Papers R.498/101, PRO Ed. 86/94)

McNair's views received a resolute endorsement from the committee of university vice-chancellors. While the latter were prepared to recognize that 'public opinion looks to the university for a lead in raising the standards of the teaching profession as a whole . . .', they flatly refused to countenance any strengthening of the university-training college link:

. . . the universities are *not* adequately staffed for closer relationships with the training colleges . . .
We feel that the disadvantage which the training colleges suffer from segregation cannot be cured by the universities. The numbers involved and the geographical facts force us to think that the remedy must lie in one or other of two directions. Either the training colleges must cease to be monotechnic and must link up with the polytechnic work of their own areas or the policy of recruiting teachers from those with some other previous experience (including experience of marriage and motherhood) must be carried so far that it will no longer be necessary to staff our schools with those who have only two segregated years between leaving schools and returning to them as teachers.
(McNair Papers, Committee Paper No. 81)

Opinions such as these led McNair and his group of supporters to propose that the existing joint boards should remain in a strengthened form and 'that the Joint Board thus reconstituted should become responsible for the organisation of an area training service in which there will be a university training department and training colleges preserving their identity and being in direct relation with the Board of Education and the Central Training Council . . .'[16]

The issue, then, was whether the training colleges should be integrated in 'an organic federation' with the proposed university schools of education ('Scheme A') or whether they should 'preserve their identity' under the joint boards ('Scheme B'). Among those in favour of the schools of education concept were the representatives on the committee of the Board of

Education and the National Union of Teachers; their views were additionally endorsed by the influential Association of Directors and Secretaries for Education, whose secretary considered that 'The training of teachers had now reached a stage which demanded the abolition of the Training Colleges in their present form.'[17] Nor was university support entirely lacking: Lord Eustace Percy, speaking as vice-chancellor of Durham University, stated that he 'would like to make Training Colleges in suitable geographical positions actually a part of Universities . . .'[18]

But the weight of university opinion was decisively against any extension of the joint board kind of relationship, the committee of vice-chancellors proposing an alternative formula for the future development of training colleges which would involve their abandonment of the monotechnic idea in favour of a link-up with the polytechnics.

The training colleges themselves took up an interesting position on these issues. Even they were prepared to abandon (at least partially) their monotechnic character, agreeing that 'There should be a wider conception of the function of the colleges, which should not be limited to training teachers only but to social workers generally . . . .' They also sought 'a closer and more integral' relationship with the universities. But at the same time they vigorously rejected suggestions that teachers generally should receive a university education:

One thing was clear and that was that the training of teachers – all teachers – could not be and ought not to be handed over to the Universities. It could not be, because the Universities would not be able to deal with the numbers . . . and it ought not to be, because of the aloofness of the Universities from the education of the people. The Universities have no contact with the Elementary Schools;* they do not speak the same language. By contrast the Training Colleges are at home with every kind of school except the Preparatory and Public Schools.
(McNair Committee Paper 21: evidence from the Standing Committee of the Training College Association and Council of Principals, PRO Ed. 86/94)

It has already been noted that the McNair Committee insisted that teacher training was in need of 'drastic reforms'. The 22 university departments of education had their own peculiar difficulties, arising 'partly from the poor regard in which Education has in the past been held by some universities and partly from the related fact that training departments tend to be conducted as self-contained units.' By the time of the McNair Report, the university departments of education had, however, long shed their original day training college image;[19] although, as the report emphasized, they had not obtained total integration with the universities, they had achieved a decisive separation from the training colleges themselves. From 1895

---

*In fact, as the McNair Report was itself to point out, 60 percent of the students from university departments of education subsequently taught in elementary schools.

onwards a number of university professorships had been established in education, first in Wales at Aberystwyth and Bangor and then, after the turn of the century, in England.* The close connection between universities and departments had been acknowledged in the 1904 and the 1911 Regulations for the Training of Teachers. The latter carefully defined the 3 + 1 course pattern (three years of undergraduate subject studies followed by one year of professional training) which was eventually to become characteristic of the graduate teacher. In the late 1930s and early 1940s the annual output of the university training departments was about 1500 teachers (compared with about 5000 from the colleges). Most of these were four-year students who had 'signed the pledge' to enter teaching after their university education and had in return received a state grant. This procedure was condemned by the committee, which observed that

It is common knowledge . . . that many students in receipt of earmarked grants for the recognised four-year course at universities are not there because they have freely chosen to be teachers but because the Declaration and its attendant grants offer them a chance which would otherwise be denied to them of obtaining a university education and particularly a university degree.
(The McNair Report, Teachers and Youth Leaders, 1944, p. 90)

The McNair Committee in fact recommended the abolition of the 'pledge' for all students, whether at training college or university and, following a further request from the National Advisory Council on the Training and Supply of Teachers in 1948, the last batch of students for the old four-year course was admitted to university in 1950. The postgraduate certificate, however, was not to become compulsory (and then in a rather desultory way) for graduates entering the teaching profession until the early 1970s.

The McNair Committee discerned problems and inadequacies of a different order in the 83 teacher training colleges. On one hand, there existed the perennial criticism that their narrow vocationalism made them incompatible with the general pattern of education: '. . . any proposal,' suggested the committee, 'in response to an effective demand, to provide courses for students preparing for another profession should be encouraged.' But even within their own circumscribed aims, the colleges were defective on a number of material and ethical grounds: 'What is chiefly wrong with the majority of the training colleges is their poverty and all that flows from it.'[20] In a later passage the report drew attention to

. . . the comparatively poor estimation in which training colleages have been held. They have never ranked in the public mind as institutions which have a duty as regards the promotion of research and investigation in the field of education, and they have been financed according to the cheap standards to which we have already referred. The remedy for this is to lift the colleges to a higher plane by, among other

---

*Chairs of education had been established at Edinburgh and St. Andrews as early as 1876.

things, offering conditions of service as regards teaching hours comparable with those which prevail in the universities. Only so will the colleges extricate themselves from their present position and fit themselves for their new tasks.
(The McNair Report, Teachers and Youth Leaders, 1944, p. 73)

This poverty was, in the committee's opinion, reflected in the colleges' unimpressive material condition:

In 50 per cent of the colleges the laboratories, studios, workshops and gymnasia are inadequate. More than 50 per cent have no music room. In more than 25 per cent of the colleges the assembly halls, libraries, lecture rooms or dining accommodation are inadequate. Nearly 60 per cent have no cinema projector and more than 30 per cent have no broadcasting reception equipment for teaching purposes . . .[21]

They had difficulty in attracting good staff:

To transfer from a secondary school to a training college often means . . . to transfer from a reasonable prospect of promotion to a service which is a blind alley . . .[22]

And they tended to constrict the development of their students in both an academic and a social sense:

Many students in training colleges do not mature by living: they survive by hurrying.[23]

The N.U.T. (one of the more scathing of the training colleges' critics) had alleged in its evidence that 'There were colleges where the students seemed to have to fight continually against the Principal for the ordinary rights of men and women';[24] the McNair Committee rejected this charge so far as the majority were concerned and indeed commented favourably upon the 'vigorous social life' of many colleges, noting only that

There are, however, some that have not emancipated themselves from the narrow and inflexible traditions of the past. Their attitude results both in stunting the development of the students in their charge and in deterring other young people from adopting a profession, the training for which appears to involve an amount of control and of interference with their private lives which separates them from the vast majority of their own generation.
(The McNair Report, Teachers and Youth Leaders, 1944, p. 77)

McNair to Robbins (1944-1963)

The alternative schemes of training organization recommended in the McNair Report were correctly interpreted as evidence of division within the educational world. The board, for its part, made no secret of its preference for the university-orientated Scheme A; the university vice-chancellors, however, inasmuch as they favoured either alternative, preferred Scheme B, which would have ensured a continued state of separation between colleges and universities. Compromise was necessary, and the urbane president of the board, R. A. Butler, was able to achieve this by assuring the universities that in a Scheme A situation they alone would have the crucial prerogative to define the nature of the 'organic federation'[25] between training colleges and universities.

Thus within a decade sixteen area training organizations had been established. All but one of these were based upon McNair's Scheme A. But whether many of them actually represented much more than a cosmetic alteration to the preexisting joint board relationship was open to doubt. In 1963 the Robbins Committee on Higher Education found it necessary to 'recommend a return' to the basic McNair Scheme A doctrine, and, in surveying the intervening period, referred to

> the view that the link between the universities and the Training Colleges had not proved as beneficial to the colleges as might have been hoped. The Colleges were not in the main stream of university life, hardly any of their students could get degrees and in many cases students and staff did not share in the activities of the university. At the same time their semi-dependence on the universities had in the eyes of some people inhibited the leading colleges from developing to the stature that they might have achieved in different circumstances. They did not enjoy in this country the same sort of esteem as, say, the Leningrad Pedagogical Institute does in the Soviet Union, and the reluctance to introduce the kind of distinctions between colleges that has become a feature of technical education in recent years has prevented any of them emerging with the same vigour and effectiveness as the Colleges of Advanced Technology.
> *(The Robbins Report, Higher Education, 1963, para. 348)*

But in the surge of expansiveness which followed its assumption that 'reserves of untapped ability' existed in the higher education age-group, the Robbins Committee made a determined attempt to clinch the McNair package, recommending that

> The colleges should have independent governing bodies and should be financed by earmarked grants made through the Grants Commission . . . through universities to the Schools of Education.[26]

and that the more able students of the newly autonomous colleges should be allowed that ultimate accolade of academic respectability, a university degree. As a further bonus the committee suggested that the colleges should be individually expanded to accommodate 750 or more students and that they should be given the more impressive title (imported from Scotland) of colleges of education.[27] There was no mention of diversification or absorption. It seemed as though the training college as an institution had finally made the grade as a permanent, *bona fide* feature of the university scene: a truly Cinderella-like transformation; and one which, it should be added, was to prove scarcely more durable.

One standard comment upon the proposals of the Robbins Committee has been that their implementation tended to be quantitative rather than qualitative.[28] This was certainly applicable to the colleges of education during the 1960s. In 1962-1963 they had a total of 48,400 places; by 1967-1968 these had increased to 94,800[29] – a figure well in excess of the Robbins recommendation of 75,200. But qualitatively the status of the colleges remained largely unaltered. Despite the increasing number of Bachelor of Education degrees being awarded from 1968 on, they signally failed to obtain integration with the universities. And the simultaneous evolution of the binary concept of higher education, together with the emergence of a new generation of academically privileged and expansionist L.E.A.-owned polytechnics, was opening up the possibility of an alternative kind of connection – and one in many ways more attractive to L.E.A.s and government alike.

Perhaps unexpectedly, the most cogent objections to the college-university link-up envisaged by Robbins do not appear to have come from the universities. Within a year of the report's appearance, every university senate (except those of London, Sussex, Oxford, and Cambridge) had in principle accepted its proposals for schools of education (though in many cases without much enthusiasm). The university departments of education themselves were more active in their support. The hard core of opposition in fact originated from central and local authorities – especially the latter. The L.E.A.s, as owners of 98 out of the 146 colleges of education[30] (and, of course, as the employers of the teachers that they produced), tended to be reluctant to relinquish possession and control of their colleges. They had already, as a result of Robbins, lost the colleges of advanced technology to the autonomous sector and indeed the only member of the Robbins Committee itself to add a note of reservation to the report had been H. C. Shearman, who had strong L.E.A. connections. He argued cogently against college-university integration:

The pressing need in this sector of higher education is not only to consolidate and extend the academic gains of the three-year course* (a bold and far-sighted venture) but also to carry through the great expansion of numbers on which we have embarked. In most of the cases with which we are concerned the local education authorities have the staffs and technical resources to contribute to this development as they are already demonstrating and as they have done in the past. They know the need better than most and they have a vital interest in the supply of teachers of suitable quality and in adequate numbers. I believe their resources, both of know-how and of goodwill, could be harnessed to the common task if the universities would consent to create their Schools of Education and provide for degrees at the earliest possible date without disrupting the administrative partnership which already exists.

(The Robbins Report, Higher Education, 1963, p. 295)

Shearman's view was ultimately to be endorsed both by the Labour

---

*A McNair recommendation introduced in 1960.

government in 1964 (acting upon the advice of the University Grants Committee) and by the Conservative opposition, the separation of teacher training from the L.E.A.s being considered, in the words of Edward Boyle

. . . quite out of the question, in the middle of a large expansion of colleges and at a time when the problem of teacher supply clearly requires the closest contact between the training system and those responsible for staffing the schools.[31]

As a concession to college independence, the government in 1965 set up a study group under the prominent civil servant Toby Weaver to investigate the administration and control of colleges of education. The Weaver Report's subsequent recommendations did result in the colleges obtaining a measure of administrative independence and internal autonomy, but they were unable to alleviate the fundamental problem with failure to implement Robbins had once more brought into prominence – the incongruity of the colleges' position within an increasingly formalized and structured system of higher education.

Prelude to the James Report

In considering the top ability band of training college students, the Robbins Committee had estimated that by the mid-1970s about 25 percent of the total intake might be taking the four-year Bachelor of Education courses. But it said little about the quality of the concurrent certificate course which would remain for the rest. The standard of this had long been open to criticism. The departmental committee of 1925 had tended to equate its academic level with that of the Higher School Certificate, while the McNair Report had recommended that it should be strengthened by an extra year's study. But the sharply increased demand for teachers in the postwar period had compelled the government to introduce an Emergency Training Scheme which not only reduced course length, but also lowered entry qualification. Between 1946 and 1951, some 35,000 teachers (about 15 percent of the total teaching force) qualified after a drastically shortened course of one year. Less than half of those new entrants to the profession had initially possessed the School Certificate or equivalent qualifications.[32]

The eventual introduction of the three-year certificate course did not, seemingly, disperse all suspicion that standards were not what they should be. By the end of 1970, the Conservative government felt justified in appointing a committee headed by Lord James to investigate the whole question of teacher training; its terms of reference, which were to include a consideration of 'whether a larger proportion of intending teachers should be educated with students who have not chosen their careers or chosen other careers', were not calculated to reassure supporters of the training college ethos.

Symptomatic of the disquiet expressed in some quarters concerning the quality of teacher education was an influential article written by Harry Rée (then Professor of Education at York) which appeared in the *Times Educational Supplement* a few weeks before the appointment of the James Committee:

The marking season is over, external examiners have lugged their big suitcases full of scripts across the country, recommended 96⅔ per cent of the students as 'passes', made their reports to the institute, and got back to their families and their books. Probably most of us have had qualms of conscience. (Were we really right to fail that girl whose mother had been so ill?) But we filled in our expense sheet and sometime this autumn we'll get our cheques. But have we earned them?

. . .

Embarrassing questions arise. Has the three years' work of the college staff, and of the students, which was induced by these final exams contributed in any assessable or convincing way to converting novices into potentially better teachers than they would have been without having done the courses 'prescribed' by our exams?

In some important ways and for some students, the answer is 'Yes'. Some courses are demonstrably successful. The main course, for some, has opened up fields of interest and enjoyment which will make them more interesting and cheerful people – and therefore more interesting and confident teachers. But in some cases, let us be honest, the same course has turned out pedantic bores. And the study of philosophy, psychology, sociology and history of education will result in a few, a very few, students adopting a more understanding approach to children, parents and even to their colleagues. It is in connection with these, the so-called 'education' subjects, that we need to look most searchingly at what we are doing.

Is there a single one of us who can state confidently that the papers we have been marking in these subjects – with very occasional exceptions – have given evidence of 'good learning', that is, that students have taken in the concepts required for the exam, and assimilated them so that they could criticize them and use them? In fact, if we are honest, is there not plenty of evidence that the contrary is the case? For every student who has understood Peters or Piaget, Bernstein or Bloom there are surely 10 or even 20 who have memorized the notes they have written under these dutifully underlined names, but have failed entirely to receive their messages. For some, memorization is based on hearing about not on reading the work done by those names: thus we read of 'Gene Flood' and of 'Froballs'. Sometimes there is an accolade: 'Professor Peters is a man of great statue as an educational philosopher'.

But all of us could produce a bookful of howlers. Four learning weaknesses are much more worrying: the unconscious misunderstandings and misinterpretations; the huge unqualified generalizations; the repeated presentation of undigested and inert ideas; and the sloppy and uncritical use of language . . .

(Harry Rée, in 'The real exam results', Times Educational Supplement, 6 November 1970, p. 2)

Rée further accused the system of 'conniving at and even encouraging a form of academic dishonesty' which would be carried over into the schools. Criticisms such as these accentuated the exposed and vulnerable position of the colleges of education: the latter had, as a group, been repeatedly cold-shouldered by the universities; at the same time the creation of the new polytechnics (equipped to award degrees validated by C.N.A.A.) increasingly seemed to offer a logical and final solution to the long-standing problem of their academic and professional isolation. Hints to this effect emanating from governmental sources and from the polytechnics themselves combined, by the end of the decade, to give the L.E.A. colleges at least a feeling not unlike that of the Young Lady of Riga; in the tendentious words of Eric Robinson (deputy director of the North East London Polytechnic)

. . . as it becomes generally recognized that the future of most of the colleges of education must lie in assimilation with larger, more comprehensive institutions, it is very likely that some of them will find their way into polytechnics. The case for the immediate assimilation of the four colleges of education (technical) is obvious. Other colleges of education located in cities that have a polytechnic but no university are strong candidates for this.

Finally, I hope that education departments will play a full part in the development of polytechnics as a whole. . . . Perhaps they could become so important that they could be abolished by absorption!
(Eric Robinson, in Times Educational Supplement, 4 December 1970, p. 33)

To many in the colleges such threats to their independent existence seemed particularly unfair in view of the apparent new start given by the B.Ed. degree and the Weaver Report: 'there is a very real danger, as we see it,' wrote one college principal, 'that the clean new baby born of Weaver will be washed down with everyone else's dirty bath water.'[33] It was with some apprehension, therefore, that the teacher training world awaited the report of the James Committee, which appeared (with commendable expedition) in early 1972.

The James Report and the phasing-out of the colleges

Like its predecessor, the James Report was outspoken in its assessment of the existing pattern of teacher training: 'Criticisms of the present system, which we hold to be justified, point to the need for a radical solution.'[34] Unlike McNair, however, James inflexibly recommended a truly drastic revision of the education of college-trained teachers – a revision which was openly aimed at sweeping away the barriers which had traditionally segregated non-graduate student teachers from the mainstream of higher education. The foundations of training college separatism had for long lain in the concurrent certificate course, which, by almost inextricably combining professional training with academic learning, and by leading to the award of a highly vocational qualification, had effectively excluded all students other than those intending to teach. The James Committee resolved that on balance the inherent inadequacies of the concurrent certificate course outweighed its advantages; its first recommendation, therefore, required that the traditional certificate course structure should effectively be scrapped:

The education and training of teachers should be seen as falling into three consecutive stages or 'cycles': the first, personal education, the second pre-service training and induction, the third, inservice education and training.

Intending teachers, therefore, should devote the first part of their course to academic study; all professional training was to be excluded. This 'first cycle' might take the form of a three-year university or polytechnic degree course. Alternatively, the committee recommended the creation of an entirely new two-year academic qualification, the Diploma of Higher Education. Thus, after two years in a college of education, a student would have a nonvocational qualification of (hoped the committee) wide potential application:

For some students, the Dip. H.E. would be the basis for subsequent professional teacher training, but for others it would be a perfectly acceptable terminal qualification. Some might go on to train for certain other professions, and some might move on to degree courses in universities, polytechnics or within the college system.

The colleges would contain a large range of students who, on completing the diploma course, would proceed on a number of different paths. The colleges would therefore no longer be training teachers in isolation.

(The James Report, Teacher Education and Training, 1972, paragraphs 6.7-6.8)

The first cycle proposed by the James Committee meant, quite simply, the death of the traditional training college course; by implication it meant also the end of the training college. The professional element of the training course, rigidly screened from the first cycle, was to be confined to the second and third cycles and would thus be supernumary to the initial qualification. There was no implication, however, that professional work was to be regarded as being in any way of less significance to the training of teachers than the academic content of the first cycle Dip.H.E. course. For the James Committee regarded the successful completion of the professionally orientated second cycle as justifying the conversion of the Dip.H.E. to full degree status. It recommended that after the first year of the second cycle – one in which 'the emphasis should be unashamedly specialised and functional'[35] – a student should be designated a 'licensed teacher'; and that upon completion of the second year he would receive the degree of B.A. (Ed.):

For all intending teachers, the second cycle would consist of two years of professional preparation. The first year would normally be in a professional institution, whether a college of education or the education department of a university or polytechnic, and would cover both the theoretical exploration of disciplines contributing to the study of education, and practical work. The training would be specifically related to the teacher's prospective needs in his first appointment. . . . At the end of the first year, successful students would be recommended to the Secretary of State for recognition as 'licensed teachers' and would proceed to the second year of the cycle, which would consist of largely school-based training.

At the beginning of this second year, a licensed teacher would take up his first teaching assignment, but with a deliberately reduced timetable. He would be released for the equivalent of not less than one day a week, for attendance at a professional institution or 'professional centre' . . . where he would take part in discussions and seminars and have the opportunity for further study. He would be able to look for help and advice to a teacher on the staff of his school who would be designated a 'professional tutor', with particular responsibilities for helping new teachers on the staff and students-in-training receiving practical experience, as well as for co-ordinating the inservice training arrangements for all teachers in his school. The second year of the second cycle would thus combine the first year of service and the last year of initial training. Teachers successfully completing this year would become 'registered teacher', i.e. full members of the profession.
(The James Report, Teacher Education and Training, 1972, paragraphs 6.10-6.11)

With the introduction of the B.A. (Education) degree it was proposed that the post-Robbins B.Ed. 'should cease to exist in its present form as an initial qualification'. Students of good ability would have the opportunity to pursue courses of study leading to the further degree of M.A. (Education) either at the end of the second cycle or after teaching for a while.

The third cycle of teacher training, which the James Committee repeatedly (and largely unavailingly) emphasized as being crucial to the whole process, was based on Recommendations 10 and 15:

10   All teachers in schools and full-time staff in F.E. colleges should be entitled to release with pay for inservice education and training on a scale equivalent to not less than one school term (say, 12 weeks) in every seven years of service and, as soon as possible, the entitlement should be written into teachers' contracts of service.

. . .

15   To accommodate third cycle work, there should be a national network of 'professional centres' which would include not only the colleges and departments of education but also a number of other centres, based on existing facilities and in some cases developed from teachers' centres.

As the report explained:

The third cycle comprehends the whole range of activities by which teachers can extend their personal education, develop their professional competence and improve their understanding of educational principles and techniques. The term thus covers a wide spectrum, at one end of which are evening meetings and discussions, weekend conferences and other short-term activities, with limited and specific objectives and taking place usually, but not always, in the teachers' own time. At the other end are long courses leading to higher degrees or advanced qualifications, and requiring the release of teachers for full-time attendance at suitable establishments . . .
(The James Report, Teacher Education and Training, 1972, paragraph 2.2)

The final section of the report's proposal determinedly attempted to dissolve the A.T.O. connection between colleges and universities. What Lord James himself was later to describe as the bluff regarding the 'bogus business about close links with the universities'[36] was to be called: the university-centred A.T.O. system of McNair was to be replaced by a network of fifteen suggested regional councils; a National Council for Teacher Education and Training was to be linked with these and empowered to award the Dip.H.E., B.A., (Ed.) and M.A. (Ed.). The university departments of education, shorn of their central A.T.O. role, were to specialize 'in the teaching of certain subjects or groups of subjects, in which they would become centres of excellence, especially in the development of third cycle courses'.

Action on the James Report

Official reaction to the James Report appeared in the form of a White Paper, *Education: A Framework for Expansion*, almost exactly a year after its publication. The principle of creating new nonuniversity-centred regional councils was accepted, though the government refused to countenance any change in the validating agencies for teaching qualifications. The James third cycle recommendations were accepted – and then put into storage on account of the financial cutbacks of the early and mid-1970s: 'I hope the storage will not prove too cold,' reflected one of the committee members, Dr. Judge, in 1976, while another, James Porter, claimed that inservice education had been almost cynically rejected in the years following the report.[37] The suggestions for the induction year (the second year of the second cycle) were largely accepted (again in principle): five government-sponsored pilot schemes were planned.[38] Three of these were subsequently cancelled due to financial difficulties and two – in Liverpool and Northumberland – were initiated in the academic year 1973-1974. In all, 976 probationary teachers were involved, and in 1976 the D.E.S. phlegmatically reported that:

It appears . . . that the majority of the new teachers taking part have found the Liverpool and Northumberland schemes helpful and believe they should be maintained. They have reservations about certain aspects. . . . These largely stem from their strongly-felt need for help with their immediate classroom problems: the support offered has not always seemed to provide this.
(D.E.S. Reports on Education, No. 84, 1976, p. 7)

Individual L.E.A.s also started up schemes of their own – many of which were soon curtailed owing to lack of funds. The proposed second cycle award of B.A. (Ed.) fell flat, and the James Report's insistence upon the exclusion of concurrent teacher training courses was not endorsed by the government. Teacher training institutions displayed a dogged and occasionally surly attachment to concurrency: according to the *Times Higher Educational Supplement* by mid-1976 virtually only one college in England had followed the pattern suggested by James – and that was Bulmershe College of Higher Education, whose principal, James Porter, had been a member of the James Committee.[39]

Originally, however, the first cycle award of Dip.H.E. had been enthusiastically welcomed by the D.E.S., which devoted a whole section of the White Paper (ominously, perhaps, Section 13) to its future, considering that it deserved 'to serve a wider purpose than that envisaged' by the James Report and stating that 'courses on the lines proposed should be seen as a new option to be offered by institutions in each of the main sectors of higher education'. The decision to extend the availability of the Dip.H.E. (which had originally been designed by James mainly – though not exclusively – for colleges of education) meant in effect that the government had decided to phase out the colleges of education as such: as *Education: A Framework for Expansion* put it:

> The logic of the conclusions recorded in this White Paper is that, leaving aside those colleges which find their eventual home in a university, the substantial broadening of function proposed for the great majority of colleges of education will involve their much closer assimilation into the rest of the non-university sector of further and higher education. Put another way, a college which expands and diversifies, either alone or by joining forces with a sister college or a further education institution – enlarging the range of its courses and extending its clientele – will not be easily distinguishable by function from a polytechnic or other further education college.
> *(Education: A Framework for Expansion, 1972, paragraph 160)*

In a subsequent Circular (7/73) the D.E.S. was even more explicit: although it was prepared to tolerate the continued existence of a few colleges of education, it insisted that 'the number of such monotechnics cannot be large. . . . Some small colleges may need to be retained, perhaps on a reduced scale, as professional centres while others not so needed or badly located for such a purpose may have to close.'[40] The monotechnic college of education had, according to one prominent administrator, become 'an embarrassment' to the plans of the D.E.S.

But by 1973 the future of teaching training courses of any description seemed problematic. The reduced birth rate was making disastrous inroads into the need for new teachers. According to the 1972 White Paper, 'the number of initial training places required in the colleges and polytechnic departments of education by 1981 will be 60,000-70,000 compared with the 1971-72 figure of about 114,000.'[41] By 1977 further D.E.S. calculations estimated that the total number of training places needed by 1981 would be down to 46,670, of which over 20 percent would be allocated to induction and in-service courses.[42] The educational press appeared to take a lugubrious pleasure in devising gloomy headlines: 'Will anyone apply for teacher training in future?' rhetorically demanded the *Times Higher Education Supplement* in April 1976. A few months later the same journal (on this occasion under the heading of 'Teacher education: the worst is yet to come') analysed the combined effects of the James Report, the 1972 White Paper and the birth pill upon the 151 colleges of education: 5 of them had finally succeeded in merging with universities; 33 had (with varying degrees of reluctance) combined with polytechnics; 63 had been amalgamated into 44 colleges of higher and further education; 21 had been closed or were due for closure. Only 29 colleges of education (4 of which had been merged into 2 institutions) had precariously managed to survive as monotechnic teacher training establishments.[43] The Green Paper of 1977 underlined the official view: 'The Secretary of State,' it affirmed, 'shares the widespread view that teacher education and other higher education should be more closely integrated, both institutionally and in course structures . . .' For better or for worse, the Kay Shuttleworth age of teacher education was finally drawing to a close.

Notes

1   R. W. Rich, *The Training of Teachers in England and Wales during the Nineteenth Century*, 1933, p. 19.

2   *The School and the Teacher*, 1 August, 1861, p. 203.

3   R. W. Rich, op.cit., p. 232.

4   Hansard, Fourth Series, Vol. XXXIX, p. 533 (31 March 1896).

5   F. H. Spencer, *An Inspector's Testament*, 1938, p. 148.

6   F. H. Spencer, op.cit., p. 148.

7   Ibid.

8   W. R. Niblett, D. W. Humphreys and J. R. Fairhurst, *The University Connection*, 1975, p. 152. This book gives a readable and detailed account of the relationships between training colleges and universities from 1923 onwards.

9   Report of the Departmental Committee on the Training of Teachers for Public Elementary Schools, 1925, p. 20.

10   Ibid, p. 19.

11   Ibid, p. 78. For details of 'the Westminster experiment' see F. C. Pritchard, *The Story of Westminster College*, 1951, Chapter 13.

12   McNair Report, p. 6.

13   Ibid, p. 8.

14   McNair Committee Papers (P.R.O. Ed. 86/94), No. 102.

15   McNair Report, Recommendations 10(a) and (b).

16   Ibid, Recommendation 11(b).

17   McNair Committee Papers, No. 48 (Pro Ed. 86/94).

18   Ibid, No. 74.

19   The transition of the day training colleges to university departments of education is dealt with by J. P. Tuck's chapters in D. E. Lomax (ed.), *The Education of Teachers in Britain*, 1973.

20   McNair Report, p. 13.

21   Ibid, p. 14.

22   Ibid, p. 72.

23   Ibid, p. 65.

24   McNair Committee Papers, No. 30 (PRO Ed. 86/94)

25   W. R. Niblett, et al., op. cit., pp. 125-126.

26   Robbins Report, Recommendation 39.

27   Ibid, Recommendations 33, 28, and 34.

28   R. Layard, J. King and C. Moser, *The Impact of Robbins*, 1969, p. 22.

29   Ibid, p. 66.

30   Robbins Report, p. 27.

31   W. R. Niblett et al., op.cit., p. 232.

32   P. H. J. H. Gosden, *The Evolution of a Profession*, 1972, pp. 289-290.

33   Select Committee on Education and Science (Session 1969-1970), Teacher Training (Documents), p. 509.

34   James Report, p. 67.

35   Ibid, p. 23.

36   In *Times Educational Supplement*, 25 June 1976, p. 8.

37   Ibid.

38   D.E.S. Reports on Education, No. 84, March 1976, p. 1.

39   *Times Higher Education Supplement*, 25 June 1976, 'B. Ed. comes out top in colleges'.

40   D.E.S. Circular 7/73, 1973, pp. 6-7.

41   *Education: A Framework for Expansion*, 1972, p. 43.

42   *Times Higher Education Supplement*, 12 August 1977, p. 4.

43   *Times Higher Education Supplement*, 10 September 1976, p. 4.

CHAPTER 9

THE ADMINISTRATION OF EDUCATION

The central authority in the nineteenth century

When W. E. Forster introduced his celebrated bill early in 1870, he was at pains to emphasize that the measure was designed to work within the existing financial framework of elementary education. The government, he explained, 'would keep to the present proportions – namely, of about ⅓ raised from parents, ⅓ out of the public taxes, and ⅓ out of local funds. Where the local funds are not raised by voluntary subscription the rates will come into action.'[1]

This three-part division of responsibility had originated in 1833, when the first Treasury grant of £20,000 had been made to supplement parental and local contributions. The two societies, under whose aegis the latter were generally administered, were nominated as the original agencies for the distribution of the money, which was to be available for school building only. The principle of shared responsibility was underlined from the outset by the demand that at least half the cost should be raised in each case by private subscription.[2]

Another condition was that the actual expenditure should in all instances be open to Treasury audit.[3] The relatively easygoing nature of this proviso was soon criticized by advocates of a greater government involvement in working-class education; safeguards against the misapplication of funds, it was felt, ought to be more specific. Justification for such doubts can be found in the report submitted some years later by a government inspector:

Willenhall Primitive Methodist School, or Chapel.

The grant to this place was made for an infant-school, but the trust-deed is purely for chapel uses, with the word 'school' used, almost as if in derision . . . wherever 'chapel' would appear in other deeds of the same connection.

. . .

All the middle part of the 'school-house' is filled with pews, and the spaces around are occupied solely with benches and forms for other, and perhaps, poorer, hearers.

. . .

A teacher has occasionally made a desperate effort to keep a day-school on his own account on the back benches of this 'school-house', though never with success, and yet it had, within the few weeks preceding my inquiries, been reattempted by a superseded teacher in a neighbouring Wesleyan school. Some of the trustees being described in the trust-deed to be of 'Catchems Corner', and others of 'Sodom', I sought my way as far as the former, to obtain these details.
(Minutes of the Committee of Council on Education, 1846, Vol. II, p. 208)

From 1833 onwards, then, there were continued demands both inside and outside Parliament for an increased measure of state participation and control in the area of elementary education. Yet it should be borne in mind that such politicians as Roebuck and Brougham, who repeatedly raised the question in the Commons and Lords respectively, were not particularly highly placed in the esteem of their ministerial colleagues: though Brougham was Lord Chancellor from 1830 to 1834, his vacillations of allegiance and policy earned him the nickname of 'Old Wickedshifts', while Roebuck's group – the radicals – were regarded as having, in Melbourne's oft-quoted words, 'neither ability, honesty, nor numbers'.

Education *per se,* in fact, appears to have remained something of a fringe enthusiasm in Parliament during the 1830s and indeed throughout the century. The voting on the 1833 grant, at two o'clock in the morning, involved, not surprisingly perhaps, only 76 M.P.s; over half a century later the Code of 1890, which eventually modified the principle of payment by results, attracted fewer than 30,[4] the preceding discussion of the merits of an adjournment on Derby day having apparently enervated the Members. It was, of course,principally when the explosive issues of religion and finance were incidentally involved that educational subjects seem to have attracted a full House.

Religion was intimately bound up with education: while the Church of England on one hand attempted to arrogate to itself a traditionally justified primacy in this area, its opponents, whether sectarian or not, invariably opposed any effort to secure legislative backing to these claims. At the same time Anglican leaders appeared highly sensitive to moves by the government which could be interpreted as an infringement upon their prerogatives. Thus almost any action involving a departure from the status quo tended to provoke heated opposition from one faction or the other, or indeed both.

So when the Whig government decided in 1839 to create a committee of the Privy Council to deal with education, its terms of reference, like the words of Forster's speech three decades later, were pitched in a low, evolutionary key. Upon the insistence of the Marquess of Lansdowne, who was *ex officio* to be the first president, its area of competence was fairly closely defined: 'It is proposed that the Board (i.e., the committee) should be entrusted with the application of any sums which may be voted by Parliament for the purpose of Education in England and Wales.'[5] Direct confrontation with the Tory opposition was avoided by the use of an Order in Council rather than a parliamentary vote to authorize this action.

But also embodied in the original aims of the committee was the proposal to establish a normal school (teacher training college). In April, 1839, the intention was announced of making this a state-run institution which would offer 'general and special' religious instruction. Formulated simultaneously was the principle that 'no further Grant be made, now or hereafter, for the establishment or support of . . . Schools, unless the right of inspection be retained . . . .'[6] This statement of intent was regarded not without reason by many Anglicans as a direct challenge to their church's vaunted right to a monopoly of national education. So by the time that Dr. James Phillips Kay (who had from the first been concerned with the policy making of the new committee) became secretary* the tussle between the representatives of church and state had reached an active stage. Indeed, the government had already been coerced into relinquishing its scheme for a normal school, though Lord John Russell, the Home Secretary, had stood firm on the issue of inspection when he made the concession. But even the strength of this position was to be severely eroded within little more than a year by the 'Concordat' which invested the archbishops with the power of veto over the appointment of individual government inspectors. The principle of the 'Concordat' was later extended to other religious groups. But Kay, an official of exceptional energy and persistence, had meanwhile decided upon his own future policy as secretary of the committee: 'I understood your Lordship's Government,' he later wrote, 'to determine in 1839 to assert the claims of civil power to control the education of the Country.'[7] Throughout his ten years of office he was to remain faithful to this aim.

Religious sensitivities, however, compelled Kay (he changed his name to Kay Shuttleworth in 1842) to employ a policy of infiltration rather than one of frontal assault. By a series of regulations which prefaced the successive annual *Minutes* of the Committee of Council, he was able to augment the power of the Education Office in certain directions without having to confront directly the representatives of the various religious interests. This was accomplished by placing the proposed regulations upon the tables of the Houses of Parliament for a specific period, after which they became valid. A useful expedient, this was ultimately to prove double-edged, for Robert Lowe later used the same device to gain authorization for the Revised Code, remarking subsequently that he did not think that he could have carried a clause of it in Parliament.[8] †

Under Kay Shuttleworth's guidance, the Committee of Council offered in 1843 to pay grants through the Education Office towards the building of teachers' houses and the purchase of school furniture and apparatus; from 1846 payments were made to pupil teachers and those who instructed them, to stipendiary monitors, and to college-trained teachers, and in 1847 supplementary grants were announced for the purchase of approved school books and maps.

---

*Officially assistant secretary (see A. S. Bishop, *The Rise of a Central Authority for English Education*, 1971, p. 25).

†Schools regulations are still laid before Parliament in this way.

The net result of Kay Shuttleworth's various *Minutes* was to make the Committee of Council, together with its executive Education Office, a very real force in elementary education. The managers of individual schools could, of course, refuse part or indeed all of the proffered aid, as did the dissenting Voluntaryists; but to do so would have in many cases entailed an intolerable degree of financial sacrifice. So government aid (and its concomitant conditions) was widely accepted, though often not very graciously.

Bureaucracy, viewed with an increasingly jaundiced eye by cost-conscious and *laissez-faire* politicians, was an inevitable by-product of this process. During Kay Shuttleworth's time, the staff (excluding the inspectors) of the Education Office increased from one to just over forty.[9] Kay Shuttleworth himself was chronically overworked: his son later recalled how '. . . at a time of special pressure, he would dictate three or more letters simultaneously to as many clerks or secretaries'.[10] Robert Lowe, whose approach to the administrative problems of education differed profoundly from that of Kay Shuttleworth, at least shared his opinion on this point, complaining in 1862 that

The number of persons with whom we have to deal at this moment is almost incredible. For the year which has just terminated the number of schools under inspection was 9,957; the number of certified teachers receiving grants, 8,698; of probationary teachers, 491; of assistant teachers, 381; pupil teachers, 16,277; and the number of Queen's scholars, 2,527; making altogether, if we count one manager for every school, the very respectable army of 38,331 persons, all engaging the attention of the Privy Council, and most of them receiving money directly from it. We pay money directly by Post office orders to the whole 16,277 pupil teachers, whose salaries, moreover, are variable, beginning at £10, and rising gradually to £20. We pay money directly to the whole 8,698 principal teachers, and the amounts vary, owing to all sorts of circumstances. We are, besides, in correspondence with 9,957 sets of managers, so that the correspondence and payments of the Department* are exceedingly large and complicated.

(R. Lowe, in Hansard, Third Series, Vol. CLXV, pp. 199-200, 13 February 1862)

Successive writers have firmly established Kay Shuttleworth on the side of the angels; his undoubted devotion to the cause of education led to a nervous breakdown in 1848 and to his premature resignation in the following year. Ambition for himself and for his work, however, sometimes caused him to seem a little disingenuous. Charlotte Brontë noticed this and so did Mrs. Gaskell, who described him in 1850 as '. . . that eminently practical man, Sir James,† who has never indulged in the exercise of any talent which could not bring him a tangible and speedy return',[11] adding later that 'he has generally a double set of motives for all his actions'.[12]

---

*The Education Office was designated a department in 1856.

†He was made a baronet after his retirement in 1849.

Above all Kay Shuttleworth was accused of deviousness in his relationship with the National Society; some of its supporters actually became convinced that his whole aim was to infiltrate the movement and surreptitiously convert it into a front organization for the Committee of Council. High churchmen such as Archdeacon Denison regarded the 1846 *Minutes* with grave suspicion and the subsequent model trust deeds (which sought to modify the power of the clergy in the management of grant-aided National schools) with extreme distaste:

It would seem, then, that the Government having had forced upon them the conviction that it was only through the instrumentality of the Church schools that it would be possible to do any thing on an extended scale for the education of the people, were, nevertheless, very unwilling to part with the hope of bringing these schools, by a gradual process, to be so mixed up with, and so dependent upon, State assistance, that it would, at no distant time, be comparatively easy to engraft upon them a State character, and that the Minutes of 1846, as explained by the Secretary of the Committee of Council, were the first fruit of these joint considerations.
(G. A. Denison, Church Schools and State Interference, 1847, pp. 18-19)

Kay Shuttleworth's successor as secretary to the Committee of Council was R. R. W. Lingen, whose own tenure of office was to last until 1869. Lingen's first years saw a continuation of his predecessor's policies: in 1853 and 1855 a new kind of annual payment to schools – the capitation grant – was introduced first in rural and then in urban areas. Assessed at 5/- for boys and 4/- for girls, this was to be dependent not only upon a yearly attendance of 192 days but – prophetically – upon 'such examination . . . as might be set forth in a separate minute of details'.[13]

In 1856 important changes were made within the central administration of education. The Science and Art Department at Kensington was brought into association under the president of the Committee of Council with the Education Office, which was elevated to the status of department. More important, the committee itself was given a vice president whose status as an M.P. would, it was hoped, ensure a greater degree of correlation with the Commons in subsequent policy making. This new position became a key one, with Robert Lowe, W. E. Forster, Viscount Sandon, A. J. Mundella, and Sir John Gorst being among those who later held it.

In his evidence to the Select Committee on Education of 1865-1866, Lingen gave an account of the day-to-day working of the department. Partly for personal reasons and partly because he was felt in some parliamentary circles to exercise too wide and independent an authority, his exchanges with the chairman of the committee, Sir John Pakington, tended to assume an abrasive tone. It has in fact been surmised that Lingen himself, rather than Lowe, was the real object of the resentment which had led to the latter's resignation following the Commons vote of censure in 1864. As the *Saturday Review*[14] put it:

> Mr. Lingen is quite as powerful, and a good deal more offensive. It is from Mr. Lingen that all the sharp, snubbing replies proceed, which have imprinted upon half the rural parishes in the country the deep conviction that the Education Department is their natural enemy, whom it is their first duty to elude, baffle, and despoil . . .

Lingen was first asked to catalogue his duties both before and after the changes of 1856; next the functions of the president, vice president and the other members of the committee were discussed, together with the procedure by which minutes were formulated and authorized; and then the conception and preparliamentary career of the Revised Code were specifically examined:

11 Will you be so good as to describe to the Committee the system under which the business of the office was transacted from the time when you accepted the secretaryship up to the time of the passing of that Act in 1856, by which the Vice President was appointed? – The daily correspondence of the office was conducted by the Secretary; he signed all the letters and was responsible for all the letters; any letter which he considered of sufficient importance he used to take himself or send, according to the circumstances, to the Lord President; and orders for the payments of grants were made by the Lord President. That was the state of the business before the appointment of the Vice President.

. . .

19 During that period did the various Lord Presidents attend regularly at the office? – There were no fixed times at which they should come; but, during the Session of Parliament, a day would scarcely pass without the Lord President's being at the office during the afternoon; and the Secretary could at any time see him at his own residence, if for a day or two he were not at the office, or could communicate with him by letter; but there never were any fixed hours of attendance.

. . .

36 Can you explain to the Committee what have been the separate functions and duties of those two offices, the Lord President and the Vice President, since the creation of the latter office? – To myself, as Secretary, the immediate chief has been the Vice President. I may say, I think, that I have transacted all business with the Vice President, with the most trifling exceptions, and those quite accidental, such as appointments, or things of that kind. I have taken my orders from him.

. . .

38 . . . The Lord President has been the controlling officer, so far as I have had the means of knowing, beyond the Vice President.

. . .

58 Will you be so good as to state what has been the practice with regard to the attendance of those other Members of the Committee, during the time you have held the office of Secretary, as to what extent they have taken an active share in the business of that Department? – Only to the extent of deliberating upon Minutes, or upon draft Minutes, or upon questions of importance which were laid before them by the Lord President; but they have taken no part whatsoever in the current business of the office.

. . .

60   Can you tell me how often, in the earlier days of your secretaryship, before there was a Vice President, the other Members of the Committee attended to transact education business? – I could ascertain the number of meetings by referring to the Court Circular; but, speaking from general impression, I should think that the Committee met three or four times every Session at least, in the earlier periods of my secretaryship, and, of late years, if there has been any question of great public importance under consideration (as, for instance, the changes of the Code lately), the Committee has met frequently at such times.*

. . .

71   What has been the system of the office with regard to the preparation of Minutes; can you describe the history of a Minute before it is submitted to the House of Commons? – It would usually arise from either an apparent need of a greater measure of assistance to schools, or from the need of settling some question which had provoked a great deal of correspondence. A certain number of letters would probably be received from private correspondents, or the official correspondence might raise the question. The Lord President, after a certain length of time, would give instructions, probably to the Secretary, to draw up the draft of a Minute, which would be confidentially printed and circulated among the members of the Committee, and very often remarks would be made upon it, and when finally settled a Committee would be called at which that Minute would be passed, and then laid upon the table of the House of Commons.

. . .

82   When once the sanction of the Committee has been obtained to a Minute it is laid upon the tables of the Houses of Parliament in the usual way, is it not? – Yes.

83   Do you remember, since you have been Secretary, any change in the practice with regard to the mode of placing those Minutes upon the tables of the Houses of Parliament; was it at any time the practice of the Minister responsible for the Department to accompany the laying of a Minute on the table by an explanation of its purpose? – Generally speaking, it was not; but with regard to important Minutes like those of 1846, which first began to give annual aid to schools, statements were made upon the subject of those Minutes; but whether that was done upon the actual occasion of laying them upon the table I cannot say.

. . .

380   To go to facts, who initiated the Revised Code? – The Royal Commissioners of 1858, I suppose, were the first cause of it.

381   That was the groundwork for the great step that was then taken; but who framed the Revised Code? – I did.

382   Did you frame it under instructions from the Lord President? – The direct instructions that came to me were from the Vice President.

383   Are you of your own knowledge able to state whether he acted under the instructions of the Lord President? – There was a repeated and continued discussion after that Report of the Royal Education Commissioners, as to what should be done upon it; and when the decision had been arrived at that something in the nature of the Revised Code should be prepared, concerning which I had general instructions, putting me in possession of what were the views of my superiors, I drew it just as, if I had remained at my old profession, I might have drawn a man's will or his marriage settlement.

---

*Lingen later stated that there were 6-10 committee meetings in connection with the Revised Code. Normally the committee met 'Certainly once every year' (414).

384   When it was framed by yourself, was a Committee of Council convened to consider it? – Yes, several Committees.
(Parl. Papers, 1865, Vol. VI, Minutes of Evidence taken before the Select Committee on Education, pp. 1-6 passim and 21)

The provisions of the Revised Code, whatever their educational consequences, were to some extent justified from a purely administrative angle. Despite an increase of about 40 percent in the number of schools dealt with, the 'indoor' staff of the Education Department showed no increase in numbers between 1864 and 1870.[15] Indeed the question to what extent the need for basic administrative efficiency motivated the policy making of Lowe and Lingen is a key one. In his major parliamentary speech of 13 February 1862, Lowe was at pains to stress the difficulties which his department experienced in paying annual grants to school staff. Then he aired his reservations concerning the efficacy of the pre-Revised Code system:

Once we pay over the money, we cannot follow it to the uses to which it is applied; but we can be satisfied that it is well applied on the whole, and make our grants dependent upon that. I believe that the only substitute for this circumlocution and red tape – the only check on managers – is not to be had by the payment of the teachers, but by the examination of the pupils.
(R. Lowe, in Hansard, Third Series, Vol. CLXV, p. 202, 13 February 1862)

The rebarbative team of Lowe and Lingen was broken up, as far as education was concerned,* by the former's resignation in 1864. Lingen remained until 1869, so his career and that of George Kekewich, who became an examiner in 1867, form a continuum from the days of the first secretary, Kay Shuttleworth, to those of the Board of Education Act of 1899, which finally abolished the Committee of Council. Kekewich eventually rose to become its last secretary; his eminently readable autobiography *The Education Department and After*, superficially humorous, has an underlying sense of bitterness, for his position as secretary during the last years of the century was to be undermined by the internal dissentions within the central authority which were eventually to contribute in no small measure to his resignation. Kekewich's own resentment, and the passage of time, may have caused him to portray some of his contemporaries in an excessively uncharitable light. Both Sir John Gorst (the Committee of Council's last vice president) and Robert Morant (who eventually replaced Kekewich) were to record privately their own misgivings about him. Recent research into the working of the department has tended to show it in a fairly mundane light, with both Sir John Gorst and the Duke of Devonshire appearing as more constructive entities than Kekewich implies in the extracts given below.[16]

---

*They worked together in the Treasury when Lowe subsequently became Chancellor of the Exchequer.

Writing, however, of his early days in the department, Kekewich recalled that

. . . as might be imagined, we had plenty of leisure, and we came late and left early. There is a story of a Treasury clerk who, when he was asked by one of his friends how he liked the Civil Service, replied that he 'liked it very well, only it cut up his day so'. Our case was similar. The hour for attendance was eleven o'clock, but it was not often that any of us put in an appearance before half-past eleven or twelve; and we were supposed to leave at five, but most of us usually disappeared long before that hour. Included in the day's attendance was, of course, the necessary period for reading the *Times*, which was provided for us at the public expense, and the hour's interval for luncheon, which was generally prolonged. In fact, we attended practically as much or as little as we liked. Some of us (and I amongst them) were even guilty on occasion of going to the Office late in the afternoon, sometimes after office hours, and putting in the one or two hours' work which were necessary; and sometimes, but rarely, a full holiday was taken on French leave without discovery.

. . .

At the time when I first entered the Office the number of reports . . . which the Examiners* agreed to regard as a day's work was, I think, eight. When the schools to be dealt with were small, these might represent an hour or an hour and a half's work, and unless they were exceptionally large, eight reports were not exactly back-breaking, as they could usually be got through on an average in three hours or less, without any undue pressure on the brain. . . . I remember that once, when there was a considerable arrear, I despatched seventy of these 'cases' (as they were called) in a day . . .

(Sir George Kekewich, The Education Department and After, 1920, pp. 16 and 17)

No great sense of gravity was apparent in the department's work at an individual level:

. . . there was at no time any hurry about answering letters. If a man had the temerity to write to the Office, we felt that he ought to take his chance of an answer, and the greater difficulty he was in . . . the less likely he was to get it.

I remember that in the time of my predecessor, Patrick Cumin, at the Education Office, he and Mundella, who was then Vice-President of the Committee of Council on Education, were once discussing what was to be said to a deputation which was expected to present a good case and to be difficult to appease, and Mundella vehemently declared that it was absolutely impossible for him to concede anything. But when the deputation arrived he gave them a sample of his very best wind-bag oratory and a world of sympathy, and they marched off under the impression that they were going to get everything they wanted. Cumin said, 'How you did humbug them!' 'Yes,' said Mundella in his fine open-mouthed style, 'we are all humbugs, you know; that is part of our stock in trade.'

(Sir George Kekewich, The Education Department and After, 1920, pp. 21 and 289)

Lingen had revealed in 1865 that no official records were kept of the committee's proceedings. He did assert, however, that one meeting at least

---

*Examiners were permanent officials of the Education Department immediately below the secretary and assistant secretaries in rank.

took place each year. If this were so, the frequency appears subsequently to have declined. In the next passage, Kekewich describes the consideration by the committee of the 1890 Code, which greatly modified the principle of Payment by Results, and the reception in Parliament of the new regulations:

The framing of the Code produced a phenomenon – the only meeting of the Committee of Council on Education that I remember. . . . It was an extremely odd, and very perfunctory, proceeding. The Code, or part of it, was read out to the Committee by Lord Cranbrook, but apparently few of them understood it or took the smallest interest in it. Lord Salisbury, however, who was present by way, I suppose, of saying something, criticised an article which provided that a proper supply of lavatories should be supplied for the use of the children. He insisted on a reduction of the grant if the school lavatories were out of repair. As he was Prime Minister, there was nothing for it but to gratify his wish, and the alteration was duly made. (But it was wholly opposed to the spirit of the Code, which had abolished all reductions of the grant, and was afterwards removed from it at the first opportunity.) Lord Cranbrook then took alarm, as he obviously feared that if the Committee began really to consider the Code in detail, they might from sheer ignorance play havoc with it. So he said that there was nothing more of importance, and as Lord Salisbury was in a hurry, the meeting ended. Lord Cranbrook was obviously delighted that we had got off so cheaply.

The Code was presented to Parliament, and was debated on the Education Estimates. I was in attendance under the gallery. The discussion on the Estimates was preceded by one on the question whether Parliament should adjourn over Derby Day. The greatest interest was taken in the debate, and the House was full to overflowing, as if the issue was of vital importance to the State. The speeches were clever and amusing. The moment, however, the result of the division was known, members rose like a covey of partridges, and the House emptied, education being neither interesting nor amusing. Only a select few remained (less than thirty, I think) to hear Sir W. Hart Dyke move the Estimates and explain the Code.

(Sir George Kekewich, The Education Department and After, 1920, pp. 59-60)

In 1895 the committee's last president and vice president were appointed; these were the Duke of Devonshire and Sir John Gorst respectively. In the words of Kekewich, 'The Duke was dull, silent, and impassive, Sir John Gorst active and mischievous. Puck was forever dancing round Jupiter. . . .' Nor was there any love lost between the two, one observer[17] describing Gorst's attitude towards his chief as one of 'slumbering rebellion'. Kekewich found them equally irritating as this final extract from his book shows:

The Duke came to the office at Whitehall comparatively rarely; in such intervals, no doubt, as he could spare from social engagements and the pleasing diversions of racing and bridge. Occasionally he would send a message in the morning, saying that he was going to look in on his way to the House of Lords. Soon after there would arrive another message to the effect that he was coming on his way back from the House of Lords; then again another saying that he was not coming at all. The attractions elsewhere were doubtless too great to be sacrificed. As to his attendance at the Science and Art Department at South Kensington (of which he was also the

Parliamentary head) it was limited, I believe, to one or two visits during his eight years of office.

. . .

Sir John had remarkable habits. He used to ride to the Department on a bicycle* of brilliant red, and he was probably often mistaken for a Post Office official.

. . .

In his room at the House of Commons it was his custom to employ his spare time, of which he had plenty, in copying pictures. The room was on the ground floor, looking on the Terrace, and inspection of his work through the window appeared to delight the younger and more frivolous Members, especially when it consisted, as it often did, in copying from the nude. Deputations and visitors seemed to be equally susceptible.

(Sir George Kekewich, The Education Department and After, 1920, pp. 98-99 and 103-104)

Local control in the nineteenth century

At a purely local level, the administration of elementary education in the nineteenth century was a more parochial business than it is today. Before 1870 schools were generally run by their managers; only links of correspondence and inspection joined them to the central government. There was, of course, no equivalent to the modern local education authority.

The 1870 Act extended rather than modified this arrangement. The school boards which it brought into being were elective and had considerable legal power but their status vis-à-vis the Education Department was essentially the same as that of the voluntary school managers whose efforts they had been called into existence to supplement.

By the end of the century there were some 14,200 voluntary managements as opposed to just over 2,500 school boards. Of these about 12,000 were affiliated to the National Society. It may be supposed, therefore, that Anglican interests tended to predominate in this field – an inference which might certainly be drawn from the contemporary writings of James Runciman and Francis Adams. The latter, in his book *History of the Elementary School Contest in England,* took a strongly nonconformist line, while Runciman lashed out with an engaging impartiality at all those connected with education except the teachers themselves.[18] Perhaps this should be kept in mind when the following passages are read.

Townspeople can hardly form an idea of the way in which an ordinary country school is managed. There is a committee, of which the clergyman is chairman; but the committee is rarely called, except when the schedules required by Government have to be signed at the end of the year. Farmer Jones and Churchwarden Giles are nominally managers; but those excellent men have nothing whatever to do with the real business, and the clergyman is almost invariably an autocrat. He assumes the

---

*A more recent minister, Quintin Hogg (the present Lord Hailsham), also apparently employed this mode of transport.

right to rule the teachers; he lets the children see that a schoolmaster is a very inferior sort of creature. He never dreams of reckoning the teacher's position as being worthy of exaltation. He talks about 'my' schools in a proprietary sort of style; and he puts on such extravagant airs of domination that an independent humourist is driven to laugh. But the clerical mastery is by no means a laughing matter for the teachers, and many good men and women live from day to day under a galling tyranny, which they must endure unless they care to risk social and professional ruin. For the teacher has no appeal when he is unjustly treated, and if some insolent priest inflicts the deadliest outrage on the feelings of a master or mistress the injured person can only apply for redress through the agency of the very man who did the wrong. Suppose that the Reverend John Robinson enters a school and says to the master, 'Thompson, you are teaching that class in a most disgracefully stupid way; sit down, and let me take charge,' then Thompson may pull the reverend man's nose, or he may say, 'I must request you to send a report on your own conduct to the proper quarter,' Is it likely that Mr. Robinson will be severe in reporting his own indiscretions?
(*James Runciman, Schools and Scholars, 1887, pp. 94-96*)

. . .

The social position of the Church teacher in the country districts was that of a menial Church officer. A Church schoolmaster wrote that many teachers of his class were subjected to a worse slavery than the most dependent labourer in the parish. Rest and relaxation, except for brief periods of the year, were almost unknown to them. After an exacting week's work in the school, they were generally compelled to undergo a similar drudgery on the Sunday. Fifty per cent. of the advertisements for Church teachers stipulated that they should assist in Church offices. From quasi-curate to beadle and gravedigger, there was no employment which the schoolmaster was not expected to undertake. Some of the inducements offered to them may be gathered from the advertisements in the National Society's Paper. 'To officiate as parish clerk;' as 'collector of charity and Church funds', as 'choirmaster and precentor'. 'To attend Sunday school and take charge of the children at Church, and to and from Church.' 'An organist, willing to assist in Church matters.' 'Parish clerkship, with liberty to take private pupils.' 'Clerkship and sexton.' 'Ability to manage and train a surpliced choir indispensable.' Situations were offered to certificated mistresses whose husbands or brothers 'followed agricultural pursuits,' or could undertake, 'at stipulated wages, the management of a kitchen garden and two or three cows.' The social standing of the rural schoolmaster was little above that of the agricultural labourer, and the only ambition he was encouraged to entertain was that of 'the charity boy who longs to be a beadle.'
(*Francis Adams, History of the Elementary School Contest in England, 1882, pp. 304-305*)

The managers of voluntary schools were not always the ciphers that Runciman believed them to be. In some instances at least they helped with the clerical work, sorted out rows between parents and teachers, organized lunches and school treats. Most of all they tried to keep their schools' finances in order,[19] though not always successfully. At East Bergholt, for example, a feud between Abram Constable (the painter's brother) and his colleagues over the possession of the account books was only resolved after a Chancery case costing the charity almost £100 – a sum greatly in excess of a year's salary for their teacher.

School boards sometimes had an equally rough treatment from contemporary commentators. Though originally welcomed by nonconformists – Dr. Rigg, the principal of Westminster Training College, enthusiastically asserting that 'The School Boards will be pervaded with a Christian spirit. . . . The Bible will be taught, will in general be intelligently and reverently taught, will often be affectionately and prayerfully taught, in the new Board schools' – their formation does not seem to have been generally viewed with approbation; only 1189 (fewer than half, that is) of them were actually created as a result of popular demand. Despite the expansionist aspirations of the more progressive school boards towards secondary education, the writing was on the wall from at least the time of the Cross Commission, which saw fit to include as 'worthy of consideration' a scheme produced by one of its members 'to abolish all school boards and attendance committees, and to transfer their functions to county councils and borough councils'.[20]

It was as repositories of bucolic prejudice and ineptitude that school boards were frequently criticized. Writing of the 1870 Act, H.M.I. Sneyd-Kynnersley opined that:

The disadvantage was that it put technical, skilled labour into the hands of men from whom no proof of skill was required; and in very many places into the hands of men who were manifestly skill-less. In the large towns the Board might become a Debating Society, but if it escaped this snare, it often did well. In small villages sometimes it was a farce, sometimes a tragedy. In most places, whether large or small, the real power fell into the hands of one man, either the clerk or the chairman, who managed both School Board and Board School.

Do you ask for an instance? At a Board School inspection, noticing that there were not enough desks for the children, I asked the chairman, who was present, to see that the deficiency was made good at once. He assured me that it would be done without delay.

'When does the Board meet?' I asked.

'Oh, we don't meet: I get what is wanted and then on market-day I go down to the town, where I am sure to find the members; they are all farmers. I say to Brown, "The Inspector was here last week; wants some more desks; always asking for something; suppose you agree?" And he says, "Whatever you think is right, Mr. Chairman." Then I go on to Jones, and Robinson, and Snooks, and they all agree. We don't bother about a meeting, except once a year to make up Form IX for your inspection.'[21]

What admirable discipline!
(E. M. Sneyd-Kynnersley, H.M.I., Some passages in the life of one of H.M. Inspectors of Schools, 1908, p. 172)

A. J. Swinburne's book tends to confirm Sneyd-Kynnersley's opinion that school boards in villages were 'sometimes . . . a farce, sometimes a tragedy':

A small rural board in my district convened a meeting to consider the gravity of the situation revealed by the startling fact that their school had won the excellent merit mark. . . . Summoning their master they explained how it had fallen upon them like an unexpected blow. That they had no idea an excellent school was forming in their midst, and finally that with the highest opinions of his powers and fidelity, they advised him to seek an opening elsewhere.

. . .

And there was the small rural board which said, 'We all know the school is unsatisfactory in every possible way, but you see this is the difficulty, (the mistress) is related to four out of the seven of the Committee.'

. . .

'Gentlemen,' said the chairman of a village school board, alluding to a mistress who, to save her fuel, took a bath and performed her toilet in the class room – while she kept the children waiting outside – 'as she must go, let us give her a very good testimonial.'

. . .

. . . a member of a small Suffolk Board, soliciting my help in the choice of a mistress, added – 'But she must be over forty, sir, as the chairman is – well – yer see, sir – he's a bit amorous like.'
(A. J. Swinburne, Memories of a School Inspector, 1912, pp. 262, 78, 84 and 143-144)

But it was in the large urban areas that the school boards really came into their own. By the end of the century, two-fifths of all children of school age were to be found in London and in the county boroughs which had their own school boards. The latter bore little resemblence to the ones described by Sneyd-Kynnersley and Swinburne; in London, for example, the board could justifiably employ a full-time architect of national repute (E. R. Robson) at the considerable salary of £1,000 p.a. and, towards the end of its existence, recruit as many as 1000 teachers[22] annually for the 550,000 children in its schools. The relative effectiveness of the instruction given by the major school boards can be gauged from some of the speeches delivered during the debates on the 1902 Education Bill, which was of course designed to replace them with local education authorities. In the first of the extracts given below, Mr. H. Broadhurst (Leicester) stressed the high scholastic quality of urban board school education, while in the second Sir Henry Campbell-Bannerman (within a few years himself destined to become Prime Minister) emphasized the achievements of the boards in the field of post-elementary education. Although in 1898 there were almost half as many children in the London voluntary schools as there were in the board schools, claimed Mr. Broadhurst,

. . . of the junior scholarships given by the Technical Instruction Committee to all elementary schools, the board school children carried off 299, while the children of the voluntary schools only gained 26. . . . In Manchester . . . the board school children numbered 42,000 and the voluntary school children 52,000; but the board school children carried off forty Owen scholarships to Manchester Grammar School, and the voluntary school children only two. In Liverpool, where there were 37,000 board school children, and 74,000 voluntary school children, the former carried off sixteen scholarships and the latter only two. That was the result of a system which this Bill was intended to destroy . . .

. . .

What was without doubt the best, the most efficient, the most successful part of the previously existing educational machinery? The continuation schools and the higher grade schools,* and the higher schools conducted by the great School Boards. They were far more efficient than your Universities, which, for all their enormous funds and traditional advantages, educate only a fraction of the community, or than your public schools, of which we are so proud, where also learning is the last thing that is considered to be of much importance. It was these humble but earnest men in the board schools who were doing the very best work for you, and it is because they did it that you have destroyed them.

(H. Broadhurst and Sir. H. Campbell-Bannerman in Hansard, Fourth Series, Vols. 109 and 115, pp. 897-898 and 939 respectively, 17 June 1902 and 2 December 1902)

'Exhortation, stimulation, criticism and propaganda': the central authority in the twentieth century

By the mid-1890s it was becoming evident that the fabric of the central administration of education was in need of drastic revision and overhaul. In the first place, the department's accommodation was haphazard to an almost insufferable degree. A departmental committee appointed to investigate the problem reported in 1896 that five buildings were in use. In one of them six clerks shared a room measuring 11 feet 3 inches by 13 feet 9 inches, while in another 'The lavatory is now turned into a library, and rows of folio returns confront the washing-basins.'

More damaging in the long term, however, was the fragmented and inadequate structure of the Committee of Council's executive. Here, increasingly, the critical area was that of secondary education. The committee's involvement in this sphere was through the agency of the Science and Art Department at South Kensington, which it had controlled since 1856. The officials there, jealously independent of the Whitehall-based Education Department, were responsible for the financing of specific postelementary courses on a payment by results basis. These tended to be of a technical or scientific nature, and indeed the utilitarian philosophy of the Science and Art Department was destined to become the centre of a profound controversy in the years around the turn of the century. There was by this date a general consensus that the central authority's jurisdiction should be extended to encompass secondary education as a whole rather

---

*F. H. Spencer, who at one stage taught in a Nottingham higher grade school, later wrote that 'The educated middle-class public has no notion how famous some "Board Schools" were. Grown men to-day will talk of Ithaca Road, or Stenhouse Street School with insolent pride . . .' (*An Inspector's Testament*, 1938, p. 157). For an account of the higher grade schools in Nottingham, see D. Wardle, *Education and Society in Nineteenth-Century Nottingham*, 1971, pp. 133-135.

than only certain aspects of it. The point at issue, however, was a fundamental one; it sprang from the lack of an agreed definition of what actually constituted secondary education. Michael Sadler of the Office of Special Inquiries attempted to analyse the difficulty in 1896. As he saw it, although the Bryce Commissioners of the previous year had strongly recommended that secondary education should be administered by a unified central government authority, they

. . . had not clearly explained what kind of secondary education they wished to see compulsorily provided everywhere. And the more the matter was considered, the more obvious it became that two very different things are meant by the words secondary education – namely instruction which has for its fundamental aim the formation of character, and that of which the primary purpose is the production of some dexterity or form of technical skill. The first kind of secondary education is not the second, though the second may accidentally produce in certain cases the effect aimed at by the first. The same school cannot make each of the two aims its fundamental and determining purpose. . . . No satisfaction will come from a jumble of the two . . .
(M. E. Sadler, Minute Paper 189, Sadler Papers)

In organizational terms this conflict resolved itself into the question of whether secondary education was to be administered by an expanded version of the technically orientated Science and Art Department or by an entirely new civil service department biased towards what Sadler referred to as 'character formation'. Sadler himself and his assistant Robert Morant were particularly alarmed by the possibility that the officials of the Science and Art Department might make a successful take-over bid for the secondary sector. Such an eventuality, wrote Morant, would be 'too ghastly for words'[23] * and he and Sadler subsequently committed themselves to a vigorous campaign aimed at transferring responsibility for secondary education to a new department to be created for the purpose. In this they were bitterly opposed by Captain Abney of the Science and Art Department, who saw their policy as one under which 'modern secondary education is to be made subordinate to literary and classical education with the natural result that it would wither and become practically extinct.'[24] Nevertheless, in 1903 a tripartite organization of elementary, secondary and technological branches was finally to be established within the Board of Education.

Michael Sadler, to the dismay of many of his supporters, was not offered the new secondary branch. His backstairs diplomacy had alienated Sir George Kekewich; Gorst had conceived an intense dislike for him and even the Duke of Devonshire considered his views to be unduly partisan.[25] At the

---

*In this instance he was in agreement with the N.U.T., whose president in 1898 described the Science and Art Department as 'a deservedly tottering institution'. (See A. S. Bishop, op.cit., p. 197.)

end of 1899, moreover, Sadler's right-hand man Robert Morant had consented to become Gorst's secretary ('running Gorst's rotten ideas' was how he unenthusiastically described his new job).[26] Morant's subsequent rise to power was paralleled by a deterioration in his friendship with Sadler. In 1903 he supplanted Kekewich as secretary to the Board of Education and in the same year an acrimonious and well-publicized quarrel between Sadler himself and Morant led to the former's resignation.

But although the board's new secretary may have been prepared to sacrifice personal allegiances, the definitive Regulations of 1904 were to demonstrate his unswerving rejection of the concept of a technically based secondary curriculum.

The fierce captiousness which had marked the internal affairs of the Committee of Council and its successor the Board of Education during the decade at the turn of the century appeared to die down after the departures of Gorst, Kekewich, and Sadler. The period had, however, been significantly illustrative of the permissive interpretation which senior officials were on occasion prepared to apply to their theoretically apolitical and impartial roles. The tradition appears to have been an enduring one. As Amherst Selby-Bigge (Morant's successor) was later diplomatically to express it:

> . . . though, broadly speaking, policy is the concern of Ministers and administration the concern of Civil Servants, policy and administration are, in so large and complicated a service as that of Education, so mixed up that the line between them is very indistinct.
> (Sir L. A. Selby-Bigge, The Board of Education, 1927, pp. 70-71)

Similarly, as recently as 1971, a senior civil servant could put forward a claim that 'I can honestly say that there is not one new policy in my sector of responsibility that I have not either started or substantially contributed to over the last twenty years',[27] while a report by the Organization for Economic Cooperation and Development has defined the part played by the officials of the D.E.S. in the following terms:

> A permanent officialdom possessing such external protections and internal disciplines becomes a power in its own right. A British department composed of professional civil servants who have watched the ministers come and go is an entity that only an extremely foolish or powerful politician will persistently challenge or ignore.

> The prestige, acquaintanceships, and natural authority of leading civil servants give them a standing in the civil forum often superior to that of their *de jure* political superiors . . .
> (O.E.C.D: Educational Development Strategy in England and Wales, quoted in Times Higher Education Supplement, 9 May 1975, p. 8)

The Board of Education and its work

The Board of Education Act of 1899 was a relatively unspecific measure:

1 (1) There shall be established a Board of Education charged with the superintendence of matters relating to education in England and Wales.

(2) The Board shall consist of a President, and of the Lord President of the Council . . ., Her Majesty's Principal Secretaries of State, the First Commissioner of Her Majesty's Treasury, and the Chancellor of Her Majesty's Exchequer.

. . .

2 (1) The Board of Education shall take the place of the Education Department (including the Department of Science and Art) . . .

. . .

4 It shall be lawful for Her Majesty in Council, by Order, to establish a Consultative Committee consisting, as to not less than two-thirds, of persons qualified to represent the views of Universities and other bodies interested in education.[28]

The key word of the act's first section – superintendence – has a ring of passivity about it; some indication of the board's self-depreciatory attitude may indeed be seen in the approach adopted by Selby-Bigge, who prefaced his description of the board's functions by enumerating at some length all the things that it did *not* do:

The Board does not itself directly provide, manage or administer any schools . . .

Generally speaking, the Board has no authority over universities, university colleges, or university education.* . . .

The Board does not engage, pay, promote or dismiss the teachers in grant-aided schools and institutions . . .

The Board does not supply or prescribe or proscribe any textbooks for use in grant-aided schools . . .

It has not for many years been the practice of the Board to prescribe in its Regulations, except in general terms, the curriculum of grant-aided schools or the methods of teaching . . .

The Board has no general power to interpret the Education Acts . . .

The Board does not provide school buildings, and the raising of loans by Local Education Authorities for erection of buildings, purchase of land, etc., is not sanctioned by the Board but by the Ministry of Health. The Ministry will not sanction a loan unless the Board supports the application . . .

The audit of the expenditure of Local Education Authorities is not performed by the Board . . .

(L. A. Selby-Bigge, *The Board of Education*, 1927, *pp. 22-28 passim*)

Selby-Bigge, of course, was perfectly aware that the board's power centred largely upon its ability 'to obtain money from Parliament and distribute it locally for the support of education on certain conditions'.[29] From the time of Kay Shuttleworth the central authority had pursued with notable success

---

*The U.G.C. had assumed this duty in 1919.

a policy of influencing school authorities by means of financial pressure. A threat by the committee to withhold financial aid (for example in the form of payment to pupil teachers under the 1846 *Minutes* or the annual examination-assessed grant of the Revised Code) usually sufficed to bring uncooperative managements or boards into line. But, as has been mentioned, whereas in the nineteenth century the central authority's attention had been generally focused upon elementary school organization, it tended to shift at around the turn of the century to that of the secondary school. The apparent change of emphasis did not prevent the board from widening its interests in other areas – the development of the School Health Service[30] is an obvious example – but an increased concern with secondary education (reflected in the relatively numerous reports on the subject) seems to have become a feature of the central authority's policy.

The controversial Regulations for Secondary Schools of 1904 provide a classic illustration of how the central authority could exert pressure upon one particular sector of education when it really desired to. They have been interpreted as the codified expression of the Sadler-Morant concept of public secondary education and Selby-Bigge himself was later prepared to admit that they were excessively exclusive. Under their terms a secondary school could earn a grant from the board in respect of each of its pupils following an approved course. The sum varied between 40s and 100s a year, but in return for this the school concerned had to follow a specified teaching programme which preempted about eighteen hours of the weekly timetable.[31] Set out below are some of the additional regulations which dealt with school organization:

The curriculum of the school must include an approved Course of general instruction extending over at least four years. (1)

The average age of the scholars in any class commencing the Course must be not less than 12 years . . . (3)

Scholars in the first and second year of the Course may not, except by the express permission of the Board, sit for any external examination except one which comprises the whole school, or one held solely for the award of scholarships or exhibitions. (9)

The school year will be held to begin on 1st August and end on 31st July. On special application, however, from the Governors, the Board will be prepared to recognise a school year beginning on 1st January and ending on 31st December. (10)

The school must be efficient; must not compete unduly with a neighbouring school . . . (14)

No scholar shall be required . . . to attend or abstain from attending any Sunday school, place of religious workship, religious observance, or instruction in religious subjects in the school or elsewhere . . . (15)

. . . The constitution and functions of the Governing Body, and their relation to the teaching staff and the Local Education Authority, must be such as the Board can approve . . . (16)

A full account of the income and expenditure of the school must be furnished annually, and any grants made must be expended to the satisfaction of the Board. (22)

The school fees must be approved by the Board as suitable. Unless local circumstances can be proved to require exceptional treatment, the Board will not recognise a school in which no fees are charged . . . (23)

The teaching staff must be sufficient in number and qualification . . . (24)

The school premises must be . . . provided with adequate equipment and appliances for the approved course of instruction. The plans of both site and buildings for new schools or enlargement of existing schools must be submitted to the Board for approval. (25)

The school must meet regularly . . . during not less than 36 weeks in the course of the school year. (26)

The school must be open at all times to inspection by the Board . . . (31)

The mechanism of grant payment after 1918

The 1918 Education Act radically changed the method of grant payment. Under Section 44 of the act it was guaranteed that 'not less than one half of the net expenditure of the authority recognised by the Board of Education' would be paid from government funds. This was a tidier arrangement than the old specific grants, but the vital power of approval remained firmly with the board: 'the payment of grant,' emphasized Selby-Bigge, ' . . . is dependent on the absolute discretion of the Board unfettered by any previous declaration of the way in which it will be exercised . . .'[32]

Normally, however, the board was solicitous in seeking 'advice and criticism from interested bodies or competent persons . . . before embarking upon important changes in their administrative regulations'.[33] But on occasion urgency could rule out consultation. Economic crisis might cause the Treasury to demand a reduction in educational spending – 'If you knew the *unspeakable* fights one has with the Treasury!!!' an exasperated Morant had written in 1909.[34] Cabinet and Treasury pressure could cause the abrupt reversal of long-established policy. Perhaps the best-publicized example of this was the notorious Circular 1421, which in 1932 unabashedly informed L.E.A.s that the principle of free scholarships to grammar schools was about to be abrogated and that consequently the parents of children successful in a new 'special place' examination would be required to pay fees.* Such action was contrary to a long, explicit, and highly valued tradition in British secondary education. Yet despite a deluge of protests, only minimal changes were made prior to the enforcement of the Circular's proposals; the 'special

---

*Partial or total exemption would be granted to low-income families.

place' fees remained until the 1944 Act consigned them, in Brian Simon's words, to the dustbin of history.[35]

The 1944 Education Act and the central authority in the postwar period

The 1944 Act was in part a legislative response to the long-standing demand for the abandonment of the all-age elementary school embodied in the Hadow, Spens, and Norwood Reports. It was also the reflection of a wartime determination to create a more egalitarian society. It sharply emphasized the role of the central authority. The latter had been created in 1839 'for the consideration of all matters affecting the Education of the People';[36] the 1870 Act had subsequently given the Education Department powers of compulsion for initiating school boards. The 1899 Board of Education Act had adopted the term 'superintendence' to describe the central authority's function, while the 1918 Act authorized it to 'approve' L.E.A. schemes for education and envisaged the board's 'withholding or reducing' grants in the case of disagreement.[37] The Act of 1944 was more explicit. The board was transformed into a ministry and the new minister, for his part, was

. . . to promote the education of the people of England and Wales and the progressive development of institutions devoted to that purpose, and to secure the effective execution by local authorities, under his control and direction, of the national policy for providing a varied and comprehensive educational service in every area.
(Education Act, 1944, Part I, Section 1(1))

In the view of one commentator at least, 'A foreign lawyer, politician or educationist might regard Section 1 of the Act of 1944 as an unambiguous statement of a highly centralized system . . . '[38] The minister, moreover, was given specific jurisdiction by certain sections of the act. For example, he was empowered by Section 10 to 'make regulations prescribing the standards to which the premises of schools maintained by local education authorities are to conform'. Section 11 enabled him to make any 'necessary or expedient' modifications to the plans submitted to him by individual L.E.A.s, while Section 13 allowed him to impose 'such modifications . . . as appear to him to be desirable' upon any proposals by an L.E.A. to establish a new county school or to change the status of an existing one. The minister was in addition given powers of direct intervention:

If the Minister is satisfied, either on complaint by any person or otherwise, that any local education authority or the managers or governors of any county or voluntary school have acted or are proposing to act unreasonably . . . he may . . . give such directions as to the exercise of the power or the performance of the duty as appear to him to be expedient. (Section 68)

. . .

If the Minister is satisfied, either upon complaint by any person interested or otherwise, that any local education authority, or the managers or governors of any county school or voluntary school, have failed to discharge any duty imposed upon them by or for the purposes of this Act, the Minister may make an order declaring the authority, or the managers or governors, as the case may be, to be in default in respect of that duty, and giving such directions for the purpose of enforcing the execution thereof as appear to the Minister to be expedient; and any such directions shall be enforceable, on an application made on behalf of the Minister, by mandamus. * (Section 99, clause 1)

For several decades after 1944, L.E.A.s appeared generally to concede that Section 68 in particular constituted a heavily coercive sanction. Even the threat of its use by the minister was 'enough to bring them grumbling to heel'. [39] The section had been worded to allow the minister to adopt his own criteria in defining 'unreasonable' behaviour; no guidelines were laid down. When, therefore, Mr. Mulley intervened in June, 1976, to prevent the newly elected Conservative council of Tameside from reversing their Labour predecessors' comprehensive policies, it was assumed by many that he would get his way. One of his principal contentions was that there would be insufficient time to select pupils for the 240 grammar school places available in the following September. There was little surprise, therefore, when his action was upheld by the Divisional Court. The Tameside Council, however, appealed, convinced the Appeal Court that they could carry out 11 + selection efficiently within the available time, and thus succeeded in reversing the decision. The Appeal Court's judgement was subsequently upheld by the Law Lords. Nor were the terms in which the Appeal Court judges couched their verdict calculated to mollify the secretary or his D.E.S. advisers: 'misdirected', 'misinformed', and 'misunderstood' were some of the words used. As *Education* observed, the judgement left 'Mr. Mulley and the D.E.S. legal branch with egg on their faces'. In future an L.E.A. would have to be shown to be 'utterly wrong' before it could be condemned for acting 'unreasonably' within the context of Section 68. The dent in the Secretary of State's powers resulting from the Tameside decision appeared likely to prove a large and enduring one. [40]

The 1944 Education Act did, however, invest the minister with indisputable authority in certain matters. Section 4 enabled him to nominate the members of the two Central Advisory Councils (one for England and one for Wales) which were to replace the Consultative Committee; Section 55 gave him powers of direction regarding the transport of children to and from school; and Section 88 allowed him to veto the appointment of unsuitable candidates to the post of Chief Education Officer. More controversial, in the long run, was Section 89, which gave the minister authority to 'approve' the

---

* i.e., by court writ.

salary scales periodically submitted to him by the Burnham Committee and to secure their adoption by the L.E.A.s. *

The powers of strategic direction outlined above were originally supplemented by the traditional means of control through grant regulations. These were exercised until 1959 by means of the percentage grant, by which date the original 1918 government contribution of 50 percent had increased to the region of 60 percent. The Local Government Act of 1958, however, fundamentally altered the minister's power in this area. From April 1959 onwards, most grants to local authorities (for example those covering town planning and child care as well as education) were consolidated into one general grant made through the agency of the Ministry of Housing and Local Government. Individual authorities were thus permitted to determine their own priorities and to make their own allocation of funds: the Minister of Education's powers under Section 100 of the 1944 Act were restricted, rather incongruously, to payments in respect of milk, mid-day meals and the demolition of air-raid shelters.[41] The 1958 system (though not the principle behind it) was modified in 1967 with the institution of the rate support grant. *Prima facie* these alterations might appear to represent a very real diminution in the power of the central authority; on the other hand J. A. G. Griffith, the author of the standard work on the relationship between central and local government, has assessed the impact of the 1958 Local Government Act in very reserved terms:

The effect of this change is that local education authorities are no longer dependent on departmental approval of individual items of expenditure before grant is payable. . . . In practice, however, the relationship between the Department† and the local authorities is affected only slightly. For the administrative controls of the Department over the building programmes of local education authorities remain and are, as they were between 1944 and 1958, the basis of the relationship.
(*J. A. G. Griffith, Central Governments and Local Authorities, 1966, p. 100*)

How powerful, then, is the central authority today? Its relationship with the local education authorities has been habitually described as 'a partnership', but this is not really saying much. Bonnie and Clyde were partners and so, in a sense, are Tom and Jerry. In the passage below Anthony Crosland (Secretary of State for Education and Science from January 1965 until August 1967) is questioned by Professor Maurice Kogan about the function of the D.E.S.:

(Kogan) . . . What is the role of the central Department in relation to local education authorities and schools? Is it really the top of a managerial system, of a single organization with authority and accountability running through it?

---

* This section was subsequently amended by the Remuneration of Teachers Acts of 1963 and 1965. Both strengthened the minister's power.
† The Ministry of Education became the Department of Education and Science on 1 April 1964.

(Crosland) No, you couldn't conceivably describe it in these terms – there is in no sense a single organization with a managerial chain of command. On the other hand I was very struck by how much influence, control, power, or whatever the right word is, the Department has. There are all the constraints I mentioned earlier, yet despite them a Minister can have a huge influence on the system . . . .

. . .

(Kogan) What views did you develop about the relationship between the D.E.S. and local authorities?

(Crosland) All governments and Ministers are a bit schizophrenic about their relationship with local authorities. On one hand they genuinely believe the ringing phrases they use about how local government should have more power and freedom, and that's why we all want local government reform. On the other hand a Labour government hates it when Tory councils pursue education or housing policies of which it disapproves, and exactly the same is true of a Tory government with Labour councils. This ambivalence exists in everybody I know who is concerned with relations between central and local government.

(E. Boyle and A. Crosland, The Politics of Education, 1971, pp. 169 and 171)

The O.E.C.D. report of 1975[42] emphasized the paradox which appeared to characterize the position of the D.E.S.: 'It is true to say that it has extremely limited authority and that it has great power,' it observed, noting that

The Government meets 60 per cent of the costs of primary, secondary and further education, but the department must leave to the local education authorities the final decision as to the way in which the monies it dispenses will be spent. In relation to institutions like the universities, the department's authority is similarly but even further restricted; it provides funds to the autonomous University Grants Committee which makes the decisions concerning the distribution of these funds. . . .

This, however, is only one side of the coin. The actual powers of the D.E.S. are nonetheless considerable. Since the government is the largest single source of educational financing in Britain, the department's advice commands attention in any case, but it has powers that run beyond the purely advisory. It has direct control over capital* expenditures at the local level and thus has the final say with regard to the direction of educational growth. Further, its consent is required by statute in every case in which a local authority wishes to introduce a course at advanced level, to build a school or to close or change the character of an existing secondary school, for example by converting it from a grammar school into a comprehensive school.

The department also controls both the size norms and the price limits for school building . . . .

In sum, although the powers of government with regard to educational planning are formally limited, and British planning does not go so far as to be described even as 'indicative planning', the central Department of Education and Science is undoubtedly the most important single force in determining the direction and tempo of educational development.

And in their concluding summary the O.E.C.D. examiners dealt harshly with the department's planning strategies. They alleged, moreover, that it

---

*(e.g., over school building)

displayed a measure of disingenuousness in attempting to conceal the true extent of its administrative ambitions:

The chief features of the bases for its policy formation seem to be characterised by attempts to: minimize the degree of controversiality in the planning process and its results; reduce possible alternatives to matters of choice of resource allocation; limit the planning process to those parts of the educational services and functions strictly controlled by the D.E.S.; exploit as fully as possible the powers, prerogatives and responsibilities given to the D.E.S. under the 1944 Education Act; understate as much as possible the full role of the government in the determination of the future course of educational policy and even minimize it in the eyes of the general public.

The preservation of this powerful position, by combining the task of coherent planning with defensive tactics, excluding an open planning process, public hearings or, even, participation, seems to an outside observer as a mixture of strength and weakness.
(O.E.C.D: Educational Development Strategy in England and Wales, quoted in Times Higher Education Supplement, 9 May 1975, pp. 8 and 11)

The emergence of the modern L.E.A.
The report of the Bryce Commission in 1895 underlined the need for a local administrative unit for secondary education. This would have to be larger than the civil or ecclesiastical parishes upon which the school boards and voluntary managements were commonly based. The Conservative government's initial response to the Bryce Report's recommendations was the ill-fated bill of 1896 which, as Sir John Gorst explained in his introductory speech, aimed to establish a two-tier system in which county authorities would be imposed upon the existing school boards.

. . . The proposal is not novel. It was recommended by the Duke of Newcastle's Committee in 1861; by the Schools Inquiry Commission of 1868, as regards secondary education; by the Technical Instruction Commission of 1884, as regards technical and secondary education; in a memorandum issued by Lord Cross's Commission in 1888; and, finally by the Secondary Education Commission which has just reported. It is proposed in the Bill that the Education Authority shall be the County Council, acting through a statutory Education Committee . . .

. . .

As regards secondary education, the new authority will be able to aid schools out of the money at their disposal, to aid schools for secondary education and to establish them; and with the consent of the Education Department they may make a transfer from the School Boards of their higher-grade schools and so become managers of higher-grade schools.
(Sir J. E. Gorst, in Hansard, Fourth Series, Vol. XXXIX, pp. 538-539 and 542, 31 March 1896)

The bill of 1896 failed, partly at least on the religious issue. By 1902, however, the situation had to some extent changed. The Cockerton Judgements had given bad publicity to the London School Board while the county Technical Instruction Committees had had an opportunity to establish themselves further as a major force in secondary education.[43] At the same time, despite the special Aid Grant of 1897,[44] the financial problems of the poorer voluntary schools had become more acute: a memorandum prepared by Robert Morant early in 1902 revealed that 56 percent of church schools had had an adverse financial balance in the previous year.[45]

The 1902 measure, therefore, was more uncompromising than its predecessor. School boards were to be abolished and voluntary schools to receive rate aid. The act has frequently been regarded as a monument to Robert Morant who had apparently been assiduous in making friends and influencing the right people since his departure from the Office of Special Inquiries in 1899: 'the indefatigable Morant flies from one Cabinet Minister to another,' recorded Almeric Fitzroy[46] 'and receives the frankest confessions from them all . . .' By late 1901 he had eclipsed his titular master, Sir John Gorst;[47] by March 1902, when the soon-to-be Prime Minister, A. J. Balfour, introduced the bill ('a timely attack of influenza,' noted Fitzroy, 'having withdrawn Gorst into obscurity')[48] Morant's influence had apparently become dominant.

Part I
Local Education Authority

1   For the purposes of this Act, the council of every county and of every county borough shall be the local education authority:
Provided that the council of a borough with a population of over ten thousand or of an urban district with a population of over twenty thousand shall . . . be the local education authority for the purpose of Part III of this Act . . . .

Part II
Higher Education

2   (1) The local education authority shall consider the educational needs of their area and take such steps as seem to them desirable, after consultation with the Board of Education, to supply or aid the supply of education other than elementary, and to promote the general co-ordination of all forms of education . . . .

Part III
Elementary Education

5   The local education authority shall, throughout their area, have the powers and duties of a school board and school attendance committee . . . and shall also be responsible for and have control of all secular instruction in public elementary schools not provided by them;* and school boards and school attendance committees shall be abolished.

The 1902 Act greatly reduced the number of local authorities providing elementary education: Selby-Bigge, writing in 1927, claimed that the 2,568 school boards and 14,238 voluntary school managements of the pre-1902 era had been replaced by 63 county L.E.A.s, 82 county boroughs, and 173

---

*i.e., voluntary schools.

boroughs and urban districts. The latter constituted the 'Part III authorities' which had initially been limited to the administration of elementary schools. In the course of time, some of these (for example Rhondda and Glossop) were delegated by their county L.E.A. to control secondary and technical education,[49] while by 1927 about 85 boroughs and urban districts had assumed limited powers to finance higher education under Section 3 of Part II of the act.

The provisions of the 1902 Act relating to voluntary schools were anathema to many nonconformists. The bill itself was debated on 59 days before receiving royal assent and under such emotive slogans as 'Rome on the Rates' and 'No control – no cash' the spirit of resistance soon permeated some of the new Welsh L.E.A.s. In Carmarthen, for example,[50] the local education authority refused to pay rate aid to 48 voluntary schools, most of which were Anglican. It was to short-circuit such action that the 1904 Education (Local Authority Default) Act was passed. The Liberal government of 1906 onwards introduced three bills aimed at modifying the status of nonprovided schools,[51] but all proved abortive and the 1902 settlement remained.

The acts of 1918 and 1944
The 1918 Education Act widened and at the same time defined more closely the responsibilities of individual L.E.A.s:

1 With a view to the establishment of a national system of public education available for all persons capable of profiting thereby, it shall be the duty of the council of every county and county borough, so far as their powers extend, to contribute thereto by providing for the progressive development and comprehensive organisation of education in respect of their area, and with that object any such council from time to time may, and shall when required by the Board of Education, submit to the Board schemes showing the mode in which their duties and powers under the Education Acts are to be performed and exercised . . .

In other words the Board of Education was to perform a watchdog function to ensure the adequacy of educational provision while initiative was to remain with the L.E.A. 'It is no exaggeration,' wrote the secretary to the board, 'to say that the Act of 1918 embodies not only a greatly enlarged conception of the service of education but also a new conception of the relation of the Central and Local Authorities.'[52]

The process of definition was continued in the 1944 Act:

8   (1) It shall be the duty of every local education authority to secure that there shall be available for their area sufficient schools –
(a) for providing primary education . . .
(b) for providing secondary education . . .
and the schools available for an area shall not be deemed to be sufficient unless they are sufficient in number, character, and equipment to afford for all pupils

opportunities for education offering such variety of instruction and training as may be desirable in view of their different ages, abilities, and apititudes, and of the different periods for which they may be expected to remain at school, including practical instruction and training appropriate to their respective needs.

The 1944 Act explicitly guaranteed the autonomy of the L.E.A. in the crucial area of secular instruction:

23   (1) In every county school and, subject to the conditions hereinafter contained as to religious education, in every voluntary school except an aided secondary school, the secular instruction to be given to the pupils shall, save in so far as may be otherwise provided by the rules of management or articles of government for the school, be under the control of the local education authority . . . .

The county and county boroughs retained their L.E.A. status under the 1944 Act. The Part III authorities were, however, abolished and a novel kind of subsidiary local organization, the divisional executive, was established to act on behalf of the L.E.A. in certain matters concerned with primary and secondary education. In most cases the divisional committee was to be made up of representatives of minor local councils, the county authority itself, and various coopted members.[53] Large boroughs and urban districts could claim to be excepted from L.E.A. schemes and to constitute their own divisional executives. In all, a total of 35 Part III authorities were successful in achieving 'excepted district' status immediately after 1944,[54] while a number of others formed the nucleus of ordinary divisional executives. This rather complex situation prevailed until 1974 when, as a result of the Local Government Act (1972), the 164 major L.E.A.s and 174 excepted districts and divisional executives in England and Wales were condensed into 104 metropolitan, county, and London L.E.A.s.

The machinery of local government

The bill of 1896, it will be remembered, sought to create an education committee for each local authority. This policy was confirmed in Part IV of the 1902 Act. Education committees were to include a number (normally a majority) of councillors and some 'persons with experience in education' appointed by the council upon the recommendation of other educational bodies. In the first instance, ex-members of school boards could be coopted. The education committees thus established were to deal with all matters concerning the exercise of local powers under the act with the exception of raising money, subject to the overruling control of the council itself.

The chairmanship of an education committee was inevitably to prove an exacting and time-consuming task. It carried considerable influence and responsibility and was, like the presidency of the Board of Education, a political appointment. Like the presidency, too, it required administrative support in the form of permanent officials. Principal among these was the committee's permanent secretary, the chief education officer.

Local authorities in the form of school boards had been in existence since 1870. Following the Technical Instruction Act of 1889 they had been paralleled by the technical instruction committees of the new county and county borough authorities.* Many of the new L.E.A.s appointed officials from one or the other of these preexisting organizations. The chief education officers (C.E.O.s) of the immediate post-1902 period were consequently often either the ex-clerks to defunct school boards or ex-secretaries to technical instruction committees.[55] A. E. Ikin, the director of education at Blackpool, described the C.E.O.'s function in these words:

. . . the secretary or director has what might be described as a 'continuing responsibility'. He is responsible for the proper working of the whole Education Department both in the office and in the schools.

He must take the responsibility of summoning committee meetings and of attending all the more important. The preparation of agendas for the meetings must be carefully thought out, and the minutes and reports of the meetings must be accurate and clear. In addition he must take the *responsibility* for all correspondence from the office, even if sent out by an officer working under him.
(A. E. Ikin, Organization and Administration of the Education Department, 1926, pp. 42-43)

The above is what might be termed a 'soft' definition of the C.E.O.'s duties; there is no mention of the policy-making function apparently fulfilled by his central authority counterparts. Sir Arthur Binns (ex-C.E.O. of Lancashire) initially described his work in much the same terms as Ikin; but then significantly added:

In giving advice he should be very careful not to 'throw his weight about'. Whenever possible his advice should be so given that his employers do not realise that they are getting it. They should be led to the right conclusion under the impression that they are arriving at it under their own steam.

Under these circumstances clashes of will between chairman and C.E.O. were on occasion unavoidable; here Binns describes one such confrontation:

I remember one chairman who was inclined to be over-strong. He wanted me to take an instruction from him which I said I would only take from the Education Committee. He said, 'Very well then, we will go to the Committee.' We did, but I was rather astonished at the way the chairman put the problem to the Committee. He said 'I wanted to do the straightforward and honest thing, but Mr. Binns thought otherwise.' I never knew him have a remark greeted with such terrific applause . . .
(A. L. Binns, 'The C.E.O. and his task', in Journal of Education, April 1957, pp. 140 and 141)

In the above instance Binns refused to accept orders direct from the chairman of the education committee. George Taylor, C.E.O. of Leeds for

---

*Initially empowered to raise and spend a maximum rate of 1d in the £ upon technical and manual instruction, these committees also disbursed 'Whisky Money' after 1890.

fifteen years, was similarly prepared to take a hard line when faced with what he regarded as presumptuousness on the part of councillors. The quarrel retailed in the next passage was the result of a decision of the chairman of the service of youth subcommittee to write a letter to the D.E.S. without consulting him:

I rang up the chairman of the education committee and said: 'I'm proposing to send for the chairman of the service of youth sub-committee and try to establish demarkation of responsibility. As C.E.O. it is my role to write to the D.E.S. I am sure you will agree that it is my responsibility to deal with decisions of the committee and all correspondence arising from them.'

I then sent for the chairman, I invited him to come and see me. I didn't tell him why. When he came in I said, 'It was very kind of you to help me, particularly as I wasn't able to attend the meeting, but it is my responsibility to deal with correspondence.'

He said, 'This is absurd. I'm chairman of the works committee. I go along every morning at nine o'clock. I open the letters and tell the Chief Officer what replies he must make.'

So I said, 'Well, you wouldn't if you were chairman of the education committee because I wouldn't tolerate it . . .'

(M. Kogan and W. van der Eyken (eds.), County Hall, 1973, p. 150)

Taylor believed that the 1944 Act effectively differentiated between the status of a C.E.O. and that of other local government officers (Section 88 of the act makes the appointment of the C.E.O. mandatory to every L.E.A.). But problems originating from a lack of demarkation appear real, fundamental, and indeed unresolved. The Maud Report on Management of Local Government concluded that 'the lack of clear recognition of what can and should be done by officers, and of what should be reserved for decision by members, lies at the root of the difficulties in the internal organisation of local authorities',[56] and went on to recommend that authorities should consider a division of functions by which strategic decisions and aims should be determined by committee members while routine control should be exercised and day-to-day decisions made by officials. Rene Saran, commenting upon policy making for secondary education in one particular area,[57] observed that officials were generally prepared to take initiative but that 'on issues which were subject to party political controversy, they preferred to be formally instructed'. In fact, of the ten decisions analysed by Saran, five were principally initiated by councillors, three by the C.E.O., and two (concerned with the status of a direct grant/independent school) by governors.

A recent account of a C.E.O.'s work has been written by Derek Birley, whose opening sentence – 'Becoming an administrator is not the only way of incurring odium, but it is as effective as most'[58] – at least shows realism. In Birley's opinion, however, rivalry between C.E.O. and committee chairman is not the main problem: rather 'the chief danger is that they will work so closely together as to appear to carve anything up between them, leaving nothing of any importance for the committee to decide.'[59]

Exactly what there might be to carve up in this way appears open to dispute. Earlier in his book Birley examined L.E.A. responsibilities from a purely financial angle and argued that current educational expenditure was anyway largely predetermined by factors outside the control of the education committee:

Item	Expenditure	Comments
Teachers' salaries including superannuation and national insurance	45.0%	The Burnham Committee determines salary levels (with some local discretion over above-scale allowances). The number of teachers employed (in schools) is largely determined by a quota fixed by the D.E.S.
Other salaries and wages	15.0%	Most scales are fixed by national bodies. Numbers are controlled by Establishment Committee.
Premises and grounds: repair and maintenance	02.5%	To some extent discretionary but a certain minimum is of course essential.
Fuel, Light, Water, Cleaning Materials	03.5%	To some extend discretionary but a certain minimum is of course essential.
Rent and rates	03.5%	Inevitable
Debt Charges	10.5%	Inevitable
Food, milk, etc.	04.0%	Inevitable
Adjustments with other authorities	01.0%	Inevitable
Aid to pupils and students	07.5%	Mostly paid according to national scales: in large part according to national regulation.
Equipment; books, stationery and materials	04.5%	
Furniture, repair and replacement	00.3%	
Improvements to buildings and furniture	00.7%	
Other expenses	02.0%	
	100.0%	

(D. Birley, *The Education Officer and his World*, 1970, p. 30)

Yet an undue emphasis upon the financial aspects of control could lead to a distortion of the overall picture. Any system which has allowed tripartite-minded L.E.A.s to resist the expressed policy of successive Labour administrations must have within it a by no means negligible measure of local autonomy. It is perhaps worth noting that all three of the C.E.O.s interviewed in the book *County Hall* expressed general approval of the D.E.S. and its personnel; as Claire Pratt (from 1964 to 1971 C.E.O. for Hillingdon) pointed out:

> Certainly, you are constrained as far as your major projects are concerned, such as building a whole new school or greatly extending a school. We are also more constrained nowadays on minor works. But on other things, on the real stuff of education within the buildings, there are no constraints. The authority can spend as much as it likes on equipment (except fixed equipment), various categories of staff, clerical assistants, welfare assistants, and it can send teachers on as many in-service training courses as it wants to.
> *(M. Kogan and W. van der Eyken, eds., County Hall, 1973, p. 121)*

It remains to be seen whether such attitudes of mutual tolerance will remain unaffected by the policies of the D.E.S. during the middle and later 1970s. Within six months of the Tameside judgement the new secretary, Mrs. Shirley Williams, was reported to be pressing for legal revisions which would allow the central authority to resume at least some of its traditional direct powers of control over L.E.A. spending.[60] The National Union of Teachers, for its part, was quick to discern D.E.S. expansionist intentions behind the 'great debate' which followed the Prime Minister's speech at Ruskin College: ' . . . I must make it abundantly clear,' announced the chairman of the union's education committee, 'that we would bitterly oppose any attempt to impose syllabus details on the schools . . .'[61] The report of the Taylor Committee, which appeared in September 1977, seemed to contain a further threat to the curricular power of teachers. Dismissed by the general secretary of the N.U.T. as a 'busybodies' charter', the Taylor Report *(A New Partnership)* proposed that a quarter of the governors of a school (some of them pupils) should be elected by the parents and, in some cases, by the pupils themselves and that a further quarter should be coopted to represent the local community. The governing body as a whole should be empowered to establish the school's objectives, share in the formation of the learning structure, keep the progress of the school under review, and regularly produce appraisals of its performance.[62]

The government Green Paper *Education in Schools,* published in July, 1977, had, however, for its part already taken a pointedly conciliatory line towards the L.E.A.s generally, stressing that the authorities themselves would initially carry out the review of curricular arrangements which it proposed and that the Secretaries of State would seek 'a broad agreement with their partners in the education service' on any subsequent decisions affecting the curriculum.[63] Only time – and, no doubt, a certain amount of argument and compromise – would determine whether the balance of power within the administration of education was moving towards any significant alteration.

Notes

1   Forster's words tended to gloss over several areas of controversy. It has been argued that his policy of 'filling up gaps' in the provision of schools owed much to the ideas and suggestions of Robert Lowe. Whether or not gaps actually existed on a really substantial scale at the time, and whether, if this was indeed the case, voluntary effort had significantly reduced the deficiencies within a few years, are points which still remain open to discussion. See D. W. Sylvester, *Robert Lowe and Education*, 1974, pp. 126-133 and 'Robert Lowe and the 1870 Education Act', in *History of Education*, Vol. 3, No. 2 (Summer 1974) for an appraisal of Lowe's contributions to the terms of the 1870 Act. E. G. West, *Education and the State*, 1965, claims (pp. 153-154) that in the years after 1870 the board schools, far from alleviating deficiencies, actually enlarged the gaps in the provision of education by destroying 'the hitherto healthily growing structure of private education'. Norman Morris, '1870 – the Rating Option', in *History of Education*, Vol. 1, No. 1 (January 1972), also examines the extent of voluntary school provision in the years immediately following 1870 and considers the significance of the rate issue at the time of the act.

2   Parl. Papers, 1837-1838, Vol. VII, *Report from the Select Committee on the Education of the Poorer Classes*, p. x.

3   Ibid.

4   See below, p. 206.

5   J. S. Maclure, *Educational Documents, England and Wales 1816-1968*, 1969, p. 4.

6   Parl. Papers, 1839, Vol. XLI, pp. 259-263.

7   Quoted by G. A. N. Lowndes, *The Silent Social Revolution*, 1937, p. 9.

8   Parl. Papers, 1865, Vol. VI, *Minutes of Evidence taken before the Select Committee on Education*, p. 43.

9   A. S. Bishop, *The Rise of a Central Authority for English Education*, 1971, p. 29.

10   Quoted in F. Smith, *The Life and Work of Sir James Kay-Shuttleworth*, 1923, p. 339.

11   *Letters of Mrs. Gaskell*, edited by J. A. V. Chappel and A. Pollard, 1966, p. 130.

12   Ibid., p. 611.

13   See M. Sturt, *The Education of the People*, 1967, pp. 208-209.

14   *The Saturday Review*, 16 April 1864, p. 465.

15   A. S. Bishop, op.cit., p. 55.

16   John Hurt, *Education in Evolution*, 1971, p. 9, actually goes so far as to give 'the bulk of the credit' for the establishment of the elementary education system to 'that much-maligned figure, the Victorian civil servant'. The structure and working of the Education Department are closely examined in Gillian Sutherland's book, *Policy-Making in Elementary Education 1870-1895*, 1973, while the roles of Sir John Gorst and the Duke of Devonshire are the subject of theses by N. D. Daglish (*The Educational Work of Sir John Gorst*, Durham University, 1974) and J. R. Fairhurst (*Some aspects of the relationship between education, politics and religion from 1895 to 1906*, Oxford University, 1974).

17   *Memoirs of Sir Almeric Fitzroy*, 1925, Vol. I, p. 28.

18   He did, however, spare Mundella a word of praise – for censuring a particularly objectionable H.M.I.

19   Peter Gordon, *The Victorian School Manager*, 1974, pp. 24-29.

20   The Local Government Act of 1888 created the county and borough councils of the pre-1974 period. See Cross Report, 1888, pp. 204-207, for Sir Francis Sandford's scheme.

21   R. R. Sellman, *Devon Schools in the Nineteenth Century*, 1967, p. 64, gives further examples of school boards persistently neglecting to hold their statutory monthly meetings.

22   M. Seaborne in *Local Studies and the History of Education*, ed. by T. G. Cook, 1972, p. 66, and S. Maclure, *One Hundred Years of London Education*, 1970, p. 59.

23   R. L. Morant to M. E. Sadler, undated, ? March 1898. Sadler Papers, Bodleian Library.

24   P.R.O. Ed 24/64, 26 February 1900, W. de W. Abney to G. Kekewich. The incompatibilities which existed between the policies of the Education Department and those of the Department of Science and Art are discussed in Harry Butterworth's article, 'South Kensington and Whitehall: A Conflict of Educational Purpose', *Journal of Educational Administration and History*, Vol. IV, No. 1 (December 1971).

25   P.R.O. Ed 24/64, 20 January 1900, Devonshire to G. Kekewich.

26   R. L. Morant to M. E. Sadler, ? 21 November 1899, Sadler Papers, Bodleian Library.

27   E. Boyle and A. Crosland, *The Politics of Education*, 1971, p. 41.

28   Michael Sadler, for one, was sceptical about the value of the Consultative Committee: 'I fear the Consultative Committee may be ill contrived through the choice of flatterers and bigwigs rather than men who have really tried to think the educational question out' he wrote in March 1900. (Bod. Lib. Eng. Misc. C. 551).

29   L. A. Selby-Bigge, *The Board of Education*, 1927, p. 29.

30   The development of the school welfare services is a major subject in itself. A concise account of their origins and history is given in *The School Health Service 1908-1974*, by the Chief Medical Officer of the D.E.S., 1975, pp. 5-8:

In Britain the London School Board, in 1890, was the first to appoint a school doctor; the second was the Bradford Board in 1893. By 1905 school doctors had been appointed by 85 local education authorities and medical inspection of school children was being carried out in 48 areas. About 300 special schools with 17,000 handicapped children had also been established.

The reports of these school doctors on the amount of ill-health, malnutrition and disability among school children were reinforced by the highly critical authoritative Reports from a Royal Commission and two Interdepartmental Committees . . .

Following the publication of these three Reports the Government decided that a School Medical Service (renamed School Health Service in 1945) should be organized on a national basis and that local education authorities should be empowered to provide, or to assist voluntary school canteen committees to provide, meals for children attending elementary schools who were unable to take full advantage of the education provided owing to lack of food. In 1906 the Education (Provision of Meals) Act, and in 1907 the Education (Administrative Provisions) Act were passed by Parliament.

The latter Act gave local education authorities the duty to provide for the medical inspection of children in public elementary schools and the power to make arrangements, with the sanction of the Board of Education, for attending to their health and physical condition. In 1907 a Medical Branch (renamed Special Services Branch in 1945 and Medical Services Branch in 1972) was formed in the Board of Education. Later that year Circular 576 (probably the most influential in the history of the service) was sent to local education authorities giving them general guidance on the aims of the school medical service. The circular stated that ' . . . the work of medical inspection should be carried out in intimate conjunction with the Public Health Authorities and under direct supervision of the Medical Officer of Health. . . . One of the objects of the new legislation is to stimulate a sense of duty in matters affecting health in the homes of the people, to enlist the best services and interests of parents. . . . It is in the home, in fact, that both the seed and the fruit of public health are to be found . . .'

Regulations made under the Education Act of 1918 gave local education authorities the duty (previously they had only the power) to make arrangements for the treatment of children attending public elementary schools, and for the medical inspection of children in secondary schools; they were also given the power, not the duty, to arrange for the treatment of children in secondary schools.

In 1919, the Ministry of Health Act established the Ministry of Health 'to promote the health of the people'. This Act transferred to the Minister of Health all the powers and duties of the Board of Education for the medical inspection and treatment of children and young persons, with the proviso that these powers and duties might by arrangement be exercised by the Board of Education on behalf of the Minister of Health. The proviso was, in fact, adopted, and the Chief Medical Officer of the Ministry of Health became also Chief Medical Officer of the Board of Education and of its successors . . .

Although the development of the school health service was seriously interrupted by the two World Wars it expanded rapidly after each of them, particularly after the War of 1939-1945. The Education Act of 1944, gave local education authorities the duty to provide school meals and milk for pupils at schools maintained by them; the duty to provide medical and dental inspection in all types of maintained primary and secondary schools; and the duty to provide or secure for children attending maintained schools all forms of medical and dental treatment, other than domiciliary treatment, without cost to the parents. The National Health Service Act of 1946, that came into force in 1948, enabled local education authorities to make arrangements with regional hospital boards and the Governors of Teaching Hospitals for free specialist and hospital treatment for children attending maintained schools . . .

The National Health Service Reorganization Act of 1973 . . . transferred the statutory responsibility for providing school health services from the local education authorities to the Secretary of State for Social Services . . .

A longer but less up-to-date work on the subject is S. and V. Leff, *The School Health Service*, 1959.

31   Details of the times specified for each subject are given on p. 84.

32   L. A. Selby-Bigge, op.cit., p. 172.

33   Ibid., p. 161.

34   R. L. Morant to E. Marvin, 10 March 1909 (Bod. Lib., M. S. Eng.Lett. C. 257).

35   B. Simon, *The Politics of Educational Reform*, 1974, p. 354.

36   J. S. Maclure, op.cit., p. 43.

37   Education Act, 1918, 8 and 9 Geo. V., Ch. 39, sect. 5, paras. 1 and 3.

38   J. A. G. Griffith, *Central Governments and Local Authorities*, 1966, p. 98.

39   *Education*, 30 July 1976, p. 104.

40   Ibid., pp. 102-104 passim.

41   M. M. Wells and P. S. Taylor (eds), *The New Law of Education*, 1961, pp. 227-228.

42   See above, p. 213.

43   M. E. Sadler to Devonshire, 7 July 1899 (P.R.O. Ed 24/64) and A. H. D. Acland to G. Kekewich, 13 July 1899 (P.R.O. Ed 26/64).

44   M. Cruickshank, *Church and State in English Education*, 1963, p. 70.

45   B. Sacks, *The Religious Issue in the State Schools of England and Wales*, 1961, p. 16.

46   Sir Almeric Fitzroy, op.cit., p. 74.

47   Ibid., p. 67.

48   Ibid., p. 81

49   N. B. Mortimer in *Education*, 15 September 1950, pp. 306-307.

50   B. Sacks, op.cit., p. 53

51   M. Cruickshank, op.cit., pp. 90-112.

52   L. A. Selby-Bigge, op.cit., p. 187. For a detailed consideration of the 1918 Act, see Lawrence Andrews, *The Education Act, 1918*, 1976 and G. E. Sherington, 'The 1918 Education Act: Origins, Aims and Development', in *British Journal of Educational Studies*, Vol. XXIV, No. 1 (February 1976).

53   For further details see H. C. Dent, *The Educational System of England and Wales*, 1961, pp. 84-85 and B. Lawrence, *The Administration of Education in Britain*, 1972, pp. 108-113.

54   N. B. Mortimer in *Education*, 11 August 1950, p. 177.

55   A. E. Ikin, *Organization and Administration of the Education Department*, 1926, pp. 40-41.

56   *Management of Local Government*, 1967, Vol. I, para. 101.

57   R. Saran, *Policy-Making in Secondary Education*, 1973, p. 257 and appendix to chapter 6.

58   D. Birley, *The education officer and his world*, 1970, p. 1.

59   Ibid., p. 135.

60   *Times Educational Supplement*, 19 November 1976, p. 1.

61   Ibid., 21 January 1977, p. 13.

62   Ibid., 23 September 1977, pp. 1, 7, and 8.

63   Ibid., 22 July 1977, p. 5.

CHAPTER 10

A CHRONOLOGICAL FRAMEWORK

1762	Jean Jacques Rousseau: *Emile*.
1773-5	David Williams' academy at Laurence Street, Chelsea.
1776	Adam Smith: *The Wealth of Nations*.
1780	R. Raikes opened his first Sunday Schools at Gloucester.
1783	Thomas Day: *Sandford and Merton*.
1789	More sisters opened school at Cheddar.
	David Williams: *Lectures on Education*.
1797	Andrew Bell: *An Experiment in Education*.
1798	Joseph Lancaster opened school at Borough Road.
	M. and R. L. Edgeworth: *Practical Education*.
1802	Health and Morals of Apprentices Act:
	(i) Religious teaching obligatory for apprentices in factories.
	(ii) Reading, writing, and arithmetic to be taught for first four years of apprenticeship.
1803	Joseph Lancaster: *Improvements in Education*.
1805	Pestalozzi founded his school at Yverdon, Switzerland.
	Leeds Grammar School decision: grammar school curriculum legally defined as classical.
1807	Parochial Schools Bill (S. Whitbread): proposed *inter alia* the establishment of parish schools supported by rates and supervised by clergy.
1810	Royal Lancasterian Association (later British and Foreign School Society) founded.
1811	National Society founded.
1816	Robert Owen's Infant School opened at New Lanark.
	Jeremy Bentham: *Chrestomathia*.
1819	Hill brothers' school at Hazelwood opened.
1820	Parish Schools Bill (H. Brougham):
	(i) Parish schools to be established and supervised by clergy.
	(ii) Parish clerks to be encouraged to become teachers.
	(iii) Denominational teaching not necessary.
1823	S. Wilderspin: *Education of Infant Children of the Poor*.
1826	David Stow founded Glasgow Infant School Society.
1828	Thomas Arnold became headmaster of Rugby School.
1832	Parliamentary Reform Act.
1833	Factory Act: factory children to have two hours instruction daily.
	Education Resolution by J. A. Roebuck, who advocated:
	(i) Provision of education as a state obligation.
	(ii) Compulsory education for children aged 6-12.
	(iii) State training colleges to award teaching certificates.

(iv) Country to be partitioned into school districts, each administered by elected school committee.

(v) Minister of Public Instruction to be appointed.

Government grant of £20,000 for 'the Erection of School Houses' in Great Britain. Considerable subsidies (about £2½ million between 1811 and 1828) had already been paid to assist education in Ireland.

1836   Kennedy became headmaster of Shrewsbury School.

Home and Colonial Infant School Society founded.

Glasgow Normal Seminary founded by David Stow.

1837   School of Design founded.

1838   J. P. Kay (Shuttleworth) started training school at Norwood.

1839   Committee of Council for Education set up.

1840   Grammar Schools Act: new subjects permitted in curriculum of grammar schools.

Battersea training college opened.

1841   Cheltenham College founded.

1842   Richard Dawes opened school at King's Somborne.

1843   Sir James Graham's Factory Bill:

(i) Children under 13 in factories to be instructed for 3 hours a day.

(ii) Government loans to build new factory schools.

(iii) Fees to be a maximum of 3d. a week and finance from poor rates.

(iv) Committees of 7 to administer schools: local Anglican clergyman, 2 churchwardens + 4 members elected by magistrates.

(v) Religious instruction to be based on Book of Common Prayer; church attendance compulsory; conscience clause for dissenters.

Committee of Council grants for teachers' houses and school apparatus.

Governesses' Benevolent Institution founded.

Marlborough College founded.

1846   Pupil teacher system initiated by Committee of Council.

1847   Reports of the Commissioners of Inquiry into the State of Education in Wales.

Supplementary grants (for purchase of approved school books) made available by Committee of Council.

1849   College of Preceptors incorporated.

1850   North London Collegiate School founded by Frances Mary Buss.

1851   School of Mines founded.

1852-3   Reports of Royal Commissions on the Universities of Oxford and Cambridge.

1853   Lord John Russell's Education Bill proposed *inter alia* that school committees be established in boroughs.

Capitation grants first offered.   PTO

Department of Science and Art founded.

Charity Commission set up.

Edward Thring became headmaster of Uppingham School.

Local examinations started by College of Preceptors.

Cheltenham Ladies' College founded.

1854   First kindergarten opened in England.

1855   Sir John Pakington's Education Bill (No. 2)

(i)   Assumed that 'voluntary system has broken down'

(ii)   Borough councils or poor law unions to be permitted to provide educational facilities.

1856   Education Department set up.

1857   T. Hughes: *Tom Brown's Schooldays*.

1858   Oxford and Cambridge local examinations started.

Dorothea Beale became headmistress of Cheltenham Ladies' College.

1859   Robert Lowe became vice-president of Committee of Council.

1861   The Report of Newcastle Commission (on Popular Education in England):

(i)   Terms of reference: . . . to Inquire into the Present State of Popular Education in England, and to consider and report what Measures, if any, are required for the Extension of sound and cheap elementary Instruction to all Classes of the People.

(ii)   Main recommendations: the commission suggested that elementary schools should receive two kinds of grant – one for attendance from the state and a county rate grant based upon the principle of payment by results.

(a) There should be an annual grant from the state of 4s.6d. to 6s. per child for average attendance and 'discipline, efficiency, and general character of the school'.

(b) There should be an additional state grant of 2s.6d. per child for average attendance dependent upon correct ratio of pupil teachers (1:30) or assistant teachers (1:60).

(c) School managers to receive a county rate grant of 22s.6d. to 21s. for 'every child who has attended the school during 140 days in the year preceding the day of the examination and who passes an examination before the county examiner in reading, writing, arithmetic and who, if a girl, also passes an examination in plain work . . . '

(d) Children under 7 not to be examined, but a 20s. grant to be made for each child in average daily attendance.

(e) 'The two grants together are never to exceed the fees and subscriptions, or 15s. per child on the average attendance.'

(f) County and Borough Boards of Education to be set up.

(g) 'The Boards of Education shall appoint examiners, being certificated masters of at least seven years standing.'

H. Spencer: *Education*.

1862   The Revised Code: this measure swept away the existing system of central government grants and replaced it by a yearly payment to

	Standard I	Standard II	Standard III	Standard IV	Standard V	Standard VI
Reading	Narrative in monosyllables	One of the narratives next in order after monosyllables in an elementary reading book used in the school.	A short paragraph from an elementary reading book used in the school.	A short paragraph from a more advanced reading book used in the school.	A few lines of poetry from a reading book used in the first class of the school.	A short ordinary paragraph in a newspaper, or other modern narrative.
Writing	Form on black-board or slate, from dictation, letters, capital and small, manuscript.	Copy in manuscript character a line of print.	A sentence from the same paragraph, slowly read once, and then dictated in single words.	A sentence slowly dictated once by a few words at a time, from the same book, but not from the paragraph read.	A sentence slowly dictated once, by a few words at a time, from a reading book used in the first class of the school.	Another short ordinary paragraph in a newspaper, or other modern narrative slowly dictated once by a few words at a time.
Arithmetic	Form on black-board or slate, from dictation, figures up to 20; name at sight figures up to 20; add and subtract figures up to 10, orally, from examples on black-board.	A sum in simple addition or subtraction, and the multiplication table.	A sum in any simple rule as far as short division (inclusive).	A sum in compound rules (money).	A sum in compound rules (common weights and measures).	A sum in practice or bills of parcels.

Revised Code Standards

each school based upon attendance and individual examination in reading, writing, and arithmetic.

(i)   Payment by Results.

(ii) 4/- grant to managers for each scholar according to the average number in attendance throughout the year at the morning and afternoon meetings of their school.

(iii) Each child over 6 with more than 200 half-day attendances to gain a further grant of 8/-; 2/8d of this to be forfeited for examination failure in each of the following: reading, writing and arithmetic.

(iv) Children aged 6-12 to be examined under 6 standards.

(v)   Children under 6 with more than 200 attendances to gain 6/6d without individual examination.

1864 The Report of Clarendon Commission (on principal public schools):

(i)   Terms of reference: . . . for the Purpose of inquiring into the Nature and Application of the Endowments, Funds, and Revenues belonging to or received by the herein-after mentioned Colleges, Schools, and Foundations, namely the College of the Blessed Mary of Eton, near Windsor (commonly called Eton College), Saint Mary College, Winchester (commonly called Winchester College), the Collegiate School of Saint Peter, Westminster, . . . the Charterhouse, St. Paul's School in the City of London, the Merchant Taylor's School in the City of London, the Free Grammar School . . . at Harrow-on-the-Hill, . . . the School founded by Lawrence Sheriff, at Rugby, . . . the Free Grammar School of King Edward the Sixth at Shrewsbury; and also to inquire into the Administration and Management of the said Colleges, Schools, and Foundations, and into the System and Course of Studies respectively pursued therein . . .

(ii) Main recommendations:

(a)   'The Governing Bodies of the several colleges and schools should be reformed, so far as may be necessary, in order to render them thoroughly suitable and efficient for the purposes and duties which they are designed to fulfil.' (I)

(b)   'The Head Master should have the uncontrolled power of selecting and dismissing assistant masters; of regulating the arrangement of the school in classes or divisions, the hours of school work, and the holidays and half holidays, . . . of maintaining discipline, prescribing bounds, and laying down other rules for the government of the boys; . . . of administering punishment, and of expulsion.' (V)

(c)   There should be a School Council of masters to meet at least once a month. (VI)

(d)   'The classical languages and literature should continue to hold the principal place in the course of study.' (VIII)

(e)   'In addition to the study of the classics and to religious teaching, every boy . . . should receive instruction in arithmetic and mathematics; in one modern language at least, which should be either French or German; in some one branch at least of natural science, and in either drawing or music. Care should also be taken to ensure that the boys acquire a good general knowledge of geography and of ancient history, some acquaintance with modern history, and a command of pure grammatical English.' (IX)

(f)   There should be arrangements for boys 'after arriving at a certain place in the school, and upon the request of their parents or guardians to specialise in non-classical or classical subjects'. (XIII)

1866	Cambridge local examinations opened to girls.
1867	Parliamentary Reform Act.
1867-8	Revised Code modified: additional grant for specific subjects.
1868	Public Schools Act.

The Report of the Schools Inquiry (or Taunton) Commission:

(i)   Terms of reference: . . . for inquiring into the Education given in Schools not comprised within the Scope of (the Newcastle and Clarendon Commissions), and also to consider and report what Measures (if any) are required for the Improvement of such Education, having especial Regard to all Endowments applicable, or which can rightly be made applicable thereto.

(ii)   Main recommendations: these dealt principally with the organization, administration, and financing of a three-tier system of endowed secondary schools.

(a)   'The first requisite is to adapt the schools to the work which is now required of them, by prescribing such a course of study as is demanded by the needs of the country.'

(b)   'We need schools of the first grade, which propose to continue school work to the age of 18 or 19; schools of the second grade, which suppose it to stop about 16; and schools of the third grade, which suppose it to stop about 14.'

(c)   'We are of opinion, that, in all arrangements relating to education, it will be expedient to provide, that it shall be possible eventually to allow each county, subject still to superior authority, to have the control of its own schools.' But in the first place the 11 regional divisions of the Registrar General should be adopted as Provincial Authorities; these should determine the grade of individual schools and suggest how to reform endowments.

(d)   A Central Authority should be created to arrange the resettlement of trusts, the inspection of endowed secondary schools and the audit of their accounts. It should also check endowments for elementary education.

(e)   Parliament should regulate the purposes to which endowments should be applied.

(f)   Indiscriminate free instruction should be abolished; it should only be given in future as a reward for merit.

(g)   '. . . we are of opinion, that, if any town or parish should desire to rate itself for the establishment of a school or schools above the elementary, it should be allowed to do so.' Rate aid should only be used for land purchase, school building and fees for 'meritorious boys selected from the elementary school of the parish or town'.

(h)   '. . . we should suggest the creation of a Council of Examinations to consist of twelve members, two to be elected by each of the Universities of Oxford, Cambridge, and London, and six to be appointed by the Crown . . .

To this Council should be assigned the duty of drawing up the general rules for the examination of schools, and of appointing the examiners . . .'

T. H. Huxley: *Essay on a Liberal Education*.

1869   Endowed Schools Act: created commission to reform endowed schools.
Cambridge higher local examinations started.
Beginnings of Headmasters' Conference.

1870   Education Act (W. E. Forster): this act assumed that the voluntary societies had insufficient resources to provide an adequate network of elementary schools. It therefore created governmental machinery by which state schools (controlled by school boards) could be founded in areas where there was a need 'to fill up gaps'.

(i)   Education Department empowered to initiate school boards which were to be elected by rate payers.

(ii)   No rate aid to denominational schools.

(iii) Provision for by-laws enforcing compulsory attendance.

(iv)   Forster anticipated that a 3d. rate would suffice to finance school board expenditure. In fact it later reached an exceptional 30d. in West Ham.

(v)   Religious instruction no longer to be inspected by department; board schools to give only undenominational religious teaching (Cowper-Temple clause).

(vi)   All schools in receipt of grant to adopt conscience clause.

(vii) Section 16 empowered Education Department ('whose decision thereon shall be final') to declare a school board in default.

National Union of Elementary Teachers founded.

1871   New Code:

(i)   Secular (i.e., board) schools eligible for grants.

(ii)   Old Standard I abolished; new Standard VI established.

(iii) 6/- attendance grant; 4/- for each of 3 Rs.

(iv)   8/- to 10/- grant for infants.

1872   Girls' Public Day School Trust instituted.

1874	Froebel Society founded.
	Oxford and Cambridge Joint Board examinations instituted.

1875   Grants introduced for class subjects.
The Devonshire Report (Royal Commission on Scientific Instruction and the Advancement of Science): basically concerned with higher education, this report also considered science teaching in schools and urged that more attention should be paid to the subject. The commissioners felt 'compelled . . . to record our opinion that the Present State of Scientific Instruction in our Schools is extremely unsatisfactory', and concluded that the 'almost total exclusion (of science) from the training of the upper and middle classes' amounted to 'little less than a national misfortune'.

1876   Education Act (Lord Sandon):
(i)   Parents required to ensure their children received efficient education.
(ii)   No child under ten allowed to undertake paid employment.
(iii)   Certificates of attendance or proficiency in '3 Rs' required before children aged 10-14 could leave school.
(iv)   School attendance committess to be set up where no school board existed to carry out provisions of act.
(v)   'Pound for pound' principle revoked; grant allowed to exceed income from other sources up to 17/6 per head.
(vi)   Provision to be made for day industrial schools for vagrant and delinquent children.

1877   Maria Grey Training College founded.

1880   Education Act: A. J. Mundella's act provided for compulsory elementary education (5-10); exemption based upon attendance and attainment was allowable for children up to 14.
Regent Street Polytechnic opened.

1881   The Aberdare Report (on Intermediate and Higher Education in Wales): resulted in Welsh Intermediate Education Act (1889) which facilitated the provision of secondary school places in Wales.

1882   Code modification:
(i)   Standard VII instituted.
(ii)   Grants for examination to be worked out on a general basis.
(iii)   Merit grant introduced.

1883   Finsbury Technical College opened.

1884   Parliamentary Reform Act.
The Samuelson Report (Royal Commission on Technical Instruction): urged that more attention should be paid to technical instruction in schools.
Toynbee Hall founded 'to link the universities with East London'.
Central Technical College opened.

1885   Roedean (girls' residential public school) founded.

1888   Local Government Act: county and county borough councils created.
                The Cross Report (on elementary education):
                Terms of reference: . . . to inquire into the working of the
                Elementary Education Acts, England and Wales.

Main findings and recommendations: one of the most controversial recommendations was No. 183 of the Majority Report, which sought a fundamental revision of the 1870 principle that rate aid should be available to board schools and not to their denominational rivals.

Majority Report

(a)   '. . . on the whole the demand for school accommodation has been fairly met.' (1)

(b)   '. . . it is neither fair nor wise to prevent elementary teachers from rising to the rank of inspectors . . .' (14)

(c)   'That the employment of women of superior social position and general culture has a refining and an excellent effect upon schools.'(25)

(d)   'That the salaries of teachers ought to be fixed, and should not fluctuate with the grant.'(26)

(e)   'That, having regard to moral qualifications, there is no other available, or, as we prefer to say, equally trustworthy source as that of pupil teachers, from which an adequate supply of teachers is likely to be forthcoming; and that, with modifications tending to the improvement of the education of pupil-teachers, the system of apprenticeship ought to be upheld.'(28)

(f)   '. . . an experiment should be made of training non-residential students in connection with local university colleges . . .'(42)

(g)   'That, however desirable higher elementary schools may be, the principle involved in their addition to our system should, if approved, be avowedly adopted; and that their indirect inclusion in the present system is injurious to both primary and secondary instruction.'(148)

(h)   '. . . the present system of "payment by results" is carried too far and is too rigidly applied . . .'(162)

(i)   (1)   that the fixed grant be increased to 10s. per child in average attendance.
      (2)   that the conditions on which the variable portion of the grant are now made be so far modified as to secure that the amount shall depend on the good character of the school and on the quality of the acquirements of the great majority of the scholars, rather than on the exact number of the children who attain the minimum standard of acquired knowledge . . .'(164)

(j)   'That the time has now come when . . . some more comprehensive system of administration should be found . . .'(181)

(k)   'That there is no reason why . . . rate aid, in respect of their secular efficiency, should not be given to voluntary schools . . .'(183)

Minority Reports

(a)   Rate aid for voluntary schools opposed as being 'unsound in principle, destructive of the settlement of 1870, and certain, if it became law, to embitter educational politics, and intensify sectarian rivalries'.

(b)   ' . . . the complaint is general that the pupil-teachers teach badly, and are badly taught.'

' . . . we strongly recommend that, wherever it is practicable, a central system of instruction of the pupil-teachers should be introduced . . .'⟩

1890   Day Training colleges founded. ⟩
'Whisky Money' for technical education.

1891   Elementary Education Act: free elementary education. ⟩

1895   The Bryce Report (on secondary education):

(i)   Terms of reference: . . . to consider what are the best methods of establishing a well-organized system of Secondary Education in England, taking into account existing deficiencies, and having regard to such local sources of revenue from endowment or otherwise as are available or may be made available for this purpose, and make recommendations accordingly.

(ii)   Main recommendations:

(a)   'We conceive . . . that some central authority is required, not in order to control, but rather to supervise the Secondary Education of the country . . . .'(1)

(b)   'The central authority ought to consist of a Department of the Executive Government, presided over by a Minister responsible to Parliament . . . .'(2)

(c)   'We . . . recommend that there shall be created a Local Education Authority for Secondary Education in every county and in every county borough . . . .'(31)

(d)   Proposed local authority to be responsible for:

1.   'The securing a due provision of secondary instruction.

2.   The re-modelling, where necessary, and supervision of the working of endowed . . . schools and other educational endowments.

3.   A watchful survey of the field of Secondary Education, with the object of bringing proprietary and private schools into the general educational system . . . .

4.   The administration of such sums, either arising from the rates levied within its area, or paid over from the National Exchequer, ⟩ as may be at its disposal for the promotion of education.'

1896   Sir John Gorst's Education Bill:

(i)   Local education authority to be estbalished in every county and county borough.

(ii)   The new authority was to channel public money to schools.

(iii)   School boards to be confined to supervising elementary education.

(iv)   4/- per head grant to necessitous Board and Voluntary schools.

(v)   17/6d. per head grant limit to be abolished.

(vi)   Managers of any elementary school to provide religious education as desired by parents.

1897   Education Act:
   (i)   17/6d. per head grant limit abolished.
  (ii)   'Aid Grant' of 5/- per head to be paid to necessitous voluntary schools through Association of Voluntary Schools.
Payment by Results finally phased out.

1899   Board of Education Act:
Central Authority (Board of Education) established to 'superintend' education.

1900   Block Grant system of teacher training introduced.
Cockerton Judgement: London School Board censured for financing postelementary education from rates.

1902   Education Act:
   (i)   Abolished school boards.
  (ii)   County and county borough councils became the local education authorities.
 (iii)   The new LEAs made responsible for provision of state elementary and secondary education.
 (iv)   Voluntary schools to be given rate aid.

1904   Regulations for Secondary Schools:
   (i)   Grant-aided secondary schools to provide a 4-year course for pupils aged 12-16.
  (ii)   Curriculum to be nonvocational: English, Geography, History, Science, Mathematics, Modern Language(s), Latin.
 (iii)   Detailed requirements concerning administration of secondary schools.

1905   Handbook of Suggestions for the Consideration of Teachers issued.

1906   Education (Provision of Meals) Act.
Birrell's Education Bill: attempted to modify the 1902 provisions relating to voluntary schools.

1907   25% Free Place Regulations: secondary schools in receipt of central government grants to offer a minimum of 25% free places to elementary school children.
Medical Branch of Board of Education established.
Welsh Department of Board of Education set up.

1908   R. McKenna's Education Bill: another attempt to modify 1902 Act.

1911   Edmond Holmes: *What Is and What Might Be.*

1912   Maria Montessori: *The Montessori Method.*

1913   Regulations for junior technical schools first issued.

1914   Rachel McMillan started nursery school at Deptford, London.

1917   Secondary School Examination Council set up: institution of School
            Certificate Examinations.

1918   Women over thirty get the vote (qualifying age lowered to twenty-
            one in 1928).
            Education Act: aimed 'to establish a national system of education'.
     (i)   Board of Education empowered to require LEAs to submit
            educational schemes.
     (ii)   Compulsory schooling 5-14.
     (iii) Continuation schools for school-leavers aged 14-16 (ultimately 18):
            320 hours attendance per year.
     (iv)   50% of approved LEA expenditure to be met by government.

1919   University Grants Committee set up.
            Burnham Committee instituted (teachers' salaries).

1920   State Scholarships begun.
            T. P. Nunn: *Education: its Data and First Principles.*

1921   Summerhill founded by A. S. Neill.

1923   Stowe School founded.

1924   Susan Isaacs started Malting House School.

1925   Report of departmental committee on training of teachers for
            elementary schools.

1926   Joint Boards for teacher training instituted.
            Circular 1381: effective establishment of direct grant school list.
            The first Hadow Report (*The Education of the Adolescent*):
     (i)   Terms of Reference:
            (a) To consider and report upon the organization, objective and
            curriculum of courses of study suitable for children who will remain
            in full-time attendance at schools, other than Secondary Schools, up
            to the age of 15, regard being had on the one hand to the
            requirements of a good general education and the desirability of
            providing a reasonable variety of curriculum, so far as is practicable,
            for children of varying tastes and abilities, and on the other hand
            the probable occupations of the pupils in commerce, industry and
            agriculture.
            (b) Incidentally thereto, to advise as to the arrangements which
            should be made:
                1. For testing the attainments of the pupils at the end of their
                course;
                2. For facilitating in suitable cases the transfer of individual
                pupils to secondary schools at an age above the normal age of
                admission.
     (ii)   Main recommendations: the Consultative Committee confirmed that
            the traditional concept of elementary education should be replaced
            by the adoption of a system of primary education ending at about

11 + and to be followed by a secondary stage which would encompass the remainder of a pupil's school career.

(a) 'All normal children should go forward to some form of post-primary education.'(4)

(b) 'It is desirable that education up to the age of 11 + should be known by the general name of Primary Education, and education after that age by the general name of Secondary Education, and that the schools . . . which are concerned with the secondary stage of education, should be called by the following designations:

    1. Schools of the "secondary" type . . . which at present pursue in the main a predominantly literary or scientific curriculum, to be known as Grammar Schools.

    2. Schools of the type of the existing selective Central Schools, which give at least a four years' course from the age of 11 + , with a "realistic" or practical trend in the last two years, to be known as Modern Schools.

    3. Schools of the type of the present non-selective Central Schools . . . also to be known as Modern Schools.

    4. Departments or classes within public elementary schools, providing post-primary education . . . to be known as "Senior Classes".'(8)

(c) The curriculum of Modern Schools was to be 'more limited in scope' than that of Grammar Schools. 'Though the subjects included . . . will be much the same as those in Grammar Schools, more time and attention will be devoted to handwork and similar pursuits . . .'(9)

(d) 'The education of children over the age of 11 in Modern Schools and Senior Classes is one species of the genus "secondary education". It is not an inferior species, and it ought not to be hampered by conditions of accommodation and equipment inferior to those of Grammar Schools.'(19)

(e) The 11 + examination should consist of 'a written examination . . . and also, wherever possible, an oral examination. A written psychological test might also be specially employed in dealing with border-line cases . . . .'(20)

(f) 'A new Leaving Examination should be framed to meet the needs of pupils in . . . Modern Schools and in the Senior classes which retain some of their pupils to the age of 15 . . .'(22)

1927   Departmental Committee report on *Welsh Education and Life* proposed policy of bilingualism.

1928   Board of Education pamphlet: *The New Prospect in Education*.

1929   Board of Education issued memorandum supporting bilingualism in Welsh primary schools.
    Godfrey Thomson: *A Modern Philosophy of Education*.

1930   Susan Isaacs: *Intellectual Growth in Young Children.*

1931   The second Hadow Report (*The Primary School*):
   (i)   Terms of reference: to inquire and report as to the courses of study
            suitable for children (other than children in infants' departments) up
            to the age of 11 in elementary schools, with special reference to the
            needs of children in rural areas.
   (ii)   Main recommendations: this report gave qualified approval to
            progressive methods of teaching.
            (a) 'We are of opinion that the curriculum of the primary school is
            to be thought of in terms of activity and experience, rather than of
            knowledge to be acquired and facts to be stored.' (30)
            (b) 'The traditional practice of dividing the matter of primary
            instruction into separate "subjects", taught in distinct lessons,
            should be reconsidered. The treatment of a series of central topics
            which have relations with many subjects, may be a useful alternative.
            It is, however, essential that provision should be made for an
            adequate amount of "drill" in reading, writing and arithmetic.' (34)
            (c) 'Carefully devised papers in English and arithmetic should be
            sufficient as a basic test of capacity and attainment at the age of
            eleven. . . . Carefully devised group intelligence tests may be a
            useful factor in selection, but in our opinion it would be inadvisable
            to rely on such tests alone.' (64-65).

1932   'Free places' at grammar schools changed to 'special places': parental
            contributions according to income.

1933   The third Hadow Report on Infant and Nursery Schools.

1938   The Spens Report (*Secondary Education*):
   (i)   Terms of reference: to consider and report upon the organization
            and interrelation of schools, other than those administered under the
            Elementary Code, which provide education for pupils beyond the
            age of 11 + ; regard being had in particular to the framework and
            content of the education of pupils who do not remain at school
            beyond the age of about sixteen.
   (ii)   Main recommendations: this report formulated a true tripartite
            system of secondary education by recommending the creation of
            technical high schools to supplement the grammar and modern
            schools of the first Hadow Report.
            (a) 'We are convinced that it is of great importance to establish a
            new type of higher school of technical character quite distinct from
            the traditional academic Grammar School. . . . We recommend that
            such schools, which would recruit their pupils at the age of 11 + and
            provide a five-year course up to the age of 16 + , should be called
            Technical High Schools . . .' (109)
            (b) The committee was unable to 'advocate the adoption of
            multilateralism as a general policy in England and Wales', but did

not wish 'to deprecate experiments for establishing multilateral schools, especially in areas of new population.' (129-130)

(c)   The committee recommended 'the adoption of 100 per cent Special Places' (scholarships) in secondary schools. (139)

(d)   The committee also considered it 'of great importance that everything possible should be done to secure parity of status for Grammar Schools, Technical High Schools, and Modern Schools'. (p. xxxv).

1939   First Ysgol Gymraeg (Welsh-language school in an anglicized area) opened privately at Aberystwyth.

1942   National Youth Advisory Council formed.

1943   White Paper: *Educational Reconstruction*.
The Norwood Report (*Curriculum and Examinations in Secondary Schools*):

(i)   Terms of reference: to consider suggested changes in the secondary school curriculum and the question of school examinations in relation thereto.

(ii)   Main recommendations: this report confirmed the theory of tripartism by postulating three 'rough groupings' of children whose respective abilities would suit them to three different kinds of education.

(a)   'Accordingly we would advocate that there should be three types of education, which we think of as the secondary Grammar, the secondary Technical, the secondary Modern, that each type should have such parity as amenities and conditions can bestow; parity of esteem in our view cannot be conferred by administrative decree nor by equality of cost per pupil; it can only be won by the school itself.' (p. 14).

(b)   'In each secondary school of whatever kind pupils of the ages 11 + to 13 + should form a "Lower School". The curriculum of the Lower School should be roughly common to all schools.' (6)

(c)   'During the years 11 + to 13 + transfer should take place as desirable; but at 13 + the pupils in each Lower School should be reviewed and be recommended to the school giving the most appropriate kind of secondary education.' (7)

1944   Education Act:

(i)   Created Ministry of Education under a minister with wide powers to 'secure the effective execution by local authorities, under his control and direction, of the national policy' concerning education.

(ii)   Two Central Advisory Councils for Education created – one for England and one for Wales.

(iii)   Public education to be organized 'in three progressive stages to be known as primary education, secondary education, and further education.' No fees to be payable in maintained schools.

(iv)   Nature of secular instruction to be under control of LEA.

(v)   Religious education to be given in all aided schools; conscience clause to allow exemption.

(vi)   LEAs to 'have regard to the general principle that, so far as is compatible with the provision of efficient instruction and training and the avoidance of unreasonable public expenditure, pupils are to be educated in accordance with the wishes of their parents'.

(vii)   Compulsory schooling to 15; to be raised when practicable to 16.

The Fleming Report (*The Public Schools and the General Educational System*):

(i)   Terms of reference: to consider means whereby the association between the public schools (by which term is meant schools which are in membership of the Governing Bodies' Association or Headmasters' Conference) and the general educational system of the country could be developed and extended; also to consider how far any measures recommended in the case of boys' public schools could be applied to comparable schools for girls.

(ii)   Main recommendations:

(a)   Scheme A: independent (day) schools to abolish fees (or grade them). Financial compensation obtainable from central or local authority.

(b)   Scheme B:
'That the Board of Education shall grant bursaries to qualified pupils who have previously been educated for at least two years at a grant-aided Primary School, to enable them to proceed to Boarding Schools accepted for inclusion in this Scheme . . . .'(16)
'That schools accepted for this Scheme shall offer in the first instance a minimum of 25 per cent of their annual admissions to pupils from grant-aided Primary Schools . . . .'(18)
'That Local Education Authorities be empowered by agreement with the Board and the Governing Bodies of the schools to reserve under this scheme a certain number of places at particular schools for pupils from their areas. . . .' (20)

The McNair Report (*Teachers and Youth Leaders*):

(i)   Terms of reference: to investigate the present sources of supply and the methods of recruitment and training of teachers and youth leaders and to report what principles should guide the board in these matters in the future.

(ii)   Main recommendations:

(a)   'that the Board of Education should ensure that teachers in grant-aided schools are not required to resign or otherwise give up their appointments solely on the ground of marriage.' (6)
(b)   'that the salaries of teachers in primary and secondary schools should be substantially increased.' (8)

(c) 'that the President of the Board of Education should appoint a Central Training Council for England and Wales . . . .' (9)

(d)   Alternative Schemes:

1.   that each university should establish one or more Schools of Education which 'should consist of an organic federation of approved training institutions . . . .' (10)

2.   that reconstituted Joint Boards 'should become responsible for the organisation of an area training service in which there will be a university training department and training colleges preserving their identity . . . .' (11)

(e)   that the "pledge" (i.e., an undertaking to become a teacher in return for a student grant) should be abandoned as soon as possible. (15)

(f)   that teaching certificate course (nongraduate) last three years. (16)

(g)   'that the salaries of the staffs of training colleges should be on a higher scale than that of the schools and should approximate to university levels.' (22)

1945   Emergency Training Scheme introduced.
National Foundation for Educational Research set up.
Ministry of Education pamphlet *The Nation's Schools* endorsed tripartite organization of state secondary education.
The Percy Report (Special Committee on Higher Technological Education): recommended development of 'a strictly limited number' of technical colleges offering courses of degree status in technology.

1946   The Barlow Report (*Scientific Manpower*): argued that 'there is clearly an ample reserve of intelligence in the country to allow both a doubling of university numbers and at the same time a raising of standards . . . .'; it recommended therefore that twice as many scientists should be accommodated in university courses. Similar expansion of nonscientific courses was also envisaged.

1947   Burnham salary scale introduced: this provided a unified scale of salaries for teachers, with additions for extra qualifications (degrees, etc.).
School-leaving age raised to 15.
First L.E.A. Ysgol Gymraeg started at Llanelli.
Ministry of Education pamphlet: *The New Secondary Education*.

1948   National Advisory Committee on Education for Industry and Commerce set up.

1949   National Advisory Council on Training and Supply of Teachers constituted.

1951   Emergency Training Scheme ended.
General Certificate of Education introduced.
Sir Eric James: *Education and Leadership*.

1953   *The Place of Welsh and English in the Schools of Wales* (Central Advisory Council for Wales): this report outlined guidelines for bilingual teaching.

1954   Central Advisory Council's report *Early Leaving*: emphasized influence of home background upon the length of a child's school career.
Michael Croft: *Spare the Rod*.

1955   Equal pay for women teachers to be phased in over seven instalments.
National Council for Technological Awards set up.
Edward Blishen: *Roaring Boys*.

1956   White Paper on Technical Education.

1958   Local Government Act introduced general grant for local authorities.
White Paper on Secondary Education.

1959   The Crowther Report (*15 to 18*):

   (i)   Terms of reference: the education of boys and girls between the ages of 15 and 18.

   (ii)   Main recommendations:

(a) 'Extended courses should be made available for all modern school pupils. By 1965 we think it possible that extended courses will be needed for half the 15 year-olds . . . .'

(b) 'Many, probably more than half, of the pupils of the modern schools would have their education deflected from its proper lines by being prepared for an external examination . . . .'

(c) 'In the examinable minority, two groups can be distinguished. One of these consists of those boys and girls who have the ability to attempt some of the subjects in the G.C.E. at Ordinary level. It is important that none of them should be denied the opportunity to do so.'

(d) 'There remains another group – consisting of about one-third or rather more of the pupils in modern schools over the age of 15 – for whom external examinations below the level of the G.C.E. may serve a useful purpose, and official policy should be modified to recognize this. . . . External examinations should . . . develop on a regional, or preferably a local, basis.'

(e) 'Both the unfulfilled provisions of the Education Act of 1944 affecting older children – the raising of the school-leaving age to 16, and the creation of county colleges for compulsory part-time day education to 18 – should be re-affirmed as objectives of national policy.'

(f) 'The country is a long way from tapping all the available supply of talent by present methods – half the National Service recruits to the Army who were rated in the two highest ability groups had left school at 15.'

E. R. Braithwaite: *To Sir, with Love*.

1960   The Beloe Report (*Secondary School Examinations other than G.C.E.*): recommended the establishment of a new category of examination (C.S.E.) for approximately 40 percent of fifth year secondary pupils whose ability range was below that required for G.C.E.

1963   The Newsom Report (*Half our Future*):

(i)   Terms of reference: to consider the education between the ages of 13 and 16 of pupils of average or less than average ability who are or will be following full-time courses either at schools or in establishments of further education. The term education shall be understood to include extra-curricular activities.

(ii)   Main recommendations:

(a)   'An immediate announcement should be made that the school-leaving age will be raised to sixteen for all pupils entering the secondary schools from September 1965 onwards.'(1)

(b)   'An interdepartmental Working Party should be set up to deal with the general social problems, including education, in slum areas. . . .' (3)

(c)   'All schools should provide a choice of programme, including a range of courses broadly related to occupational interests, for pupils in the fourth and fifth years of a five year course, and should be adequately equipped to do so.' (4)

(d)   'The schools should provide all sixteen year-old leavers with some form of internal leaving certificate . . . .
They should resist external pressures to extend public examinations to pupils for whom they are inappropriate . . . .
No pupils should be entered for any external examination before the fifth year . . . .' (10)

(e)   '. . . action should be continued and, indeed, accelerated to remedy the existing functional deficiencies of schools, especially in relation to provision for practical subjects, science and libraries . . . .' (12)

The Robbins Report (*Higher Education*):

(i)   Terms of reference: to review the pattern of full-time higher education in Great Britain and in the light of national needs and resources to advise Her Majesty's Government on what principles its long-term development should be based. In particular, to advise, in the light of these principles, whether there should be any changes in that pattern, whether any new types of institution are desirable and whether any modifications should be made in the present arrangements for planning and coordinating the development of the various types of institution.

(ii)   Main recommendations: the report endorsed 'pool of ability' arguments that 'large numbers of able young people do not at present enter higher education'.

(a)   'Compared with the 216,000 students in full-time higher education in Great Britain in 1962/63, places should be available for about 390,000 in 1973/74 and, on present estimates, for about 560,000 in 1980/81.' (1)

(b)   Teacher training colleges should (unless under exceptional circumstances), ultimately contain a minimum of 750 students (28); four year courses leading to a Bachelor of Education degree should be provided for suitable students (33); training colleges should be renamed 'Colleges of Education'. (34)

(c)   'The colleges in each university's Institute of Education and the University Department of Education should be formed into a School of Education.' (35)

(d)   'The volume of postgraduate work in science and technology should be considerably increased . . . .' (48)

(e)   Five Special Institutions for Scientific and Technological Education and Research (SISTERs) 'should be selected for rapid development'. (51)

(f)   Colleges of Advanced Technology 'should in general be designated as technological universities . . . .' (56)

(g)   Council for National Academic Awards should be established perhaps by royal charter. (74)

(h)   'Of the 392,000 places needed in 1973/74, 219,000 should be in universities, 122,000 in Colleges of Education and 51,000 in further education.' (97)

(i)   'Provision should be made for a growth in the proportion of students taking science and, particularly, technology.' (99)

(j)   'This can, and should, be achieved without reducing the proportion taking arts subjects.' (100)

1964   Ministry of Education retitled Department of Education and Science.
            Schools Council for Curriculum and Examinations.
            Council for National Academic Awards.

1964-6   Introduction of Certificate of Secondary Education.

1965   Circular 10/65: LEAs requested to prepare schemes for comprehensive reorganization of secondary education.

1966   White Paper: *Polytechnics and other colleges*.

1967   The Plowden Report (*Children and their Primary Schools*):

(i)   Terms of reference: to consider primary education in all its aspects, and the transition to secondary education.

(ii)   Main recommendations: like the 1931 Hadow Report, Plowden gave its approval to progressive methods of teaching. It also pressed for community involvement on the part of schools and their staff and formulated a policy of 'positive discrimination' to help schools in deprived areas.

(a)   'All schools should have a programme for contact with

children's homes . . . .' (1)

(b) 'As a matter of national policy, "positive discrimination" should favour schools in neighbourhoods where children are most severely handicapped by home conditions . . . .' (8)

(c) Schools in Educational Priority Areas should have improved staff ratios; staff should receive a salary addition of £120; there should be a teacher's aide for every two classes, and preferential treatment in building programmes, equipment, and nursery provision. (14)

(d) Special attention should be paid to the education of the children of immigrants. (23-27)

(e) Nursery education (3-5) should be expanded 'so that over the country as a whole provision should be made for 15 per cent of children to attend both a morning and afternoon session.' (45)

(f) Infants' schools (5-8) should be renamed 'first schools'. (57). Junior schools (8-12) should be renamed 'middle schools'. (58) Transfer to secondary school would thus be delayed for a year.

(g) 'The infliction of physical pain as a method of punishment in primary schools should be forbidden.' (94)

(h) 'We recommend a combination of individual group work and class work and welcome the trend towards individual learning.' (96)

(i) 'We welcome unstreaming in the infant school and hope that it will continue to spread through the age groups of the junior school.' (100)

(j) Trained teachers' aides should be employed under teachers' supervision (1 to 2 infant or 4 junior classes). (120)

(k) 'There should be a full enquiry into the system of training teachers.' (134)

(l) More money should be made available for minor building works and projects. (166-167)

The Gittins Report (*Primary Education in Wales*):

(i)   Terms of Reference: as for the Plowden Report.

(ii) Main recommendations: the Gittins Report accepted the principal Plowden attitudes towards primary education, which perhaps was not surprising as Professor Gittins and one of his colleagues served on the Plowden Committee. But in addition it emphasized the role of the Welsh language in primary education. The Gittins Report also recommended that the statutory 1944 requirement 'making religious education compulsory should be relaxed' (para. 20.3).

(a) 'We . . . desire at the outset to make it plain that we accept certain major aspects of the discussion and recommendations of the (Plowden Report).' These areas included nursery education, E.P.A.s and the Plowden 'philosophy of education.' (pp. 2-3)

(b) 'Each child should be given the opportunity of learning effectively his second language, Welsh or English, during the

primary stage. To create the conditions for effective bilingualism, the
second language should be introduced as early as feasible and be
used at the appropriate time and in reasonable measure as a parallel
medium of instruction.

Each child should be given sufficient opportunity to become
reasonably bilingual by the end of the primary stage, i.e. between 11
and 13 years . . .' (para. 11.11)

1968 The Public Schools Commission, First Report (boarding schools):

(i) Terms of reference: to advise on the best way of integrating the
public schools with the state system of education. For the immediate
purpose of the commission public schools are defined as those
independent schools now in membership of the Headmasters'
Conference, Governing Bodies' Association, or Governing Bodies of
Girls' Schools Association.

(ii) Main recommendations:

(a) 'Suitable and willing' independent boarding schools should
accept a minimum of 50% of their pupils from state schools. (1)
(b) Admission from state schools to be based upon criteria of
comprehensive selection and social needs. (2 and 21)

1969 First Black Paper on Education published.
R. S. Peters: *Perspectives on Plowden*.

1970 Secretary of State for Wales assumed responsibility for a range of
functions in respect of primary and secondary schools in Wales.
Circular 10/70: Conservative government withdrew circular 10/65.
The Public Schools Commission, second Report (independent day
and direct grant schools):

(i) Terms of reference: as for first Report.
(ii) Main recommendations:

(a) All grant-aided day schools should admit pupils without
charging fees and upon comprehensive principles or forgo state aid.

1971 Ivan Illich: *Deschooling Society*.
Everett Reimer: *School is Dead*.

1972 Raising of school leaving age to 16.
The James Report (*Teacher Education and Training*):

(i) Terms of reference: in the light of the review currently being
undertaken by the Area Training Organizations, and of the evidence
published by the Select Committee on Education and Science, to
enquire into the present arrangements for the education, training,
and probation of teachers in England and Wales and in particular to
examine:

(a) what should be the content and organization of courses to be
provided;
(b) whether a larger proportion of intending teachers should be

educated with students who have not chosen their careers or chosen other careers;

(c)   what, in the context of (a) and (b) above, should be the role of the maintained and voluntary colleges of education, the polytechnics, and other further education institutions maintained by local education authorities, and the universities and to make recommendations.

(ii)   Main recommendations:

(a)   The structure of teacher training courses should be radically altered.

(b)   All intending teachers should undergo at least a 4-year course of training leading to a degree.

(c)   Teacher training should consist of 3 cycles:

1.   2 years of nonvocational studies (Diploma of Higher Education) or a 3-year degree course.

2.   2 years of vocational preservice training and induction leading to qualification and to degree of B.A. (Education).

3.   In-service courses taking up equivalent of at least one term every seven years of service.

(d)   Creation of a new network of professional centres and administrative councils to supervise teacher training.

White Paper: *Education: A Framework for Expansion.*

N.F.E.R.: *A Critical Appraisal of Comprehensive Education.*

1974	Local government reorganization.
1975	Direct grant schools required to choose between comprehensivization and withdrawal of state aid.

The Bullock Report on teaching the use of English: (*A Language for Life*).

William Tyndale School controversy.

1976	Education Act – intended to compel reluctant LEAs to comprehensivize.

Tameside Judgement: central authority's powers of intervention under 1944 Act in respect of LEAs questioned.

Mr. Callaghan's speech at Ruskin College, Oxford.

N. Bennett: *Teaching Styles and Pupil Progress* (cast doubts upon relative educational efficiency of progressive primary teaching).

1977	Green Paper: *Education in Schools.*

The Taylor Report (*A New Partnership for Our Schools*): recommended equal representation of parents, teachers, representatives of L.E.A., and representatives of local community on school boards of governors. Boards of governors to have responsibility for defining the broad aims of the school and how to achieve them. Provision for pupils to serve as governors.

BIBLIOGRAPHY

Adams, F.: *History of the Elementary School Contest in England*, Chapman and Hall, London, 1882. (Reprinted 1972 by Harvester Press).

Adamson, J. W.: *English Education 1789-1902*, Cambridge University Press, 1930.

Archer, R. L.: *Secondary Education in the Nineteenth Century*, Cambridge University Press, 1921.

Argles, M.: *South Kensington to Robbins*, Longmans, London, 1964.

Armytage, W. H. G.: *Four Hundred Years of English Education*, Cambridge University Press, 1964.

Bamford, T. W.: *Thomas Arnold*, Cresset, London, 1960.

Bamford, T. W.: *The Rise of the Public Schools*, Nelson, London, 1967.

Banks, O.: *Parity and Prestige in English Secondary Education*, Routledge & Kegan Paul, London, 1955.

Barker, R.: *Education and Politics 1900-1951*, Oxford University Press, 1972.

Barnard, H. C.: *A History of English Education from 1760*, University of London Press, 1961.

Bell, R., Fowler, G., and Little, K.: *Education in Great Britain and Ireland*, Routledge & Kegan Paul, London, 1973.

Benn, C. and Simon, B.: *Half Way There*, McGraw-Hill, London, 1970.

Bennett, N., et al.: *Teaching Styles and Pupil Progress*, Open Publishing, London, 1976.

Berg, L.: *Risinghill – Death of a Comprehensive School*, Penguin, Harmondsworth, 1968.

Birley, D.: *The Education Officer and his World*, Routledge & Kegan Paul, London, 1970.

Bishop, A. S.: *The Rise of a Central Authority for English Education*, Cambridge University Press, 1971.

Blackie, I.: *Inspecting and the Inspectorate*, Routledge & Kegan Paul, London, 1970.

Blishen, E.: *Roaring Boys*, Thames & Hudson, London, 1955.

Blishen, E.: *This Right Soft Lot*, Thames & Hudson, London, 1969.

Borer, M. C.: *Willingly to School, A History of Women's Education*, Lutterworth, Guildford and London, 1976.

Boyle, E. and Crosland, A.: *The Politics of Education*, Penguin, Harmondsworth, 1971.

Boyson, R.: *Oversubscribed, The Story of Highbury Grove School*, Ward Lock Educational, London, 1974.

Braithwaite, E. R.: *To Sir, With Love*, The Bodley Head, London, 1959.

Coates, R. D.: *Teachers' Unions and Interest Group Politics*, Cambridge University Press, 1972.

Cook, T. G. (ed.): *Local Studies and the History of Education*, History of Education Society, Methuen, London, 1972.

Corbett, A.: *Much to do about Education*, Council for Educational Advance, London, 1973.

Cotgrove, S. F.: *Technical Education and Social Change*, Allen & Unwin, London, 1958.

Croft, M.: *Spare the Rod*, Longmans, London, 1954.

Cruickshank, M.: *Church and State in English Education, 1870 to the Present Day*, Macmillan, London, 1963.

Curtis, S. J.: *History of Education in Great Britain*, University Tutorial Press, London, 1967.

Dancy, J.: *The Public Schools and the Future*, Faber & Faber, London, 1963.

Davies, H.: *The Creighton Report – A Year in the Life of a Comprehensive School*, Hamish Hamilton, London, 1976.

Davis, R.: *The Grammar School*, Penguin, Harmondsworth, 1967.

Dent, H. C.: *Secondary Modern Schools, An Interim Report*, Routledge & Kegan Paul, London, 1958.

Dent, H. C.: *The Educational System of England and Wales*, University of London Press, 1961.

Dent, H. C.: *The Training of Teachers in England and Wales 1800-1975*, Hodder & Stoughton, London, 1977.

Eaglesham, E. J. R.: *From School Board to Local Authority*, Routledge & Kegan Paul, London, 1956.

Eaglesham, E. J. R.: *The Foundations of Twentieth Century Education in England*, Routledge & Kegan Paul, London, 1967.

Edmonds, E. L.: *The School Inspector,* Routledge & Kegan Paul, London, 1962.

Edwards, R.: *The Secondary Technical School,* University of London Press, 1960.

Fenwick, I. G. K.: *The Comprehensive School 1944-1970,* Methuen, London, 1976.

Ford, J. B.: *Social Class and the Comprehensive School,* Routledge & Kegan Paul, London, 1969.

Fowler, G., Morris, V. and Ozga, J.: *Decision making in British Education,* Heinemann, London, 1973.

Gathorne-Hardy, J.: *The Public School Phenomenon, 597-1977,* Hodder & Stoughton, London, 1977.

Goldstrom, J. M.: *The Social Content of Education 1808-1870,* Irish University Press, Shannon, 1972.

Gordon, P.: *The Victorian School Manager,* Woburn Press, London, 1974.

Gosden, P. H. J. H.: *The Development of Educational Administration in England and Wales,* Blackwell, Oxford, 1966.

Gosden, P. H. J. H.: *How they were Taught,* Blackwell, Oxford, 1969.

Gosden, P. H. J. H.: *The Evolution of a Profession,* Blackwell, Oxford, 1972.

Gosden, P. H. J. H.: *Education in the Second World War,* Methuen, London, 1976.

Graves, J. T. R.: *Policy and Progress in Secondary Education 1902-1942,* Nelson, London, 1943.

Hargreaves, D. H.: *Social Relations in a Secondary School,* Routledge & Kegan Paul, London, 1967.

Hewitson, J. N.: *The Grammar School Tradition in a Comprehensive World,* Routledge & Kegan Paul, London, 1969.

Honey, J. R. de S.: *Tom Brown's Universe: The Development of the Public School in the 19th Century,* Millington, London, 1977.

Hurt, J.: *Education in Evolution: Church, State, Society and Popular Education 1800-1870,* Hart-Davis, London, 1971.

Illich, I.: *Deschooling Society,* Calder & Boyars, London, 1971.

James, E. J. F.: *Education and Leadership,* Harrap, London, 1951.

Johnson, M.: *Derbyshire Village Schools in the Nineteenth Century,* David & Charles, Newton Abbot, 1970.

Kalton, G.: *The Public Schools – A Factual Survey of Headmasters' Conference Schools in England and Wales,* Longmans, London, 1966.

Kamm, J.: *How Different from Us, A Biography of Miss Buss and Miss Beale,* The Bodley Head, London, 1959.

Kamm, J.: *Hope Deferred, Girls' Education in English History,* Methuen, London, 1965.

Kazamias, A.: *Politics, Society and Secondary Education in England,* University of Philadelphia Press, 1966.

Kekewich, G. W.: *The Education Department and After,* Constable, London, 1920.

Kneebone, R. M. T.: *I Work in a Secondary Modern School,* Routledge & Kegan Paul, London, 1957.

Koerner, J. D.: *Reform in Education, England and the United States,* Weidenfeld & Nicolson, London, 1968.

Kogan, M.: *Educational Policy-Making,* Allen & Unwin, London, 1975.

Kogan, M. and van der Eyken, W.: *County Hall, The Role of the Chief Education Officer,* Penguin, Harmondsworth, 1973.

Lambert, R., et al.: *The Chance of a Lifetime? A Study of Boys' and Coeducational Boarding Schools in England and Wales,* Weidenfeld & Nicolson, London, 1975.

Laqueur, T. W.: *Religion and Respectability: Sunday Schools and English Working Class Culture 1780-1850,* Yale University Press, 1976.

Lawrence, B.: *The Administration of Education in Britain,* Batsford, London, 1972.

Lawson, J. and Silver, H.: *A Social History of Education in England,* Methuen, London, 1973.

Layard, R. and King, J. and Moser, C.: *The Impact of Robbins,* Penguin, Harmondsworth, 1969.

Leese, J.: *Personalities and Power in English Education,* Arnold, Leeds, 1950.

Leff, S. and V.: *The School Health Service*, H. K. Lewis, London, 1959.
Lister, I. (ed.): *Deschooling, A Reader*, Cambridge University Press, 1974.
Lomax, D. E. (ed.): *The Education of Teachers in Britain*, John Wiley, London, 1972.
Lowndes, G. A. N.: *The Silent Social Revolution*, Oxford University Press, 1937.
McCann, P. (ed.): *Popular Education and Socialization in the Nineteenth Century*,
   Methuen, London, 1977.
Mack, E. C.: *Public Schools and British Opinion*, Columbia University Press, New York,
   1938 and 1941 (Reprinted 1971 by Greenwood Press, Westport, Connecticut.)
Maclure, J. S. (ed.): *Educational Documents, England and Wales 1816 to the Present Day*,
   Methuen, London, 1973.
Maclure, J. S.: *One Hundred Years of London Education 1870-1970*, Penguin,
   Harmondsworth, 1970.
Middleton, N. and Weitzman, S.: *A Place for Everyone, A History of State Education*,
   Gollancz, London, 1976.
Midwinter, E. C.: *Patterns of Community Education*, Ward Lock, London, 1973.
Morrish, I.: *Education since 1800*, Allen & Unwin, London, 1970.
Neill, A. S.: *Summerhill, A Radical Approach to Education*, Gollancz, London, 1962.
Newsome, D.: *Godliness and Good Learning, Four Studies on a Victorian Ideal*, Murray,
   London, 1961.
Niblett, W. R., Humphreys, D. W. and Fairhurst, J. R.: *The University Connection*,
   N.F.E.R., Slough, 1975.
Ogilvie, V.: *The English Public School*, Batsford, London, 1957.
Parkinson, M.: *The Labour Party and the Organization of Secondary Education*, Routledge
   & Kegan Paul, London, 1970.
Parry, J. P.: *The Provision of Education in England and Wales*, Allen & Unwin, London,
   1971.
Partridge, J.: *Middle School*, Gollancz, London, 1966.
Pedley, R.: *The Comprehensive School*, Penguin, Harmondsworth, 1963.
Percival, A. C.: *Very Superior Men: Some early Public School Headmasters and their
   Achievements*, Knight, London, 1973.
Peters, R. S. (ed.): *Perspectives on Plowden*, Routledge & Kegan Paul, London, 1969.
Punch, M.: *Progressive Retreat, A Sociological Study of Dartington Hall School 1926-1957
   and Some of its Former Pupils*, Cambridge University Press, 1977.
Razzell, A.: *Juniors, A Postscript to Plowden*, Penguin, Harmondsworth, 1968.
Rée, H.: *The Essential Grammar School*, Harrap, London, 1956.
Reimer, E.: *School is Dead – An Essay on Alternatives in Education*, Penguin,
   Harmondsworth, 1971.
Rich, E. E.: *The Education Act, 1870, A Study of Public Opinion*, Longmans, London,
   1970.
Rich, R. W.: *The Training of Teachers in England and Wales in the Nineteenth Century*,
   Cambridge University Press, 1933. (Reprinted 1972 by Chivers.)
Richmond, W. K.: *The Free School*, Methuen, London, 1973.
Roach, J. P.: *Public Examinations in England, 1850-1900*, Cambridge University Press,
   1971.
Robinson, G.: *Private Schools and Public Policy*, Loughborough University, 1971.
Ross, J. M., Bunton, W. J., Evison, P. and Robertson, T. S.: *A Critical Appraisal of the
   Comprehensive School*, N.F.E.R., Slough, 1972.
Rubinstein, D. and Simon, B.: *The Evolution of the Comprehensive School 1926-1966*,
   Routledge & Kegan Paul, London, 1969.
Runciman, J.: *Schools and Scholars*, Chatto, London, 1887.
Saran, R.: *Policy-Making in Secondary Education, A Case Study*, Clarendon Press, Oxford,
   1973.
Selby-Bigge, L. A.: *The Board of Education*, Putnam, London, 1927.
Selleck, R. J. W.: *The New Education 1870-1914*, Pitman, London, 1968.
Selleck, R. J. W.: *English Primary Education and the Progressives, 1914-1939*, Routledge &
   Kegan Paul, London, 1972.

Sellman, R. R. S.: *Devon Village Schools in the Nineteenth Century*, David & Charles, Newton Abbot, 1967.

Silver, H.: *The Concept of Popular Education, A Study of Ideas and Social Movements in the Early Nineteenth Century*, McGibbon & Kee, London, 1965.

Silver, P. and Silver, H.: *The Education of the Poor*, Routledge & Kegan Paul, London, 1974.

Simon, B.: *Studies in the History of Education 1780-1870*, Lawrence & Wishart, London, 1960. (Republished as *The Two Nations and the Educational Structure 1780-1870*, 1974.)

Simon, B.: *Education and the Labour Movement 1870-1920*, Lawrence & Wishart, London 1965.

Simon, B.: *The Politics of Educational Reform, 1920-1940*, Lawrence & Wishart, London, 1974.

Simon, B. and Bradley, I. (eds.): *The Victorian Public School*, Gill & Macmillan, Dublin, 1975.

Skidelsky, R.: *English Progressive Schools*, Penguin, Harmondsworth, 1969.

Smith, P. and Summerfield, G. (eds.): *Matthew Arnold and the Education of the New Order*, Cambridge University Press, 1969.

Sneyd-Kynnersley, E. M.: *H.M.I., Some Passages in the Life of one of H.M. Inspectors of Schools*, Macmillan, London, 1908.

Stevens, F. M.: *The Living Tradition: The Social and Educational Assumptions of the Grammar School*, Hutchinson, London, 1960.

Stewart, W. A. C.: *Progressives and Radicals in English Education, 1750-1970*, Macmillan, London, 1972.

Stewart, W. A. C. and McCann, W. P.: *The Educational Innovators*, Macmillan, London, 1967.

Sturt, M.: *The Education of the People, A History of Primary Education in England and Wales in the 19th Century*, Routledge & Kegan Paul, London, 1967.

Sutherland, G. R.: *Policy-Making in Elementary Education, 1870-1895*, Oxford University Press, 1973.

Sylvester, D. W.: *Robert Lowe and Education*, Cambridge University Press, 1974.

Taylor, G. and Saunders, J. B.: *The Law of Education*, Butterworth, London, 1976.

Taylor, W.: *The Secondary Modern School*, Faber & Faber, London, 1963.

Taylor, W.: *Society and the Education of Teachers*, Faber & Faber, London, 1969.

Tropp, A.: *The School Teachers, The Growth of the Teaching Profession in England and Wales from 1800 to the Present Day*, Heinemann, London, 1957.

van der Eyken, W.: *Education, The Child and Society*, Penguin, Harmondsworth, 1973.

van der Eyken, W. and Turner, B.: *Adventures in Education*, Penguin, Harmondsworth, 1969.

Wardle, D.: *English Popular Education, 1780-1970*, Cambridge University Press, 1970.

Watts, J. (ed.): *The Countesthorpe Experience*, Allen & Unwin, London, 1977.

Waugh, A.: *The Loom of Youth*, Richards, London, 1917. (Reprinted 1972 by Bles).

West, E.G.: *Education and the State*, Institute of Economic Affairs, London, 1965.

West, E. G.: *Education and the Industrial Revolution*, Batsford, London, 1975.

Whitbread, N.: *The Evolution of the Nursery-Infant School*, Routledge & Kegan Paul, London, 1972.

Official Publications

Nineteenth-century official publications sometimes have a double relevance in that they illuminate the attitudes of their writers as well as the specific subject under investigation. The Reports of the Commissioners of Inquiry into the State of Education in Wales (1847) are a case in point. The same may also be said of twentieth-century documents, which, though perhaps less discursive, are generally more widely available for reference. Some of the more important of these are listed below in order of publication. Several of them contain concise historical accounts of the subject with which they deal: the Spens Report, for example, has an opening chapter on the development of the secondary curriculum, while the 1972 report on Educational Priority includes a consideration of the origins of compensatory education and of the governmental response to the Plowden recommendations on the subject.

The Education of the Adolescent (1st Hadow Report), 1926

The Primary School (2nd Hadow Report), 1931

Secondary Education (Spens Report), 1938

Curriculum and Examinations in Secondary Schools (Norwood Report), 1943

Educational Reconstruction (White Paper), 1943

The Public Schools and the General Educational System (Fleming Report), 1944

Teachers and Youth Leaders (McNair Report), 1944

The Nation's Schools (Ministry of Education pamphlet), 1945

The New Secondary Education (Ministry of Education pamphlet), 1947

15-18 (Crowther Report), 1959

Secondary School Examinations other than the G.C.E. (Beloe Report), 1960.

Half Our Future (Newsom Report), 1963

Higher Education (Robbins Report), 1963

Children and their Primary Schools (Plowden Report), 1967

Primary Education in Wales (Gittins Report), 1967

Public Schools Commission (first report: *Independent Boarding Schools),* 1968
Public Schools Commission (second report: *Independent Day Schools and Direct Grant Grammar Schools),* 1970

Teacher Education and Training (James Report), 1972

Education: A Framework for Expansion (White Paper), 1972

Educational Priority (EPA Problems and Policies), 1972

INDEX